JOE CELKO'S
THINKING IN SETS

The Morgan Kaufmann Series in Data Management Systems

JOE CELKO'S
THINKING IN SETS
Auxiliary, Temporal, and Virtual Tables in SQL

Joe Celko

ELSEVIER

AMSTERDAM • BOSTON HEIDELBERG • LONDON
NEW YORK • OXFORD • PARIS • SAN DIEGO
SAN FRANCISCO • SINGAPORE • SYDNEY • TOKYO
Morgan Kaufmann is an imprint of Elsevier

MORGAN KAUFMANN PUBLISHERS

Publisher	Denise E. M. Penrose
Publishing Services Manager	George Morrison
Project Manager	Marilyn E. Rash
Assistant Editor	Mary E. James
Production Management	Multiscience Press, Inc.
Design Direction	Joanne Blank
Cover Design	Dick Hannus
Typesetting/Illustrations	diacriTech
Interior Printer	Sheridan Books
Cover Printer	Phoenix Color Corp.

Morgan Kaufmann Publishers is an imprint of Elsevier.
30 Corporate Drive, Burlington, MA 01803-4255

This book is printed on acid-free paper.

Library of Congress Cataloging-in-Publication Data
Celko, Joe.
  [Thinking in sets]
  Joe Celko's thinking in sets : auxiliary, temporal, and virtual tables in SQL
  / Joe Celko.
    p.   cm.
  Includes index.
  ISBN 978-0-12-374137-0 (alk. paper)
  1. SQL (Computer program language) 2. Declarative programming.   I. Title.
    II. Title: Thinking in sets.
  QA76.73.S67C463 2008
  005.13—dc22   2007043898

For information on all Morgan Kaufmann publications, visit our Web site at
www.mkp.com or www.books.elsevier.com.

Transferred to Digital Printing in 2014

To my god-niece, Olivia. When we are finished with her board books, we can start on SQL manuals before bedtime!

CONTENTS

18 Procedural and Data Driven Solutions   323

Preface

THIS BOOK DEALS with the use of various kinds of SQL programming techniques that make use of tables rather than procedural code. I have been telling people that the biggest obstacle to learning SQL is unlearning procedural programming, but saying that does not show someone who has been thinking in files and procedural code his or her entire career how to do things in a declarative relational language. Hence this book, with actual techniques and an explanation of the thought processes that lead to them.

Like all of my other books, this one is for the working SQL programmer who wants to pick up good SQL programming techniques. It assumes that readers know the language well enough to write code that runs and that they are approaching their first year of actual SQL experience.

Why a year? My experience in teaching SQL for the past few decades is that the average SQL programmer goes through phases while moving from procedural programming languages such as FORTRAN, Cobol, Pascal, the C family, OO languages, and whatever else the "application language du jour" happens to be this year. A declarative language is totally different from anything they have done before.

Learning a new programming language is much like learning a foreign language. At first, you mispronounce words and try to use the word order and syntax of your native language. Then you can assemble a proper sentence using a template and a bit of effort. Finally, you actually think and speak that foreign language and do not have to really focus on the effort.

The initial phase in using SQL programming is just copying existing code blindly from someone else's programs. This is not really programming. You might as well be using a GUI tool that assembles SQL from text files without ever showing you the actual code.

The next step is writing new SQL code, but doing it as if it were your original or best-known language. A symptom of this mind-set is using the wrong terminology, such as calling a column a field, as if we were still using sequential filing systems. But it also shows up in the form of cursors and temporary tables used to mimic sequential file systems at great danger and expense.

Toward the end that first year of SQL programming, the programmer's mind-set starts to change. She or he has seen good SQL code, read something about RDBMS, and is finally starting to think in SQL. If the person is lucky, he or she might have taken a college or training course during this time.

The funniest example of the mindset problem was a college class I taught decades ago to engineers who knew only FORTRAN and C. They assumed that SQL must have WHILE-loops and IF-THEN constructs. The one LISP programmer in the class was actually quite happy about the lack of iterative loops and the ability to nest code modules but could not understand the lack of recursive constructs in SQL.

Developers are using databases and cannot stay in the comfort of their native language. There was an article in the IT trade press on March 22, 2007 from Evans Data about a two-year survey that showed that 40 percent of American developers are using databases in their work. A year before, only 32 percent of developers were using databases in their work, according to the study.

Auxiliary, Temporal, and Virtual Tables

There is only one data structure in SQL: the table. How tables are used often affects how they are declared. There are base, or operational, tables that persist in storage. They hold the core data of the data model, but they are not the only kind of table.

Staging tables are horrible monsters without constraints or even keys. But SQL allows you to create them. You use them as staging areas for dirty, raw data that you would never ever put in your beautiful clean base tables.

Auxiliary tables are used to compute functions and other values by joins rather than by procedural programming. Common examples are look-up tables for translating encodings and functions that cannot be computed easily. They should not appear in the ER diagrams for the data model, because they are not really entities or relationships.

Temporal tables are those that support temporal queries, historical data, and audit information. Although you can consider them to be auxiliary or base tables, they need special emphasis. This topic is complicated in both the concepts and the implementations.

Virtual tables are materialized (or appear to be materialized) by the SQL engine. They do not exist in the schema like base tables. They come in several "flavors" and can be used to improve the performance of SQL statements.

This book also contains a discussion about the Schema Information Tables that SQL uses to describe a schema in SQL itself. There is an ANSI/ISO standard for them, but most products have their own versions of them.

Corrections and Additions

Please send any corrections, additions, suggestions, improvements, or alternative solutions to me or to the publisher at Morgan Kaufmann, 30 Corporate Drive, Suite 400, Burlington, MA 01803.

CHAPTER 1

SQL Is Declarative, Not Procedural

I N THE PREFACE I told a short story about FORTRAN programmers who could only solve problems using loops and a LISP programmer who could only solve problems recursively. This is not uncommon because we love the tools we know. Let me tell a joke instead of a story: A mathematician, a physicist, and a database programmer were all given a rubber ball and told to find the volume.

The mathematician carefully measured the diameter and either evaluated the volume of sphere formula or used a triple integral if the ball was not perfectly round.

The physicist filled a beaker with water, put the ball in the water, and measured the total displacement. He does not care about the details of the shape of the ball.

The database programmer looked up the model and serial numbers in his rubber ball manufacturer's on-line database. He does not care about the actual ball. But he has information about the tolerances to which it was made, the expected shape and size, and a bunch of other things that apply to the entire rubber ball production process.

The moral of the story is: The mathematician knows how to compute. The physicist knows how to measure. The database guy knows how to look up data. Each person grabs his tools to solve the problem.

Now change the problem to an inventory of thousands of rubber balls. The mathematician and the physicist are stuck with a lot of manual labor. The database guy does a few downloads and he can produce rubber ball industry standards (assuming that there are such things) and detailed documentation in court with his answers.

1.1   Different Programming Models

Perfecting oneself is as much unlearning as it is learning.
—Edsgar Dijkstra

There are many models of programming. Procedural programming languages use a sequence of procedural steps guided by flow of control statements (`WHILE-DO`, `IF-THEN-ELSE`, and `BEGIN-END`) that change the input data to output data. This was the traditional view of programming, and it is often called the von Neumann Model after John von Neumann, the mathematician who was responsible for it. The same source code runs through the same compiler and generates the same executable module every time. The same program will work exactly the same way every time it is invoked. The keywords in this model are predictable and deterministic. It is also subject to some mathematical analysis *because* it is deterministic.

There are some variations on the theme. Some languages use different flow control statements. FORTRAN and COBOL allocated all the storage for the data at the start of the program. Later, the Algol family of languages did dynamic storage allocation based on the scope of the data within a block-structured language.

Edsgar Dijkstra (see his archives at *www.cs.utexas.edu/users/EWD/*) came up with a language that was nondeterministic. Statements, called guarded commands, have a control that either blocks or allows the statement to be executed, but there is no particular order of execution among the open statements. This model was not implemented in a commercial product, but it demonstrated that something we had thought was necessary for programming (determinism) could be dropped.

Functional programming languages are based on solving problems as a series of nested function calls. The concept of higher-order functions to change one function to another is important in these languages. The derivative and integral transforms are mathematical examples of such higher-order functions. One of the goals of such languages is to avoid a side effect in programs so they can be optimized algebraically. In particular, once you have an expression that is equal to another (in some sense of equality), they can substitute for each other without affecting the result of the computation.

APL is the most successful functional programming language and had a fad period as a teaching language when Ken Iverson wrote his book *A Programming Language* in 1962. IBM produced special keyboards that included the obscure mathematical symbols used in APL for their desktop machines. Most of the functional languages never made it out of academia, but some survive in commercial applications today. Erlang is used for concurrent applications; R is a statistical language; Mathematica is a popular symbolic mathematics product; and Kx Systems uses the K language for large-volume financial analysis. More recently, the ML and Haskell programming languages have become popular among Linux and UNIX programmers.

Here we dropped another concept that had been regarded as fundamental: There is no flow of control in these languages.

Constraint or constraint logic programming languages are a series of constraints on a problem domain. As you add more constraints, the system figures out which answers are possible and which are not. The most popular such language is PROLOG, which also had an academic fad many years ago when Borland Software (*www.borland.com*) made a cheap student version available. The website ON-LINE GUIDE TO CONSTRAINT PROGRAMMING by Roman Barták is a good place to start if you are interested in this topic (*http://kti.ms.mff.cuni.cz/~bartak/constraints/index.html*).

Here we dropped the concept of an algorithm altogether and just provided a problem specification.

Object-oriented (OO) programming is based on the ideas of objects that have both data and behavior in the same module of code. The programming model is a collection of independent cooperating objects instead of a single program invoking functions. An object is capable of receiving messages, processing data, and sending messages to other objects.

The idea is that each object can be maintained and written independently of any particular application and dropped into place where it is needed. Imagine a community of people who do particular jobs. They receive orders from their customers, process them, and return a result.

Many years ago, the INCITS H2 Database Standards Committee (née ANSI X3H2 Database Standards Committee) had a meeting in Rapid City, South Dakota. We had Mount Rushmore and Bjarne Stroustrup as special attractions. Mr. Stroustrup did his slide show with overhead transparencies (yes, this was before PowerPoint was ubiquitous!) about Bell Labs inventing C++ and OO programming, and we got to ask questions.

One of the questions was how we should put OO features into the working model of the next version of the SQL standard, which was known as SQL3 internally. His answer was that Bell Labs, with all their talent, had tried four different approaches to this problem and they came to the conclusion that it should not be done. OO was great for programming but deadly for data.

I have watched people try to force OO models into SQL, and it falls apart in about a year. Every typo becomes a new attribute or class, queries that would have been so easy in a relational model are now multitable monster outer joins, redundancy grows at an exponential rates, constraints are virtually impossible to write so you can kiss data integrity goodbye, and so forth.

With all these programming models, why should we not have different data models?

1.2   Different Data Models

Consider the humble punch card. Punch cards had been used in France to control textile looms since the early 1700s; the method was perfected by Joseph Marie Jacquard in 1801 with his Jacquard loom.

Flash forward to the year 1890, when a man named Herman Hollerith invented a punch card and tabulating machines for that year's United States Census. His census project was so successful that Mr. Hollerith left the government and started the Tabulating Machine Company in 1896. After a series of mergers and name changes, this company became IBM. You might have heard of it.

Up to the 1970s, the "IBM card" and related machinery was every-where. The most common card was the IBM 5081, and that part number became the common term for it—even across vendors! The punch card was data processing back then.

The physical characteristics of the card determined how we stored and processed data for decades afterwards. The card was the size of an 1887 United States dollar bill (3.25 inches by 7.375 inches). The reason for that size was simple; when Hollerith worked on the Census, he could get drawers to store the decks of cards from the Department of the Treasury across the street.

The cards had a grid of 80 columns of 12 rows, which could accommodate holes. This was for physical reasons again. But once the 80-column convention was established, it stuck. The early video terminals that replaced the key punch machines used screens with 80 columns of text and 24 or 25 rows—that is, two punch cards high and possibly a line for error messages.

Magnetic tapes started replacing punch cards in the 1970s, but they also mimicked the 80-column convention, although there was no longer any need. Many of the early ANSI tape standards for header records are based on this convention. Legacy systems simply replaced card readers with magnetic tape units for obvious reasons, but new applications continued to be built to this standard, too.

The physical nature of the cards meant that data was written and read from left to right in sequential order. Likewise, the deck of cards was written and read from front to back in sequential order.

A magnetic tape file is also written and read in the same way, but with the added bonus that when you drop a tape on the floor, it does not get scrambled like a deck of cards. The downside of a tape over a deck of cards is that it cannot be rearranged manually on purpose either.

Card and tape files are pretty passive creatures and will take whatever an application program throws at them without much objection. Files are also independent of each other, simply because they are connected to one application program at a time and therefore have no idea what other files look like.

Early disk systems also mimicked this model—physically contiguous storage read in a sequential order, with meaning given to the data by the program reading it.

It was a while before disk systems realized that the read/write heads could be moved to any physical position on the disk. This gave us random access storage. We still have a contiguous storage concept within each field and each record, however.

The Relational Model was a big jump, because it divorced the physical and logical models of data. If you read the specifications for many of the early programming languages, they describe physically contiguous data and storage methods. SQL describes only the behavior of the data without any reference to physical storage methods.

1.2.1 Columns Are Not Fields

A field within a record is defined by the application program that reads it. A column in a row in a table is defined independently of any application by the database schema in DDL. The data types in a column are always scalar and NULL-able.

This is a problem for files. If I mount the wrong tape on a tape drive, say a COBOL file, and read it with a FORTRAN program, it can produce meaningless output. The program simply counts the number of bytes from the start of the tape and slices off so many characters into each field from left to right.

The order of the application program variables in the READ or INPUT statements is important, because the values are read into the program variables in that order. In SQL, columns are referenced only by their names. Yes, there are shorthands like the SELECT * clause and "INSERT INTO <table name>" statements that expand into a list of column names in the physical order in which the column names appear within their table declaration, but these are shorthands that resolve to named lists. This is a leftover from the early days of SQL, when we were doing our unlearning and still had a "record-oriented" mindset.

The use of NULLs in SQL is also unique to the language. Fields do not support a missing data marker as part of the field, record, or file itself. Nor do fields have constraints that can be added to them in the record, like the DEFAULT and CHECK() clauses in SQL.

Nor do fields have a data type. Fields have meaning and are defined by the program reading them, not in themselves. Thus, four columns on a punch card containing 1223 might be an integer in one program, a string in a second program, or read as four fields instead of one in a third program.

The choice of data types is not always obvious. The sure symptom of a newbie programmer is that they blindly pick data types without any research. My favorite example is the use of a "VARCHAR (<magical length>)" declaration for almost every column, where <magical length> is an integer value that their particular implement of SQL generates as a default or maximum. In the Microsoft world, look for 255 and 50 to appear.

As an example of the difference in research versus impulse design, consider trying to sort the sections of this book that use a numeric outline for the sections. If you model the outline numbers as character strings, you lose the natural order when you sort them.

For example:

1.1
1.2
1.3
...
1.10

Sorts as:

1.1
1.10

1.2

1.3

...

When this question appeared in a newsgroup, the various solutions included a recursive function, an external function, a proprietary name parsing function, and an extra column for the sort order.

My solution is to pad each section with leading zeros and hope I never have more than 99 headings. Most publishers have an acceptable maximum depth of five levels.

00.00.

01.00.

01.01.

01.01.02.

etc.

You enforce this with SIMILAR TO predicate in the DDL rather than trying to do it in the ORDER BY clause in the DML.

```
CREATE TABLE Outline
(section_nbr VARCHAR(15) NOT NULL PRIMARY KEY,
   CHECK (section_nbr SIMILAR TO '[:digit:][:digit:]\.+'),
 ..);
```

When you want to display the section numbers without the leading zeros, use a REPLACE() or TRANSLATE function in the query. We will get to this principle in a later section.

In 25 words or less, columns are active and define themselves; fields are passive and are interpreted by the application program.

1.2.2   Rows Are Not Records

Rows are not records. A record is defined in the application program that reads it, just like the fields. The name of the field in the READ statements of the application language tells the program where to put the data. The *physical* order of the field names in the READ statement is vital. That means "READ a, b, c;" is not the same as "READ c, a, b;" because of the sequential order.

A row in a table is defined in the database schema and not by a program at all. The columns are referenced by their names in the schema and not by local program names or physical locations. That means

"SELECT a, b, c FROM..." is the same data as "SELECT c, a, b FROM..." when the data goes into a host program.

All empty files look alike; they are a directory entry in the operating system registry with a name, a length of zero bytes of storage, and a NIL pointer to their starting position. Empty tables still have columns, constraints, security privileges, and other structures, even though they have no rows. All CHECK() constraints are TRUE on an empty table, so you must use a CREATE ASSERTION statement that is external to the tables if you wish to impose business rules on potentially empty tables or among tables.

This is in keeping with the set theoretical model, in which the empty set is a perfectly good set. The difference between SQL's set model and standard mathematical set theory is that set theory has only one empty set, but in SQL each table has a different structure, so they cannot be used in places where nonempty versions of themselves could not be used.

Another characteristic of rows in a table is that they are all alike in structure and they are all the "same kind of thing" in the model. In a file system, records can vary in size, data types, and structure by having flags in the data stream that tell the program reading the data how to interpret it. The most common examples are Pascal's variant record, C's struct syntax, and COBOL's OCCURS clause.

Here is an example in COBOL-85. The syntax is fairly easy to understand, even if you do not read COBOL. The language has a data declaration section in the programs that uses a hierarchical outline numbering system. The fields are strings, described by a template or PICTURE clause. The dash serves the same purpose as the underscore in SQL.

```
01     PRIOR-PERIOD-TABLE.
  05     PERIOD-AMT PICTURE 9(6)
         OCCURS ZERO TO 12 TIMES
         DEPENDING ON PRIOR-PERIODS.
```

The PRIOR-PERIODS field holds the value that controls how many PERIOD-AMT fields we have. ZERO option was added in COBOL-85, but COBOL-74 had to have at least one occurrence.

In Pascal, consider a record for library items that can be either a book or a CD. The declarations look like this:

```
ItemClasses = (Book, CD);
LibraryItems =
RECORD
```

```
  Ref: 0..999999;
  Title: ARRAY [1..30] OF CHAR;
  Author: ARRAY [1..16] OF CHAR;
  Publisher: ARRAY [1..20] OF CHAR;
CASE Class: ItemClasses
  OF Book: (Edition: 1..50; PubYear: 1400..2099);
    CD: (Artist: ARRAY [1..30] OF CHAR;
END;
```

The ItemClasses is a flag that picks which branch of the CASE declaration is to be used. The order of the declaration is important. You might also note that the CASE *declaration* in Pascal was one of the sources for the CASE *expression* in SQL.

Unions in C are another way of doing the same thing we saw done in Pascal. This declaration:

```
union x {int ival; char j[4];} mystuff;
```

defines mystuff to be either an integer (which are 4 bytes on most modern C compilers, but this code is nonportable) or an array of 4 bytes, depending on whether you say mystuff.ival or mystuff.j [0].

As an aside, I tried to stick with the idioms of the languages—all uppercase for COBOL, capitalized name in Pascal, and lowercase in C. COBOL is all uppercase because it was first used on punch cards, which only have uppercase. C was first written on Teletype terminals for mini computers, which have a shift key, but the touch is so hard and so long that you have to hit the keys vertically; you cannot type with your fingertips. C was designed for two-finger typists, pushing the keys with strokes from their elbows rather than the wrist or fingertips. SQL and modern language idioms are based on the ease of text formatters and electronic keyboards that respond to fingertip touch.

Once more, the old technology is reflected in the next technology, until eventually the new technology finds its voice. These styles of formatting code are not the best practices for human readability, but they were the easiest way of doing the job at the time. You can get some details about human factors and readability in my other book, *SQL Programming Style* (ISBN 0-12-088797-5).

The OCCURS keyword in Cobol, union in C, and the variant records in Pascal have a number or flag that tells the program how to read a record structure you input as bytes from left to right.

In SQL the *entire row* is read and handled as the "unit of work," and it is *not* read sequentially. You UPDATE, INSERT, and DELETE *entire* rows and not columns within a row. The ANSI model of an UPDATE is that it acts as if

1. You go to the base table (updatable VIEWs are first resolved to their underlying base table). It cannot have an alias because an alias would create a working table that would be updated and then disappear after the statement is finished, thus doing nothing.

2. You go to the WHERE clause. All rows (if any!) that test TRUE are marked as a subset. If there is no WHERE clause or the search condition is always TRUE, then the entire table is marked as the subset. If the search condition is always FALSE or UNKNOWN, then the subset is empty. But an emptyset is still a set and gets treated as such. The name of this set/pseudo-table is OLD in Standard SQL, and it can be used in TRIGGERs.

3. You go to the SET clause and construct a set/pseudo-table called NEW. The rows in the NEW table are built two ways: if they are not on the left side of the SET clause, then the values from the original row are copied; if the columns are on the left side of the SET clause, then the expression on the right side determined their value. This is supposed to happen in parallel for all the columns, all at once. That is, the unit of work is a row, not one column at a time.

4. The OLD subset is deleted and the NEW set is inserted. This is why

```
UPDATE Foobar
   SET a = b, b = a;
```

swaps the values in the columns "a" and "b," while a sequence of assignment statements in a procedural file–oriented language would behave like this:

```
BEGIN
SET a = b;
SET b = a;
END;
```

and leave the original value of "b" in both columns.

5. The engine checks constraints and does a ROLLBACK if there are violations.

In full SQL-92, you can use row constructors to say things like:

```
UPDATE Foobar
  SET (a, b)
    = (SELECT x, y
         FROM Floob AS F1
          WHERE F1.keycol= Foobar.keycol);
```

Think about what a confused mess this statement is in the SQL model:

```
SELECT f(c2) AS c1, f(c1) AS c2 FROM Foobar;
```

The entire row comes into existence all at once as a single unit. That means that "c1" does not exist before the second function call. Such nonsense is illegal syntax.

1.2.3   Tables Are Not Files

There is no sequential access or ordering in table, so "first," "next," and "last" rows are totally meaningless. If you want an ordering, then you need to have a column that defines that ordering. You must use an ORDER BY clause in a cursor or in an OVER() clause.

An RDBMS seeks to maintain the correctness of all its data. The methods used are triggers, constraints, and declarative referential integrity.

Declarative referential integrity (DRI) says, in effect, that data in one table has a particular relationship with data in a second (possibly the same) table. It is also possible to have the database change itself via referential actions associated with the DRI.

For example, a business rule might be that we do not sell products that are not in inventory. This rule would be enforced by a REFERENCES clause on the Orders table that references the Inventory table and a referential action of ON DELETE CASCADE, SET DEFAULT, or whatever.

Triggers are a more general way of doing much the same thing as DRI. A trigger is a block of procedural code that is executed before, after, or instead of an INSERT INTO or UPDATE FROM statement. You can do anything with a trigger that you can do with DRI and more.

However, there are problems with triggers. While there is a standard syntax for them in the SQL-92 standard, most vendors have not implemented it. What they have is very proprietary syntax instead. Second, a trigger cannot pass information to the optimizer like DRI. In the example in this section, I know that for every product number in the Orders table, I have that same product number in the Inventory table. The optimizer can use that information in setting up EXISTS() predicates and JOINs in the queries. There is no reasonable way to parse procedural trigger code to determine this relationship.

The CREATE ASSERTION statement in SQL-92 will allow the database to enforce conditions on the entire database as a whole. An ASSERTION is not like a CHECK() clause, but the difference is subtle. A CHECK() clause is executed when there are rows in the table to which it is attached. If the table is empty, then all CHECK() clauses are effectively TRUE. Thus, if we wanted to be sure that the Inventory table is never empty, we might naively write:

```
CREATE TABLE Inventory
( ...
 CONSTRAINT inventory_not_empty
      CHECK ((SELECT COUNT(*) FROM Inventory) > 0), ... );
```

and it would not work. However, we could write:

```
CREATE ASSERTION Inventory_not_empty
      CHECK ((SELECT COUNT(*) FROM Inventory) > 0);
```

and we would get the desired results. The assertion is checked at the schema level and not at the table level.

A file is closely related to its physical storage media. A table may or may not be a physical file at all. DB2 from IBM uses one physical file per table, while Sybase puts several entire databases inside one physical file. A table is a set of rows of the same kind of thing. A set has no ordering and it makes no sense to ask for the first or last row.

A deck of punch cards is sequential, and so are magnetic tape files. Therefore, a physical file of ordered sequential records also became the mental model for data processing and it is still hard to shake. Anytime you look at data, it is in some physical ordering.

The various access methods for disk storage system came later, but even these access methods could not shake the contiguous, sequential mental model.

Another conceptual difference is that a file is usually data that deals with a whole business process. A file has to have enough data in itself to support applications for that business process. Files tend to be "mixed" data that can be described by the name of the business process to which they belong, such as "the Payroll file" or something like that.

Tables can be entities, relationships, or auxiliaries within a business process. This means the data that was held in one file is often put into several tables. Tables tend to be "pure" data that can be described by single words. The payroll would now have separate tables for time cards, employees, projects, and so forth.

1.2.4   Relational Keys Are Not Record Locators

One of the first things that a newbie does is use a proprietary autonumbering feature in their SQL product as a PRIMARY KEY. This is completely wrong, and it violates the definition of a relational key.

An attribute has to belong to an entity in the real world being modeled by the RDBMS. Autonumbering does not exist in an entity in the real world being modeled by the RDBMS. Thus, it is not an attribute and cannot be in a table, by definition.

Autonumbering is a result of the physical state of particular piece of hardware at a particular time as read by the current release of a particular database product. It is not a data type. You cannot have more than one column of this "type" in a table. It is not NULL-able, which all data types have to be in SQL. It is not a numeric; you cannot do math with it. It is what is called a "tag number"—basically, a nominal scale written with numbers instead of letters. Only equality tests make sense.

1.2.4.1   Redundant Duplicates

Assume we have a table of vehicles with some autonumbering feature as its key—I will use a function call notation here. Execute this code with the same VALUES() clause.

```
INSERT INTO Vehicles (auto_nbr(), vin, mileage, ..)
VALUES ( ..);
INSERT INTO Vehicles (auto_nbr(), vin, mileage, ..)
VALUES ( ..);
```

I now have two cars with the same VIN number. Actually, I have two copies of the same car (object) with an autonumber pseudo-key instead of the industry standard VIN as the proper relational key. This is called an insertion anomaly.

Assume that this pair of insertions led to creating vehicles with pseudo-keys 41 and 42 in the table, which are the same actual object. I can update 42's mileage without touching 41. I now have two versions of the truth in my table. This is a called an update anomaly.

Likewise, if I wreck vehicle 41, I still have copy 42 in the motor pool in spite of the fact that the actual object no longer exists. This is deletion anomaly.

1.2.4.2 *Uniqueness Is Ruined*

Before you say that you can make a key from (auto-numbering, vin), read more from Dr. E. F. Codd: "If the primary key is composite and if one of the columns is dropped from the primary key, the first property [uniqueness] is no longer guaranteed."

Assume that I have correct VINs and use (auto-numbering, vin) as a key. Dropping the pair clearly does not work—a lot of vehicles could have the same mileage and tire sizes, so I do not have unique rows guaranteed. Dropping the autonumber will leave me with a proper key that can be validated, verified, and repeated.

Dropping the VIN does not leave me with a guarantee (i.e., repeatability and predictability). If I run this code:

```
BEGIN ATOMIC
DELETE FROM Vehicles
 WHERE id = 41;
INSERT INTO Vehicles (mileage, ..)
 VALUES (<<values of #41>> );
END;
```

the relational algebra says that I should have in effect done nothing. I have dropped and reinserted the same object—an EXCEPT and UNION operation that cancel. But since autonumbering is physical and not logical, this does not work.

If I insert the same vehicle (object) into another table, the system will not guarantee me that I get the same autonumbering as the relational key in the other table. The VIN would be guaranteed constant in this schema and any other schema that needs to model a vehicle.

The guarantee requirement gets worse. SQL is a set-oriented language and allows me to write things like this:

```
INSERT INTO Vehicles (pseudo_key, vin, mileage, ..)
SELECT auto_nbr(), vin, mileage, ..
 FROM NewPurchases;
```

Since a query result is a table, and a table is a set that has no ordering, what should the autonumbers be? The entire, whole, completed set is presented to Vehicles all at once, not a row at a time. There are (n!) ways to number (n) rows. Which one did you pick? Why? The answer in such SQL products has been to use whatever the physical order of the physical table happened to be. That nonrelational phrase "physical order" again!

But it is actually worse than that. If the same query is executed again, but with new statistics or after an index has been dropped or added, the new execution plan could bring the result set back in a different physical order.

Can you explain from a logical model why the same rows in the second query get different pseudo-keys? In the relational model, they should be treated the same if all the values of all the attributes are identical and each row models the same object as it did before.

1.2.5   Kinds of Keys

Now for a little more practice than theory. Here is my classification of types of keys. It is based on common usage.

1.   A natural key is a subset of attributes that occur in a table and act as a unique identifier. They are seen by the user. You can go to the external reality or a trusted source and verify them. You would also like to have some validation rule. Example: UPC codes on consumer goods (read the package barcode), which can be validated with a check digit, a manufacturer's website, or a tool (geographical coordinates validate with a GPS tool).

2.   An artificial key is an extra attribute added to the table that is seen by the user. It does not exist in the external reality, but can be verified for syntax or check digits inside itself. It is up to the DBA to maintain a trusted source for them inside the enterprise. Example: the open codes in the UPC scheme to which a user can assign products made inside the store. The most common example is grocery stores that have bakeries or delicatessens

inside the stores. The check digits still work, but you have to define and verify them inside your own enterprise.

If you have to construct a key yourself, it takes time to design them, to invent a validation rule, set up audit trails, and so forth. Yes, doing things right takes time and work. Not like just popping an autonumbering on every table in the schema, is it?

3.   An "exposed physical locator" is not based on attributes in the data model but in the physical storage and is exposed to the user. There is no reasonable way to predict it or verify it, since it usually comes from the physical state of the hardware at the time of data insertion. The system obtains a value through some physical process in the hardware totally unrelated to the logical data model.

Just because autonumbering does not hold a track/sector address (like Oracle's ROWID) does not make it a logical key. A hash points to a table with the address. An index (the mechanism in autonumbering) resolves to the target address via pointer chains. If you rehash or reindex, the physical locator has to resolve to the new physical location.

4.   Surrogate keys were defined in a quote from Dr. E. F. Codd: "...Database users may cause the system to generate or delete a surrogate, but they have no control over its value, nor is its value ever displayed to them ..." (Dr. E. F. Codd in *ACM Transactions on Database Systems*, pp. 409–410), and in Codd, E. F., "Extending the Database Relational Model to Capture More Meaning," *ACM Transactions on Database Systems*, 4(4), 1979, pp. 397–434.

This means that a surrogate ought to act like an index: created by the user, managed by the system, and NEVER seen by a user. That means never used in queries, DRI, or anything else that a user does.

Codd also wrote the following:

There are three difficulties in employing user-controlled keys as permanent surrogates for entities.

1.   The actual values of user-controlled keys are determined by users and must therefore be subject to change by them (e.g., if two companies merge, the two employee databases might be combined with the result that some or all of the serial numbers might be changed.)

2.   Two relations may have user-controlled keys defined on distinct domains (e.g., one uses Social Security, while

the other uses employee serial numbers) and yet the entities denoted are the same.

3.   It may be necessary to carry information about an entity either before it has been assigned a user-controlled key value or after it has ceased to have one (e.g., an applicant for a job and a retiree).

These difficulties have the important consequence that an equi-join on common key values may not yield the same result as a join on common entities. A solution—proposed in Chapter 4 and more fully in Chapter 14—is to introduce entity domains that contain system-assigned surrogates.

Database users may cause the system to generate or delete a surrogate, but they have no control over its value, nor is its value ever displayed to them....

—Codd, in ACM TODS, pp. 409–410).

1.2.6   Desirable Properties of Relational Keys

In an article at *www.TDAN.com* by Mr. James P. O'Brien (Maximum Business Solutions), the author outlined desirable properties of relational keys. I agree with almost everything he had to say, but I have to take issue on some points.

I agree that natural keys can be inherent characteristics, such as DNA signatures, fingerprints, and (longitude, latitude). I also agree that the ISO-3779 Vehicle Identification Number (VIN) can be a natural key. What makes all of these natural keys is a property that Mr. O'Brien does not mention: they can be verified and validated in the real world.

When I worked for a state prison system, we moved inmates by fingerprinting them because we had to be absolutely sure that we did not let someone out before their time, or keep them in prison longer than their sentence. If I want to verify (longitude, latitude) as an attribute, I can walk to the location, pull out a GPS tool, and push a button. The same principle holds for colors, weights, and other physical measurements that can be done with instruments.

The VIN is a bit different. I can look at the format and determine if it is a valid VIN—Honda does not make a Diablo and Lamborghini does not make a Civic. However, if the parts of the VIN are in the correct format, I need to contact the automobile manufacturer and ask if the VIN was actually issued. If Honda made 1,000,000 Civics, then a VIN for the 1,000,001th Civic is a fake.

Validate internally, and verify externally. But this leads to the concept of a "trusted source" that can give us verification. And that leads to the question, "How trusted?" is my source.

My local grocery story believes that the check I cash is good and that the address on the check and driver's license number are correct. If I produced a license with a picture of Britney Spears that did not match the name on the check, they would question it. But as long as the photo ID looks good and has a bald white male who looks like "Ming the Merciless" from the old Flash Gordon comic strips on it, they will probably cash the check.

When I travel to certain countries, I need a birth certificate and a passport. This is a higher degree of trust. For some security things I need to provide fingerprints. For some medical things, I need to provide DNA—that is probably the highest degree of trust, since in theory you could make a clone from my sample, *á la* many science fiction stories.

The points I want to challenge in Mr. O'Brien's article are that a natural key

1.   Must have an invariant value

2.   Must have an invariant format

1.2.7   Unique But Not Invariant

In 2007, the retail industry in the United States switched from the 10-digit UPC barcode on products to the 13-digit EAN system, and the International Standard Book Number (ISBN) is falling under the same scheme. Clearly, this violates Mr. O'Brien's condition. But the retail industry is still alive and well in the United States. Why?

The most important property of a key is that it must ensure uniqueness. But that uniqueness does not have to be eternal. Nor does the format have to be fixed for all time. It simply has to be verifiable at the time I ask my question.

The retail industry has assured that the old and the new barcodes will identify the same products by a carefully planned migration path. This is what allowed us to change the values and the formats of one of the most common identifiers on earth. The migration path started with changing the length of the old UPC code columns from 10 to 13 and padding them with leftmost zeros.

In a well-designed RDBMS product, referenced keys are easy to change. Thus, I might have an Inventory table that is referenced in the

Orders table. The physical implementation is a pointer in the Orders table back to the single value in the Inventory table. The main problem is getting the data types correctly altered.

Mr. O'Brien argues for exposed physical locators when

- No suitable natural key for the entity exists.

- A concatenated key is so lengthy that performance is adversely affected.

The first condition—no suitable natural key exists—is a violation of Aristotle's law of identity (to be is to be something in particular) and the result of a bad RDBMS design flaw. Or the designer is too lazy to look for industry standards.

But if you honestly cannot find an industry standard and have to create an identifier, then you need to take the time to design one, with validation and verification rules, instead of returning to 1950s-style magnetic tape files' use of an exposed physical locator.

The argument that a concatenated key that is "too long" forgets that you have to ensure the uniqueness of that key to maintain data integrity anyway. Your performance choices are to either have the SQL engine produce a true surrogate or to design an encoding that is shorter for performance. The VIN has a lot of data (country, company, make, model, plant, etc.) encoded in its 17-character string for verification.

1.3   Tables as Entities

An entity is a physical or conceptual "thing" that has meaning in itself. A person, a sale, or a product would be an example. In a relational database, an entity is defined by its attributes, which are shown as values in columns in rows in a table.

To remind users that tables are sets of entities, I like to use collective or plural nouns that describe the function of the entities within the system for the names of tables. Thus "Employee" is a bad name because it is singular; "Employees" is a better name because it is plural; "Personnel" is best because it is collective noun and does not summon up a mental picture of individual persons, but of an abstraction (see *SQL Programming Style*, ISBN: 0-12088-797-5, for more details).

If you have tables with exactly the same structure, then they are sets of the same kind of elements. But you should have only one set for each kind of data element! Files, on the other hand, were physically separate units of storage that could be alike—each tape or disk file represents a step in the procedure, such as moving from raw data to edited data, sorting and splitting the data for different reports, and finally sending it to archival storage.

In SQL, this physical movement should be replaced by a logical status code in a single table. Even better, perhaps the RDBMS will change status code for you without your actions. For example, an account over 120 days past due is changed to "collections status" and we send the account holder a computer-generated letter.

1.4   Tables as Relationships

A relationship is shown in a table by columns that reference one or more entity tables. Without the entities, the relationship has no meaning, but the relationship can have attributes of its own. For example, a show business contract might have an agent, a studio, and a movie star. The method of payment is an attribute of the contract itself, and not of any of the three parties.

These tables will always have FOREIGN KEY references to the entities in the relationship and DRI actions to enforce the business rules.

1.5   Statements Are Not Procedures

Declarative programming is not like procedural programming. We seek to keep the data correct by using constraints that exclude the bad data at the start. We also want to use data rather than computations to solve problems, because SQL is a data retrieval language and not a computational one.

As an example of the difference, the PASS-2006 SQL Server group conference has a talk on Common Language Resources (CLR) in that product. This is a proprietary Microsoft "feature" that lets you embed any of several procedural or OO languages inside the database. The example the speaker used was putting a Regular Expression object to parse an e-mail address as a constraint.

The overhead was high, execution time was slow, and the regular expression parser called might or might not match the SIMILAR TO predicate in ANSI/ISO Standard SQL, depending on the CLR language used. But the real point was that needless complexity could have been avoided. Using a TRANSLATION (or nested REPLACE() functions if your SQL does not support ANSI/ISO Standard SQL) in a CHECK() constraint could have prevented bad e-mail addresses in the first place.

Declarative programming prevents bad data, while procedural programming corrects it.

1.6   Molecular, Atomic, and Subatomic Data Elements

If you grew up as a kid in the 1950s, you will remember those wonderful science fiction movies that always had the word "atomic" in the title, like *Atomic Werewolf from Mars* or worse. We were still in awe of the atomic bomb and were assured that we would soon be driving atomic cars and airplanes. It was sort of like the adjectives "extreme" or "agile" are today. Nobody knows quite what it means, but it sounds really, really cool.

Technically, "atom" is the Greek word meaning "without parts" or "indivisible." The original idea was that if you kept dividing a physical entity into smaller and smaller pieces, you would eventually hit some lower bound. If you went beyond that lower bound, you would destroy that entity.

When we describe First Normal Form (1NF) we say that a data element should hold atomic or scalar values. What we mean is that if I try to pull out "subatomic parts" from the value in a column, it loses meaning.

Scalar is used as a synonym for atomic, but it actually is a little trickier. It requires that there be a scale of measurement from which the value is drawn and from which it takes meaning. It is a bit stricter, and a good database designer will try to establish the scales of measurement in his or her data model.

Most newbies assume that if they have a column in an SQL table, this automatically makes the value atomic. A column cannot hold a data structure, like an array, linked list, or another table, and it has to be of a simple data type. Ergo, it must be an atomic value. This was very easy up to Standard SQL-92, since the language had no support for those structures. This is no longer true in SQL-99, which introduces several very nonrelational "features," and to which several vendors added their own support for arrays, nested tables, and variant data types.

Failure to understand atomic versus scalar data leads to design flaws that split the data so as to hide or destroy facts, much like splitting atomic structures destroys or changes them.

1.6.1   Table Splitting

The worst way to design a schema is probably to split an attribute along tables. If I were to design a schema with a "Male_Personnel" and a "Female_Personnel" table or one table per department, you would see the fallacy instantly. Here an attribute, gender, or department, is turned into metadata for defining tables.

In the old punch cards and tape file system days, we physically moved data to such selective files to make processing easier. It was how we got parallelism and did a selection. The most common split is based on time—one table per day, week, month, or year. The old IBM magnetic tape library systems used a label based on a "yyddd" format—Julianized day within a two-digit year. That label was used to control when a tape was refreshed—magnetic tape degrades over time due to cosmic rays and heat, so tapes had to be reread and rewritten periodically. Reports were also based on time periods, so the physical tapes served the same filtering function as a WHERE clause with a date range.

The next most common split is geographical. Each physical location in the enterprise is modeled as its own table, even though they are the same kind of entity. Again, this can be traced back to the old days, when each branch office prepared its own reports on paper, then on punch cards, and then on magnetic tapes for the central office.

A partitioned table is not the same thing. It is one logical, semantic unit of data; the system and not the applications maintain it. The fact that it is physically split across physical file structures has nothing to do with the semantics.

Perhaps the fact that DDL often has a mix of logical data descriptions mixed with physical implementations in vendor extensions confuses us. As an aside, I often wonder if SQL should have had a separate syntax for referential integrity, relational cardinality, membership, domain constraints, and so forth, rather than allowing them in the DDL.

1.6.2   Column Splitting

The other mistake is having an atomic attribute and splitting it into columns. As we all know from those 1950s science fiction movies, nothing good comes from splitting atoms—it could turn your brother into an atomic werewolf!

A phone number in the United States is displayed as three sections (area code, exchange, and number). Each part is useless by itself. In fact, you should include the international prefixes to make it more exact, but usually context is enough. You would not split this data element over three columns, because you search and use this value in the order that it is presented, and you use it as a whole unit. This is an atom and not a molecule.

You can also split a single data element across rows. Consider this absurd table:

```
CREATE TABLE Personnel
(worker_name CHAR(20) NOT NULL,
attribute_name CHAR(15) NOT NULL
   CHECK (attribute_name IN ('weight', 'height',
   'bowling score')),
attribute_value INTEGER NOT NULL,
PRIMARY KEY (worker_name, attribute_name));
```

The bad news is that you will see this kind of thing in the real world. One column gives metadata and the other gives a value.

Look at a subtler version of the same thing. Consider this table that mimics a clipboard upon which we record the start and finish of a task by an employee.

```
CREATE TABLE TaskList
(worker_name CHAR(20) NOT NULL,
task_nbr INTEGER NOT NULL,
task_time TIMESTAMP DEFAULT CURRENT_TIMESTAMP NOT NULL,
task_status CHAR(1) DEFAULT 'S' NOT NULL
   CHECK (task_status IN ('S', 'F')),
PRIMARY KEY (worker_name, task_nbr, task_status));
```

In order to know if a task is finished (task_status = 'F'), we first need to know that it was started (task_status = 'S'). That means a self-join in a constraint. A good heuristic is that a self-joined constraint means that the schema is bad, because something is split and has to be reassembled in the constraint.

Let's rewrite the DDL with the idea that a task is a data element.

```
CREATE TABLE TaskList
(worker_name CHAR(20) NOT NULL,
task_nbr INTEGER NOT NULL,
task_start_time TIMESTAMP DEFAULT CURRENT_TIMESTAMP NOT NULL,
task_end_time TIMESTAMP, -- null means in process
 PRIMARY KEY (worker_name, task_nbr));
```

Temporal split is the most common example, but there are other ways to split a data element over rows in the same table.

1.6.3   Temporal Splitting

The most common newbie error is splitting a temporal data element into (year, month, day) columns or as (year, month) or just (year) columns. There is a problem with temporal data. By its nature, it is not atomic; it is a continuum. A continuum has no atomic parts; it can infinitely subdivide. Thus, the year '2005' is shorthand for the pair ('2005-01-01 00:00:00', '2005-12-31 23:59:59.999 …') where we live with the precision that our SQL product has for the open end on the left. It includes every point in between. That means every uncountable infinite one of them.

The Greeks did not have a concept of a continuum, and this lead to Zeno's famous paradoxes. Hey, this is a database book, but you can Google Greek philosophy for yourself. In particular, look for "Resolving Zeno's Paradoxes" by W. I. McLaughin (*Scientific American*, November 1994).

1.6.4   Faking Non-1NF Data

So, how do programmers "fake it" within the syntax of SQL when they want non-1NF data semantics to mimic a familiar record layout? One way is to use a group of columns where all the members of the group have the same semantic value; that is, they represent the same data element. Consider the table of an employee and his children:

```
CREATE TABLE Employees
(emp_nbr INTEGER NOT NULL,
emp_name CHAR(30) NOT NULL,
...
child1 CHAR(30), birthday1 DATE, sex1 CHAR(1),
child2 CHAR(30), birthday2 DATE, sex2 CHAR(2),
child3 CHAR(30), birthday3 DATE, sex3 CHAR(1),
child4 CHAR(30), birthday4 DATE, sex4 CHAR(1));
```

This looks like the layouts of many existing file system records in COBOL and other 3GL languages. The birthday and sex information for each child is part of a repeated group and therefore violates 1NF. This is faking a four-element array in SQL; the index just happens to be part of the column name!

Very clearly, the dependents should have been in their own table. There would be no upper limit on family size, aggregation would be much easier, the schema would have fewer NULLs, and so forth.

Suppose I have a table with the quantity of a product sold in each month of a particular year, and I originally built the table to look like this:

```
CREATE TABLE Abnormal
(product CHAR(10) NOT NULL PRIMARY KEY,
month_01 INTEGER, -- null means
month_02 INTEGER,
...
month_12 INTEGER);
```

and I wanted to flatten it out into a more normalized form, like this:

```
CREATE TABLE Normal
(product CHAR(10) NOT NULL,
month_nbr INTEGER NOT NULL,
qty INTEGER NOT NULL,
PRIMARY KEY (product, month_nbr));
```

I can use the statement

```
INSERT INTO Normal (product, month_nbr, qty)
SELECT product, 1, month_01
  FROM Abnormal
 WHERE month_01 IS NOT NULL
UNION ALL
SELECT product, 2, month_02
  FROM Abnormal
WHERE month_02 IS NOT NULL
...
UNION ALL
SELECT product, 12, month_12
  FROM Abnormal
 WHERE bin_12 IS NOT NULL;
```

While a UNION ALL expression is usually slow, this has to be run only once to load the normalized table, and then the original table can be dropped.

1.6.5   Molecular Data Elements

A molecule is a unit of matter made up of atoms in a particular arrangement. So let me define a unit of data made up of scalar or atomic values in a particular arrangement. The principle characteristic is that the whole loses precise meaning when any part is removed. Note that I said precise meaning—it can still have some meaning, but it now refers to a set, possibly infinite, of values instead of single value or data element.

One example would be (longitude, latitude) pairs kept in separate columns. Together they give you a precise location, a geographical point (within a certain error), but apart they describe a line or a circle with an infinite number of points.

Yes, you could model a location as a single column with the pair forced inside it, but the arithmetic would be a screaming pain. You would have to write a special parser to read that column, effectively making it a user-defined data type. Making it a "two-atom molecule" makes much more sense. But the point is that semantically it is one data element, namely a geographical location.

Likewise, the most common newbie error is to put a person's name into one column, rather than having `last_name`, `first_name`, and `middle_name` columns. The error is easy to understand; a name is a (relatively) unique identifier for a person and identifiers are semantically atomic. But in practice, sorting, searching, and matching are best done with the atoms exposed.

1.6.6   Isomer Data Elements

The worst situation is isomer data elements. An isomer is a molecule that has the same atoms as another molecule but arranged a little differently. The most common examples are right- and left-handed versions of the same sugar. One creature can eat the right-handed sugar but not the left-handed isomer.

The simple example is a table with a mix of scales, say temperatures in both Celsius and Fahrenheit. This requires two columns, one for the number and one for the scale. I can then write VIEWs to display the numbers on either scale, depending on the user. Here the same semantic value is modeled dynamically by a VIEW. The correct design would have picked one and only one scale, but bear with me; things get worse.

Consider mixed currencies. On a given date, I get a deposit in one of many currencies, which I need to convert to other currencies, all based on the daily exchange rate.

```
CREATE TABLE Deposits
(..
deposit_amt DECIMAL (20,2) NOT NULL,
```

```
currency_code CHAR(3) NOT NULL, -- use ISO code
deposit_date DATE DEFAULT CURRENT_DATE NOT NULL,
..);
CREATE TABLE ExchangeRates
(..
currency_code CHAR(3) NOT NULL, -- use ISO code
exchange_date DATE DEFAULT CURRENT_DATE NOT NULL,
exchange_rate DECIMAL (8,4)NOT NULL,
..);
```

Semantically, the deposit had one and only one value at that time. But I express it in U.S. dollars, and my friend thinks in euros. There is no single hard formula for converting the currencies, so you have to use a join.

```
CREATE VIEW DepositsDollars (.., dollar_amt, )
AS
SELECT .., (D1.deposit_amt * E1.exchange_rate),
 FROM Deposits AS D1, ExchangeRates AS E1
 WHERE D1.deposit_date = E1.exchange_date;
```

and likewise there will be a "DepositsEuros" with a euro-amt column, and whatever else we need. The VIEWs are good, atomic scalar designs, but the underlying base tables are not!

Another approach would have been to find one unit of currency and only use it, doing the conversion on the front end. The bad news is that such an approach would have lost information about the relative positions among the currencies and been subject to rounding errors. This is not an easy problem.

1.6.7   Validating a Molecule

The major advantage of keeping each atomic data element in a column is that you can easily set up rules among them to validate the whole. For example, an address is a molecular unit of data. Within it, I can see if the city and state codes match the ZIP code.

Instead of putting such constraints into one CHECK() constraint, break it into separate constraints that have meaningful names that will show up in errors messages.

This leads to the next section and a solution for the storage versus processing problem.

CHAPTER 2

Hardware, Data Volume, and Maintaining Databases

AMAJOR FACTOR in data processing is that the hardware has changed radically in the last few years. Moore's Law is a rule of thumb that computing speed doubles every 18 months; but the principle applies to more than just processor speeds. All hardware is faster and cheaper than it has ever been and it continues to get faster and cheaper. Because storing data is cheaper, the volume of data is increasing. The question for a database is how to keep up with the changes.

In an article entitled "A Conversation with Jim Gray" (*Storage,* Vol. 1, No. 4, June 2003), Dave Patterson began the interview with the question "What is the state of storage today [2003]?"

Jim Gray's response was:

> We have an embarrassment of riches in that we're able to store more than we can access. Capacities continue to double each year, while access times are improving at 10 percent per year. So, we have a vastly larger storage pool, with a relatively narrow pipeline into it.
>
> We're not really geared for this. Having lots of RAM helps. We can cache a lot in main memory and reduce secondary storage access. But the fundamental problem is that we are building a larger reservoir with more or less the same diameter pipe coming out of the reservoir. We have a much harder time accessing things inside the reservoir.

2.1   Parallelism

That was 2003. In 2007, *InformationWeek* ran an article entitled "Where's the Software to Catch Up to Multicore Computing?" (*http://www.informationweek.com/news/showArticle.jhtml?articleID=197001130*) after INTEL had announced a business strategy to have 100 percent of its server processors shipped with multicore processors by end of 2007. IBM's chief architect Catherine Crawford stated that "We will never, ever return to single processor computers."

The current (this is written in 2007) dual-core processors are a response to success. Intel and AMD pushed the clock speeds towards 3 GHz. But the trade-off was more energy consumption, which lead to more heat, which lead to less efficiency and performance. Parallelism was the easy way out. We know how to make chips, and the multicore chips required no technological breakthrough. These chips, can simultaneously perform calculations on two streams of data, which increases total efficiency and speed when running multiple programs at conventional clock speeds. This approach is great for multithreaded software, such as video and audio applications.

The Relational Model is based on sets, and one of the rules of finite sets is that the union of a partition is the original set. If you want to see this in symbols:

```
(∩ᵢ Aᵢ) = Ø defines a partitioning of set A
(∪ᵢ Aᵢ) = A is the union of all the partitions of set A
```

This means that for most of the operations I do on a row in a table, I can do them in parallel. Again, if you like symbols:

```
∪ᵢ f(Aᵢ) = f(A)
```

Nothing is faster than simultaneous. Many years ago Jerry Pournelle, a columnist in *BYTE* magazine and an award-winning science fiction author, invented Pournelle's Laws and observations, one of which is: You want one CPU per task when hardware is cheap enough.

In terms of a database, the extreme of Pournelle's Law would be to have one processor handling each row of a table to either reject or pass that row to an intermediate result set managed by its own processor. Then the intermediate results sets would be joined together to produce a final result set by another group of processors.

In the above-quoted *InformationWeek* article, Catherine Crawford explained why current is not going to run well on new multicore processors, because it was never built with parallelism in mind.

About the same time as this article appeared, the April 2007 edition of *Dr. Dobb's Journal* (*www.ddj.com*) ran an article on the IBM Cell Processor ("Programming the Cell Processor," by Daniele Paolo Scarpazza, Oreste Villa, and Fabrizio Petrini), which is used in the Xbox video game machine. The Cell contains one general-purpose 64-bit processor, called the power processing element (PPE), that uses the PowerPC instruction set. Eight simpler processors, called the synergistic processor elements (SPE), are connected to it on a bus.

The SPEs have 128 registers and a "single instruction, multiple data" (SIMD) instruction set that work in parallel. Having that much register space means that you can unroll a loop in main storage for speed. Instead of having cache, there is a 256-KB scratchpad memory called the local storage (LS), and all variables have to be kept in it.

The example program used in the article was depth-first graph search. The single-processor version was written in 60 lines of C code, and the Cell version required about 1,200 lines of rather complex code. However, the single-processor program could handle 24 million edges in the graph; the parallel version processed 538 million edges.

2.2 Cheap Main Storage

Traditionally, main storage (older programmers called this "core memory" or "primary storage" and called tapes and disk "secondary storage," while younger programmers call it "memory" and "storage," respectively) was fast, but small and expensive in a computer. This is no longer true, since it is made from the same materials as the processors. The real problem today is managing the address space once you have reached a physical limit in the software and/or hardware. Here we have random access that does not require moving a physical read/write head to locate data.

There is still an open question as to when (or if) the cost of solid-state storage will become lower than magnetic media. To quote from Jim Gray's interview:

> From about 1960 to 1990, the magnetic material density improved at something like 35 percent per year—a little slower than Moore's Law. In fact, there was a lot of discussion that RAM megabyte per dollar would surpass disks because RAM was following Moore's Law and disks were evolving much more slowly.
>
> But starting about 1989, disk densities began to double each year. Rather than going slower than Moore's Law, they grew faster. Moore's Law is something like 60 percent a year, and disk densities improved 100 percent per year.

Today disk-capacity growth continues at this blistering rate, maybe a little slower. But disk access, which is to say, "Move the disk arm to the right cylinder and rotate the disk to the right block," has improved about tenfold. The rotation speed has gone up from 3,000 to 15,000 RPM, and the access times have gone from 50 milliseconds down to 5 milliseconds. That's a factor of 10. Bandwidth has improved about 40-fold, from 1 megabyte per second to 40 megabytes per second. Access times are improving about 7 to 10 percent per year. Meanwhile, densities have been improving at 100 percent per year.

2.3   Solid-State Disk

This has switched around again. The Internet added another aspect to data volume. Databases have to service high-demand networks. Databases are constantly read from or written to by multiple sources across the network. Lots of fast main storage and high-speed disks are helpful, but demand is growing even faster.

According to StorageReview.com, the fastest hard disk drives have peak access times of ~5 milliseconds. Solid-state disks have a 15-microsecond access time, or ~250 times faster than hard disk drives. The solid-state disk needs backup batteries to persist data in RAM, but battery technology has also improved. It is also not a huge power demand. For absolute safety, the data in the solid disk can be moved to permanent storage with extended redundancy checks.

2.4   Cheaper Secondary and Tertiary Storage

Bulk storage is also cheaper and faster today. Traditionally, secondary storage meant disk drives that required moving a physical read/write head to locate data. When you connected to the database, the system connected to these drives and got ready to move data in and out of primary storage to and from them.

In 2007, the traditional disk drive is being challenged by solid-state memory. When the right price point is hit, there will be little speed difference between primary and secondary data.

Tertiary or archival storage is the slowest storage on a system, and it is usually off-line. That means the user has to deliberately "mount" or "dismount" the media to get to the data. This is for data that is not often used or that has to be secured in another physical location for whatever reasons.

The use of blue lasers, vertical magnetic recording, and other technology gives us physically denser storage units, which means more can be transferred per second. We ought to be very thankful to the video industry for pushing these technologies.

2.5   The Data Changed

All of the above-mentioned technology would seem to imply that storage is not a problem any more. That is not quite true; the nature of the data we keep changed. More and more data is not being kept in text, but as video, MP3, and other media formats. Look up the bandwidth and volumes that video is using on the Internet.

These new formats require software to compact it and to convert it to other formats, as well as very specialized software to search it. For example, facial recognition is a specialized area in pattern matching. The same is true for fingerprints, maps, text, and DNA-matching software. Most of these new data formats have no ANSI/ISO Standards yet, and are not even close to a common searching language.

The traditional RDBMS will be around for a long time to come, but it quite likely to consume only a small part of the physical storage in the future with its traditional data types. Instead of selling you pairs of shoes by mimicking a paper catalog order form, websites let you zoom and rotate the product image and change the color. In a few years, you will pull up a personal avatar, walk around a virtual store, and try on a full outfit. If you have joined Second Life or other community websites, you have already gotten a taste of what is to come.

2.6   The Mindset Has Not Changed

Everyone is aware of the changes in hardware simply because they can see it is consumer goods. But people still try to "squeeze the bits" in their systems. A common application you will see posted on newsgroups is a recurrent relationship of some kind. The most common are probably temporal events, like scheduled meetings ("Every Friday at 14:00 Hrs", "First of each month", "The 15th of each month," etc.), which we will discuss in Chapter 9.

The user will try to program the formula for these events and values into one or more columns in the table itself. In the case of the temporal functions, this has to be highly proprietary, but other functions are not easy either. There are two common kludges for this approach:

1. The formula is kept as text and executed dynamically one row at a time, since it is getting parameters from each row. The formula has to be in an external procedural language that

handles dynamic execution or in the vendor's proprietary 3GL. The DBA now has to handle, maintain, and validate all of this non-SQL code.

2.   One or more columns hold the constants for the formula and plug them into the SQL statement that uses them. While this avoids dynamic execution, it is in many ways worse. When the formula was written in text, you could see all of it at once. Now, you have to gather the pieces of it from the table in the DDL and the statement in the DML.

These kludges make new SQL programmers comfortable because they can see procedural code and they are still in that mindset. They might have done that "store and change code text on the fly" trick in an interpreted language like BASIC or one of the scripting languages. It was not a good coding practice in the interpreted languages, either. But it is an old technique—and we care about both good *and bad* habits to the new environment.

The reason most often given for doing this elaborate coding is to save storage space! Personnel costs are the major expense in a modern IT system. Only cabling is cheaper than storage. To paraphrase a famous movie quotation from *The Outcast* (1954, directed by William Witney), "Here's a dime. Buy yourself a gigabyte."

The estimate is the 80 percent or more of the total cost of any of any system in the maintenance. This is probably a low estimate for a database. A database serves multiple applications and usually outlives a lot of them. It has to be ready to evolve, and that ability has to be designed into it at the start. There are four general kinds of maintenance for traditional procedural software that also apply to databases:

1.   *Corrective*. This is traditional bug fixing in the procedural world. DML code in SQL can also have bugs, but we can also screw up DDL and DCL code in the other sublanguages. We have to look for bugs in the entire system, not within a single module of code.

2.   *Adaptive*. A good database seldom stays in one release of one SQL product on one piece of hardware. People who write SQL that way are in effect saying that their enterprise is planning for stagnation or failure. This is why a good SQL programmer avoids proprietary code whenever possible.

3.   *Perfective*. This is the removal of errors in the data. In the database world, it goes by the name data quality and has

become a topic in its own right. Look for books and articles by Jack Olson, Dr. Thomas Redman, and Larry English.

4. *Preventive.* The hardware side of prevention is well understood. Software for making backups, storing log files, disk defragmenting, and physical integrity can be had from the database vendor or a third party. Preventative maintenance on the data has to come from the enterprise. This one is often a hard sell even in the procedural world. The usual slogan is "If it ain't broken, why fix it?" and we wait for the crisis that breaks the system. Planning for known changes in data, such as the switch in the United States from UPC to EAN barcodes in retail, is one example. Designing encoding schemes that can be easily extended is another.

The new SQL programmers do not see that they are in a procedural mindset any more than a fish thinks about being in water. And they do not think much beyond their immediate application (read: fishbowl). The rest of this book is a series of SQL programming examples to perhaps wake up the fish and show them the ocean.

CHAPTER 3

Data Access and Records

THE RELATIONAL MODEL and the SQL standards are not concerned with physical implementations or access methods used by actual products. Standard SQL wants to keep the language portable and predictable, no matter what the internal implementations. However, code eventually has to run on hardware, and those platforms are totally different. Programmers are mildly concerned with tricks to tune their SQL.

Job titles in IT vary with each fad, but somewhere you have a physical DBA who is very concerned with how a database is configured for performance.

In the 1980s, we attempted to create database machines such as the Britton-Lee IDM, but they never really caught on ("Database Machines: An Idea Whose Time Passed? A Critique of the Future of Database Machines" by Haran Boral and David J. DeWitt, International Workshop on Database Machines, 1983). Specialized hardware was very expensive back then, and while it is easier to make your own custom chips today, it is not in any way competitive with off-the-shelf hardware.

The SQL standard has never (and should never) specify what access method is to be used in SQL. However, the X/Open vendor consortium did issue a portability guide to try to keep the various SQLs similar enough that a user of one product would experience the least surprise when learning another. For example, we use "CREATE

INDEX ..." so that all persistent schema objects have the same "CREATE <schema object>" format, all temporary schema objects have the same "DECLARE <schema object>" format, and so forth.

3.1   Sequential Access

Many of my readers have not ever worked with or perhaps even seen a tape file system. I hope that looking at tape drives in old science fiction movies will convince you that doing random access on magnetic tape is not practical. Tapes are dying out even for archival storage today. The last major advance in the technology was a drive from IBM that archived and encrypted the data in the hardware.

So, why do I bother to mention it? Because the spirit of the magnetic tape files lives on, long after the body is gone. If you scan any SQL newsgroup, you will find newbie programmers using temporary tables and cursors to mimic tapes. This approach to data is very natural to programmers who learned to program on file systems.

3.1.1   Tape-Searching Algorithms

Imagine a sequential magnetic tape file that is in some sorted order. Your task is to locate one particular record based on the sort key. Assume that you can read forward and backward (n) records on the tape because you know the size of the records or can detect the end of one record and the beginning of the next.

How do you find one particular record? The easiest way is to read the tape from front to back and stop when you fetch it. If all records are equally likely to be requested, then you can expect to read about half the records on the tape for a request.

A better way is to go to the start of the file and jump ahead (k) records. Then see if the fetched record is the target; if not, is it ahead of or behind you? Now make a second forward or backward jump based on a new value of (k). Repeat as needed until you either get a hit or a clear failure. The problem is now to get an algorithm for finding (k); in most cases, the square root of (k) is a good guess for uniformly distributed data. You jump ahead in steps of the square root of the size of the file. If the desired value is hit, then stop. Otherwise, go past the search value. This isolates the target between the last two records probed. Since the tape drive could read backwards, you reverse direction and read in steps the size of the square root of the square of the file size. Repeat this process until you succeed or fail.

If the sort key was not uniformly distributed, then we had more complex algorithms to do probes in uneven steps based on the actual distribution. There were other tricks that involved special sorting orders on the tapes to get the most often used values toward the front of the file, but these were only for special cases.

New programmers ought to take the time to look at tape file systems to see what had to be done within the limitations of sequential access. In particular, the Polyphase Merge Sort is quite clever. It disperses the records onto several tape drives, ensuring that the count of records on each drive is a Fibonacci number, and then merges these sequences of records until only one sequence remains.

3.2 Indexes

Indexes (or indices to use another plural form) came when sequential file systems moved to disk. There is a rule in engineering that the new technology begins by mimicking the previous technology until it can find its own voice. Thus, the first movies had a fixed camera position to mimic a stage play until W. D. Griffith invented close-ups, trucking shots, dissolves, and most of the techniques we take for granted in film today. The first skyscrapers were built to look like Greek temples because that was what important public buildings looked like. You can easily add to this list or read any of the wonderful books by Henry Petroski on engineering (*The Evolution of Useful Things: How Everyday Artifacts—From Forks and Pins to Paper Clips and Zippers—Came to Be as They Are*, ISBN-0-679-74039-2, 1994).

Imagine an old-fashioned unabridged dictionary with notches or "thumb indexes" cut into the outside edge of the pages that let you quickly flip open to the start of the words that begin with a given letter.

The first computer indexes were modeled after the unabridged dictionary. The file was kept in sorted order and a small index file would have the search key value and the physical location within the master file of that record. The programmer had to explicitly maintain the index in his code. Subroutines would position the disk drive's read/write heads on or near the record desired without having to read the file starting at the first record. The assumption was that the file was in some sorted order, so the disk could mimic the tape search algorithm given in Section 3.1.1, but with a list of "jump points" held in the index.

3.2.1　Single-Table Indexes

A bit later, the index files were arranged into various tree structures to minimize the time needed to locate the records. Instead of keeping the physical locations of a subset of the records, cheaper primary and secondary storage made it possible to keep track of all the records in a file and not depend on sequential ordering at all.

However, the trade-off was that you could spend a lot of time jumping across many tracks and sectors to get a sequential result.

Since most reporting is done in some sorted order, keeping the disk file in a physical ordering that favors sequential access has advantages. This ordering is based on contiguous allocation of tracks and sectors. The idea is that the read/write head moves as little as possible—physical movement is very slow compared to electronic transfer speeds.

Indexes have other advantages. They are usually smaller than the table that they index, so if the data you need is in the index, you can avoid scanning the base table. It is a good trick to put extra columns into an index to get what is called a "covering index" to cover the most common queries in your environment.

Another advantage is that they are orderly creatures, which makes it easy to locate the extrema (MIN() and MAX()) of a column. Going one step further, the nodes in the index tree can carry other information, such as the number of rows with values less than or greater than the current node.

The trade-off is that indexes have redundant data in them and that as the size of the database grows, the depth of the tree increases and requires more and more probes to work.

3.2.2　Multiple-Table Indexes

The single-table indexes came first because a lot of SQL products were built on top of existing file systems. Today, several products such as Sybase (née WATCOM) SQL Anywhere have indexing that, in effect, "prejoins" tables in the same schema. A value appears once as a PRIMARY KEY or UNIQUE constraint in a base table. Then when it is in a REFERENCE as a foreign key, instead of putting a redundant copy of the value in the referencing table, we put a pointer to the referenced table's row.

Since a lot of joins are done with foreign keys to primary key, this is a real improvement in performance. The real payoff comes from being able to quickly do declarative referential integrity (DRI) actions such as a CASCADE ON UPDATE, CASCADE ON DELETE, and so forth. It also

means that when a PRIMARY KEY is changed, such as converting
from the old 10-digit to the new 13-digit International Standard Book
Number (ISBN) or the UPC codes to EAN, you make one and only one
change. The pointers will simply go to the new value in the PRIMARY
KEY base table and find a new data type and value. This also means
that long keys are not a real problem for accessing data.

3.2.3   Type of Indexes

From a programmer's viewpoint, there are two kinds of indexes: primary
and secondary. A primary index exists to assure uniqueness and has
to be there for the schema to have data integrity. A secondary index is
added for performance improvements.

Indexes require physical storage requirements, and if you are not
careful, they can be bigger than the raw data. Indexes require execution
time, especially noticeable during data loading and update, since they
have to be updated, too.

Performance can become unpredictable, since the queries that can
use indices are fast, but a similar or identical query without an index
can be slow. This tends to push people to write queries that are tuned to
the current configuration, rather than useful ones.

The cost of indexing everything is usually prohibitive. This means
someone has to design the indexes, and they need to design them
for the system as a whole rather than just for one application—in
short, we need a smart DBA. But even that is not enough. Finding the
optimal indexing arrangement is known to be NP-complete. For references see: D. Comer, "The Difficulty of Optimum Index Selection,"
ACM Transactions on Database Systems, 3(4):440–445, 1978; and
G. Paitetsky-Shapiro, "The Optimal Selection of Secondary Indexes is
NP-Complete," *SIGMOD Record*, 13(2):72–75, 1983.

This does not mean that you cannot optimize indexing for a
particular database schema and set of input queries, but it does mean
that you cannot write a program that will do it for all possible relational
databases and query sets.

3.3   Hashing

The basic idea of hashing is that given input values, the hashing
function will return a physical storage address. Writing hashing
functions is not easy. If you are very lucky, the function can do this
directly with your hardware, but it is more likely to return an address
inside a hash table. The hash table is an array of physical addresses

that fit into main storage which indexed by the hash function, so that "HashBucket[hash(key)]=physical location".

There are many kinds of hashing functions, and you can start with a review of them in V. Y. Lum, P. S. T. Yuen, and M. Dodd, "Key-to-Address Transformation Techniques: A Fundamental Performance Study," *Communications of the ACM,* April 1971, pp. 228–239.

3.3.1   Digit Selection

The simplest hashing algorithm is to concatenate a subset of digits in a string. This subset does not have to be contiguous, but if you know that a particular set of digits is uniformly random, the algorithm can be quite good.

This is actually used in department stores when you go to pick up an order. Instead of asking for your name or a long order number, the clerk asks for the last two digits of your telephone number. They then go to a set of pigeonhole bins numbered from "00" to "99" and sequentially search for your folder. People without phone numbers are placed in "00" by convention.

3.3.2   Division Hashing

The key value is simply divided by a prime number. The most common choice is the greatest prime that you can use to build an array in main storage that is less than the greatest key value. Surprisingly, in practice a prime with no small factors ($f < 20$) works quite well.

3.3.3   Multiplication Hashing

The key value is squared and the middle digits are used. The middle digits are the important trick in this method. The rightmost digits will be the square of the last digit in the original key value.

3.3.4   Folding

Several subsets of digits are taken from the key and added together. Consider the key 987654321. We break it into four-digit groups and total them: (0009 + 8765 + 4321) = 13095. These totals can fall between 0 and 20007. If that range is a problem, I can apply division or multiplication to the total.

3.3.5   Table Lookups

If you have a limited set of tokens, you can create a simple lookup table that gives a hashing result. For example, Cichelli created a simple minimal perfect hashing function for the keywords in the Pascal programming language that uses the length, the first letter, and the last letter of the word (R. J. Cichelli, "Minimal Perfect Hash Functions Made Simple," *Communications of the ACM,* 23(1), January 1980).

If you search the literature, you will find a lot of work being done with minimal perfect hash functions for databases. It is possible because of faster computations in the hardware as well as decades of research. It is possible to create minimal perfect hash functions in polynomial time with a single processor model of computations. Here are two references: T. J. Sager, "A Polynomial Time Generator for Minimal Perfect Hash Functions," *Communications of the ACM*, 28(5), pp. 523–532, May 1985; and Edward A. Fox, Lenwood S. Heath, Qi Fan Chen, Amjad M. Daoud, "Practical Minimal Perfect Hash Functions For Large Databases," *Communications of the ACM*, 35(1), pp. 105–121, January 1992.

3.3.6   Collisions

If two or more input values have the same hash value ("hash clash" or "collision"), then they are put into the same "bucket" in the hash table, or they are run through another hashing function.

If the index is on a unique column, a great situation is what is called a perfect hashing function—each value hashes to a unique physical storage address. But there can be some empty spaces in the hash table. If there are no empty spaces in the hash table, it is a minimal perfect hashing function. It is always possible to have a perfect hashing function for a static set of values. But computations can be complicated. Balancing this complexity, we have improved hardware and you will see more research on using perfect and minimal perfect hashing functions for general use in databases.

A hashing function for a nonunique column will always have collisions. This is a good thing when you are trying to do aggregate functions on the data.

One of the most common methods is to build a linked list that has its head in the hash table. The list is then read from head to tail to find all the rows with a nonunique value or until the desired unique value is located.

Rehashing is another method. The key is hashed several different ways and then each of the hash table locations produced is checked for availability. Producing five candidate hash keys seems to be a good choice for large amounts of data, if they all use the right choice of prime numbers.

3.4   Bit Vector Indexes

The fact that a particular occurrence of an entity has a particular value for a particular attribute is represented as a single bit in a vector or array. Predicates are handled by doing Boolean bit operations on the arrays. These techniques are very fast for large amounts of data and are used by the SAND (née Nucleus) database engine from Sand Technology and Foxpro's Rushmore indexes.

3.5   Parallel Access

As we mentioned before, there have been attempts at commercial database engines built on proprietary hardware. They have generally lost to virtual machines on standard hardware. There are various schemes for parallelizing data retrieval, updates, and insertions. But as a generalization, they depend on having a bus that connects multiple processors that are in charge of a storage device (usually a relatively cheap, smaller disk drive). Given a statement to execute, they use a proprietary algorithm to locate the data and do the work.

3.6   Row and Column Storage

There two basic ways to put a table into storage. The row storage approaches put the rows into contiguous physical locations, much like the traditional record and file systems. The database engine then extracts the columns needed for each query. The column storage approaches put the data into the database in columns and assemble the rows.

3.6.1   Row-Based Storage

Row-based storage holds the data in rows, so that you can find all the columns in one operation. The trade-off is that you have to work with a whole row at once and not just the columns you need.

However, this makes queries based on two or more columns for the same entity faster, and it improves the speed of updates, inserts, and deletes.

Row-based storage systems can be parallelized and do not have to mimic a sequential file system, although many such products do.

The bad news is that once you have architecture in place, it is not "legacy code" so much as "the family curse" code.

Teradata (*www.teradata.com*) is a very popular data warehouse product that uses hashing and was born parallel. It began as a database machine, but the current version sets up virtual machines on standard hardware. It was always designed to be parallel.

Teradata uses "shared nothing" architecture (SN). This means each node is independent and there is no single point of contention in the system. Michael Stonebraker at University of California Berkeley used the term in *Database Engineering,* 9(1), 1986. Nodes talk to each other as needed rather than being controlled from a central point. This is way the Web works, so it should not be too strange to model programmers.

Teradata uses a proprietary hashing algorithm that distributes the data values over the hardware storage as uniformly as possible, based on the number of AMPs (the nodes) in the system. If that number changes, the data is redistributed by the system. Thanks to using logical addresses rather physical addresses as you would in a conventional index model, the user never sees this. A failed node relocates its data and removes itself from the system. A new node will transfer data from the existing nodes to its local storage.

Kognitio WX_2 (née White Cross), Tandem, and Tolerant are also examples of shared nothing systems. The Kognitio WX_2 is interesting because it uses an in-memory model on 1 to 10,000 blade servers. There are no indexes; the data is scanned and kept in main storage on the servers as much as possible. The ability to drop and add nodes is much like Teradata.

3.6.2   Column-Based Storage

The trades-offs are that column-based access is usually slower to load because the source data is presented in rows or records from an external source. The payoff is that simple queries based on values in a column are very fast and require minimal internal storage.

This means a search on a particular value in a column can go directly to that column's storage and not have to scan across an entire row. This also makes data compression much easier, because a column is always of one data type. This architecture is not a problem for the bulk data loads used in data warehousing, but it is not good for OLTP with lots of row accesses and updates.

Sybase IQ is one of these databases. Given a test set of one trillion rows in 155 terabytes of input data, the built-in compression reduced actual file storage to only 55 terabytes. Clearly, this is meant for data warehouses. The trade-off for the compression and fast access is complexity for insertions.

The SAND Dynamic Nearline Architecture (SAND/DNA) engine also uses a column approach, but tokenizes the values to get speed and data compression. They use a proprietary bit vector scheme that can be searched while in compressed form. This is very good for archives, but the tokens have to be translated back into the original data values for display and to use inside expressions. But the compression encourages breaking a data column into extra columns with more detail. For example, instead of storing a full phone number as a CHAR(12) string, you can save space by splitting it into area code, exchange, and phone number columns.

3.7   JOIN Algorithms

The one operation that defines an RDBMS more than any other is a JOIN between tables. This was one of Dr. Codd's basic operators, and various forms of joins are given keywords in SQL. Every SQL engine will have internal differences, but there are some common algorithms for doing JOINs. Picking the best algorithm to use for each query is the job of the optimizer. The programmer should not spend much time worrying about those choices, but he should know something about the algorithms in the few situations where he needs to look at execution plan. All major SQL implementations have an EXPLAIN or other command that will display execution plan in a human-readable format.

In the old days, the nested-loop and the sort-merge join algorithms were the most used. Main storage was still expensive, and we were still thinking in terms of magnetic file systems. Be patient, and I will explain what those algorithms are shortly.

The research showed that the sort-merge join algorithm would be the choice when no index existed on the join columns. The nested-loop join algorithm was better when a usable index did exist.

Today, the cost, size, and speed of main storage are a fraction of what they were even a few years ago. Nobody now questions the fact that join algorithms based on hashing perform better than nested-loop or sort-merge join methods (see D. J. DeWitt and R. Gerber, "Multiprocessor Hash-Based Join Algorithms," *Proceedings of the Eleventh International Conference on Very Large Data Bases,* Stockholm, 1985: pp. 151–64).

But even today, you will find SQL Server and other products still using nested-loop and the sort-merge join algorithms. They were originally built on some existing file system and cannot escape their legacy of contiguous storage.

3.7.1 Nested-Loop Join Algorithm

The nested-loop join method is the simplest algorithm. The two tables involved are called the outer (or source) table S and the inner (or target) table T, respectively. First, each table is inspected to remove rows that cannot meet the join criteria. For example, given this skeleton query:

```
SELECT ..
  FROM T INNER JOIN S
     ON T.a = 5
        AND S.b = 7
        AND S.x = T.x;
```

we would retain only the rows in T where ($T.a = 5$) and only the rows in S where ($S.b = 7$). This filtering can be done in the first pass of the loop, or it can be done before the looping starts.

Each row of table S is compared with all the rows of the target table T against the join condition. If the join condition is satisfied, that row of S is concatenated with the matching row of T to insert a row in the result table R.

The usual way of setting up such a join is to make the source table the smaller table and the target table the larger table. The idea was that the smaller table might fit into main storage and save us disk accesses. But even if it does not, the number of accesses can be mineralized. Clearly, the time complexity of the nested-loop join algorithm is $O(S*T)$.

3.7.2 Sort-Merge Join Method

This algorithm is a little more sophisticated. First, sort the source (S) and target (T) tables on the join attributes. We know that there are $O(n * \log(n))$ nonstable sorting algorithms, such as QuickSort, and that process is well understood. It is also easy to remove rows that cannot ever match the join criteria during the sorting phase.

The two sorted streams of rows are merged together, just as if they were 1950s magnetic tapes. During the merge operation, if a row of the source table S and a row of T satisfy the join condition, they are inserted into the result table R.

The difference between nested-loop and sort-merge algorithms is that there is a sorted order that lets us advance a cursor on each table forward to the next matching row without reusing rows we know will not match. If the target and source are relatively large so that neither one of them can be put into main storage and are about the same size, then this has advantages over the simple nested-loop algorithm.

3.7.3   Hash Join Method

Just in case you are not familiar with hashing, let me give a quick explanation. A hashing function takes a parameter (or list of parameters) and returns a single value. A very simple hash function, which is too simple for real use but good for illustration, might be to convert the parameter into a binary number x and compute MOD (x, n). All of the rows that have the same hash result (0 through (n−1) in this simplified example) are put into the same "hash bucket" in working storage. In practice, the hash buckets are usually linked lists or an array (known as a hash table) containing the physical addresses of the rows in their respective tables.

If there are no empty spaces in the hash table, then the hash is called minimal. If each unique value in the table hashes to one and only one hash code, then the hash is called perfect. Finding a minimal perfect hashing function is a challenge. The best choices for (n) are usually prime numbers that are under a certain size that would keep buckets in main storage as much as possible.

In the simple hash join algorithm, the source and target tables are hashed on the join attribute values. Equal values in both tables will hash to the same bucket. The bucket will also have a lot of nonequal values if this was not a perfect hashing, but even so, the set of possible join pairs is considerably smaller. One of the advantages of hashing is that it naturally supports parallelism; each bucket can be controlled by its own processor. This algorithm works best for equi-joins, which are the vast majority joins done.

3.7.4   Shin's Algorithm

In Shin's join algorithm, the source and target tables are repeatedly hashed by a maximum of five statistically independent hash functions until a set of source rows and target rows are found to have an identical join attribute These independent hash functions can be derived from a set of prime numbers. The source and target rows that fall into the same set of alternative buckets will be equal (D. K. Shin, "A Comparative Study of Hash Functions for a New Hash-Based Table Join Algorithm," Pub #91-23423, Ann Arbor: UMI Dissertation Information Service, 1991).

Obviously, all five hashes can be computed at the same time instead of making five passes through the data. Doing math inside main storage is very fast, and most hashing functions can be expressed in very low-level assembly code for speed. The time complexity of hash-based join algorithms is $O(S+T+R)$.

The stack oriented filter technique (SOFT) is another member of this family that has a stack of pairs of hash tables, one hash table for source rows and the other hash table for target rows. The algorithm pushes five pairs on the stack to do the join operation.

CHAPTER
4

Lookup Tables

LOOKUP TABLES ARE a special case of auxiliary tables, but I wanted to treat them first since they are the most common case in real schemas. The "freshman" SQL programmer thinks that tables are the same as files and do not need to have any relationships among them enforced by declarative referential integrity (DRI) constraints. The "sophomore" SQL programmer was overly impressed by referential integrity constraints and assumes that *all* tables in a schema have to be linked via DRI. The better design for a schema lies somewhere in between.

A lookup table is used in SQL for the same purpose as a function or procedure in a computational language. For example, you can easily find the formula for the sine function and write code for it. Most procedural programming languages already have it as a built-in library function that can be invoked with a simple call.

Students today use a calculator for the sine function. The usual methods for the computations are series expansions and Chebyshev polynomials. If you want to look up references, I would go to the Internet, but for a book you can use *Mathematical Functions and Their Approximations* by M. Abramowitz (ISBN 0-12-459950-8) for the painful mathematical details.

In the old days when I was in school and dinosaurs roamed the earth (well, I exaggerate; saber-toothed tigers and mammoths were going extinct by then), we had lookup tables of sine functions in the back of our trigonometry textbooks.

Every time you want the get the sine of a number, the code in the function will be executed in a procedural language because of the sequential nature of the programming language. This is not a problem when you have a calculator or a printed lookup table and are doing one trig homework assignment at a time. But databases seldom do "one thing at a time"—they work with *sets* of data and parallelism.

They do not do one "trig problem" at a time; they do thousands, tens of thousands, or millions of them at a time. Now a good deal of the time, the same procedural call with the same parameters will be made many, many times. If there is a lookup table for the parameter values of a DETERMINISTIC function, then you can do a simple JOIN to it and get the needed values in the invoking statement.

A JOIN between columns of the same data type will execute at a constant rate, all else being equal. This is not true of a computation—it varies with input values. Faster computations were a major motivation for improvements in numerical analysis and algorithms. We do have very good techniques for the procedural programming languages because of this research. That being said, they are not faster than simultaneous joins and a simple equality test for any meaningful function.

In commercial situations, the actual range of the parameters is relatively limited. Loans tend to be made within a certain dollar range and in steps of a certain dollar value. For example, a home loan is not made in increments of a penny, but might be made in $100 increments within a range of $100,000.00 to $10,000,000.00, and the interest rates are in steps of 0.25% interest starting at some minimum rate. Not all combinations of loan amounts and interest rates are possible.

4.1   Data Element Names

This is a short list of postfixes that can be used as the name of the key column in auxiliary tables. There is a more complete list of postfixes in my book *SQL Programming Style* (ISBN: 0-12088-797-5). The most important point is that the primary key of an auxiliary table cannot be an identifier ("_id") because an identifier uniquely references an entity. Auxiliary tables do not hold entities; they deal with attribute values and computations.

"_nbr" or "_num" = `tag number`; this is a string of digits that names something. Do not use "_no" since it looks like the Boolean yes/no value. I prefer "_nbr" to "_num" since it is used as a common abbreviation in several European languages.

"_code" or "_cd" = a code, which is a standard maintained by a trusted source, usually outside of the enterprise. For example, the ZIP code is maintained by the United States Postal Service. A code is well understood in its context, so you might not have to translate it for humans.

"_cat" = category, an encoding that has an external source that has very distinct groups of entities. There should be strong formal criteria for establishing the category. The classification of kingdom in biology is an example.

"_class" = an internal encoding that does not have an external source that reflects a subclassification of the entity. There should be strong formal criteria for the classification. The classification of plants in biology is an example.

"_type" = an encoding that has a common meaning both internally and externally. Types are usually less formal than a class and might overlap. For example, a driver's license might be motorcycle, automobile, taxi, truck, and so forth.

The differences among type, class, and category are an increasing strength of the algorithm for assigning the value. A category is very distinct; you will not often have to guess if something is "animal, vegetable, or mineral" to put it in one of those categories.

A class is a set of things that have some commonality; you have rules for classifying an animal as a mammal or a reptile. You may have some cases for which it is harder to apply the rules, such as the "egg-laying mammals" in Australia, but the exceptions tend to become their own classification—"monotremes," in this example. If you really care, here is the full taxonomy:

Order Monotremata:

Family Ornithorhynchidae: Platypus

- Genus Ornithorhyncus

  - Platypus, Ornithorhyncus anatinus

Family Tachyglossidae: Echidna

- Genus Tachyglossus

  - Short-beaked Echidna, Tachyglossus aculeatus

- Genus Zaglossus

  - Western Long-beaked Echidna, Zaglossus brujinii

  - Sir David's Long-beaked Echidna, Zaglossus attenboroughi

  - Eastern Long-beaked Echidna, Zaglossus bartoni

A type is the weakest of the three, and it might call for a judgment that a can vary. For example, in some states, a three-wheeled motorcycle is licensed as a motorcycle. In other states, it is licensed as an automobile. And in some states, it is licensed as an automobile only if it has a reverse gear.

The three terms are often mixed in actual usage. Stick with the industry standard, even if it violates the definitions given above.

You can add a unique constraint on the descriptive column, but most programmers do not bother since these tables do not change much—and when they do change, it is done with data provided by a trusted source. Uniqueness constraints on the encoding are important, because they will usually create an index or other access method on the table.

A simple basic lookup table has a column with an encoding value and a translation of it into a display format, usually natural language or a human-readable abbreviation. You need to tie them to the base tables that use them with declarative referential integrity (DRI) actions. Using the oversimplified Customers table and the two-letter state codes, we might have:

```
CREATE TABLE Customers
(customer_id CHAR(9) NOT NULL PRIMARY KEY,
 ..
 state_code CHAR(2) NOT NULL
  REFERENCES StateCodes(state_code)
  ON DELETE CASCADE
  ON UPDATE CASCADE,
 ..);

CREATE TABLE StateCodes
(state_code CHAR(2) NOT NULL PRIMARY KEY,
 state_name VARCHAR(15) NOT NULL,
 ..);
```

The DRI actions on the state_code column are overkill. It is not very likely that states will drop out of the Union, since we had a

"War Between the States" (improperly called the American Civil War in many textbooks) to settle that issue. Nor it is likely states will change their names. Statehood for Puerto Rico has been discussed over the years, so we might add more states. Again, that would be a rare event and could be handled as an exceptional case.

One thought is that since we only have 64 state codes (this includes territories and military addresses overseas), we can put them into a "CHECK (state_code IN (<expression list>))" and not create another table at all. This will also keep somebody from inventing a new state code, just like a REFERENCES clause.

But the referenced table has another advantage beyond data integrity. With the referential integrity constraints, the optimizer knows that the most we can have is 64 rows, the number of unique rows in the StateCodes table. The engine can construct the first column, state_code, of the result set and begin working on the counts for each state.

A still better approach would be to use an SQL product that has CREATE DOMAIN and ALTER DOMAIN statements that would allow us to use a "user-defined data type" complete with the constraints we want.

The key for a lookup table cannot be an identifier; that is, it cannot end with a "_id" postfix. But you will often see things like "state_id" or "state_code_id" in lookup tables. Chapter 5, on auxiliary tables, has a short list of postfixes that can be used as the name of the key column in lookup or auxiliary tables. There is a more complete list of postfixes in my book *SQL Programming Style*.

4.2 Multiparameter Lookup Tables

The simple, single parameter lookup table is probably the most common kind. But you can also have lookup tables that use multiple parameters. As an example, consider a table of shipping boxes that have some standard industrial size number and three characteristics.

```
CREATE TABLE BoxSizes
(box_nbr INTEGER NOT NULL -- industry code
    PRIMARY KEY, -- see text
 box_vol DECIMAL (10,4) NOT NULL
   CHECK (box_vol > 0.00),
 content_type CHAR(3) DEFAULT 'dry' NOT NULL
   CHECK (content_type IN ('wet', 'dry')),
```

```
box_material CHAR(5) DEFAULT 'paper' NOT NULL
  CHECK (box_material IN ('paper', 'wood', 'metal')),
box_wgt DECIMAL (8,3) NOT NULL
  CHECK (box_wgt > 0.000),
box_price DECIMAL (8,3) NOT NULL
  CHECK (box_price > 0.000),
UNIQUE (box_vol, content_type, box_material));
```

If I want to ship 10 cubic centimeters of nuts in a wooden box, I can lookup the appropriate box size

```
SELECT box_size
  FROM BoxSizes
 WHERE box_vol = 10.0
   AND content_type = 'dry'
   AND box_material = 'wood';
```

If I do not care about one or more of the parameters, I can simply leave them out of the query and get a list of box sizes that will meet the other criteria. It is a good idea to have a multicolumn NOT NULL UNIQUE constraint on the parameter columns as well the result value column. This will guarantee that each combination of parameters is unique. However, it is possible that the result value actually is not unique. If we had a lookup table that took several factors from a buyer to pick, say, an automobile for them, it is possible that two different buyers with different criteria would match to the same make and model of automobile.

4.3   Constants Table

When you configure a system, you might want to have a way to set and keep constants in the schema. One method for doing this is to have a one-row table that can be set with default values at the start, and then updated only by someone with administrative privileges.

```
CREATE TABLE Constants
(lock CHAR(1) DEFAULT 'X'
     NOT NULL PRIMARY KEY
     CHECK (lock = 'X'),
 pi FLOAT DEFAULT 3.142592653 NOT NULL,
 e FLOAT DEFAULT 2.71828182 NOT NULL,
 phi FLOAT DEFAULT 1.6180339887 NOT NULL,
 ..);
```

To initialize the row, execute this statement:

```
INSERT INTO Constants VALUES DEFAULTS;
```

Most SQL programmers do not know about the VALUES DEFAULTS option in the INSERT INTO statement. The lock column ensures there is only one row and the DEFAULT values load the initial values. These defaults can include the current user and current timestamp, as well as numeric and character constant values.

   Another version of this idea that does not allow for any updates is a VIEW defined with a table constructor.

```
CREATE VIEW Constants (pi, e, phi, ..)
AS VALUES (CAST 3.142592653 AS FLOAT),
          (CAST 2.71828182 AS FLOAT),
          (CAST 1.6180339887 AS FLOAT),
   ..;
```

Please notice that you have to use CAST() operators to assure that the data types are correct. This is not a problem with INTEGER values, but could be if you wanted DOUBLE PRECISION and got a default of DECIMAL(s, p) or FLOAT.

   This idea extends to constant tables. A classic example would be lookup tables for functions in statistics and finance, such as the Student's t-distribution for small samples. The value of (r) is the size of the sample minus one, and the percentages are the confidence intervals.

   Loosely speaking, the Student's t-distribution is the best guess at the population distribution that we can make without knowing the standard deviation with a certain level of confidence. William Gosset created this statistic in 1908. His employer, Guinness Breweries, required him to publish under a pseudonym, so he chose "Student" and that name stuck. Here is a short table:

r	90%	95%	97.5%	99.5%
1	3.07766	6.31371	12.7062	63.65600
2	1.88562	2.91999	4.30265	9.92482
3	1.63774	2.35336	3.18243	5.84089
4	1.53321	2.13185	2.77644	4.60393

r	90%	95%	97.5%	99.5%
5	1.47588	2.01505	2.57058	4.03212
10	1.37218	1.81246	2.22814	3.16922
30	1.31042	1.69726	2.04227	2.74999
100	1.29007	1.66023	1.98397	2.62589
..	1.28156	1.64487	1.95999	2.57584

This becomes the VIEW:

```
CREATE VIEW Student_T(r, c900, c950, c975, c995)
AS VALUES (CAST (1 AS INTEGER),
           CAST (3.07766 AS FLOAT),
           CAST (6.31371 AS FLOAT),
           CAST (12.7062 AS FLOAT),
           CAST (63.65600 AS FLOAT)),
  (2, 1.88562, 2.91999, 4.30265, 9.92482),
  (3, 1.63774, 2.35336, 3.18243, 5.84089),
  .. ;
```

Notice that the first row has the CAST() function on all the columns. This will guarantee that all the columns in the VIEW will have the appropriate data types.

Another version of this trick in SQL-99 is to use a common table expression (CTE) instead of a VIEW:

```
WITH Student_T(r, c900, c950, c975, c995)
AS (VALUES (CAST (1 AS INTEGER), -- redundant but safe
           CAST (3.07766 AS FLOAT),
           CAST (6.31371 AS FLOAT),
           CAST (12.7062 AS FLOAT),
           CAST (63.65600 AS FLOAT)),
  (2, 1.88562, 2.91999, 4.30265, 9.92482),
  (3, 1.63774, 2.35336, 3.18243, 5.84089),
  ..)
SELECT (..) AS t, etc
  FROM <<sample table expression>>
WHERE ..;
```

Obviously you will need a SELECT that has the particular use of the t-statistic for your situation (i.e., one sample versus the population, one sample versus a second, etc.,)

The trade-offs between a constant VIEW versus a constant CTE are that a VIEW can be shared and a CTE is created locally within the scope of a query. If every user (or type of user) has a different lookup table, then this can be an advantage for security. For example, the discount schedule for Class A salesmen is different from the discount schedule for Class B salesmen, and so forth.

As a matter of programming style, table constants tend to be large amounts of text. It is not a good idea to put them into the query as a derived table, since it makes the code harder to read.

4.4 OTLT or MUCK Table Problems

I think that Paul Keister was the first person to coin the phrase "one true lookup table" (OTLT) for a common SQL programming technique that is popular with newbies. Don Peterson (*www.SQLServerCentral.com*) gave the same technique the name "massively unified code-key" or MUCK tables in one of his articles.

The technique crops up time and time again, but I will give Paul Keister credit as the first writer to give it a name. Simply put, the idea is to have one table to do all of the code lookups in the schema. It usually looks like this:

```
CREATE TABLE Look-ups
(code_type CHAR(10) NOT NULL,
 code_value VARCHAR(255) NOT NULL, -- notice size!
 code_description VARCHAR(255) NOT NULL, -- notice size!
 PRIMARY KEY (code_value, code_type));
```

So if we have Dewey Decimal Classification (library codes), International Classification of Diseases (ICD), and two-letter ISO-3166 Country Codes in the schema, we have them all in one honking big table.

Let us start with the problems in the DDL and then look at the awful queries you have to write (or hide in VIEWs). So we need to go back to the original DDL and add a CHECK() constraint on the "code_type" column. Otherwise, we might "invent" a new encoding system by typographical error.

Notice that we are already in trouble because a data element cannot be both a "<something>_code" and a "<something>_type"; it must be one or the other, and it must be the code or type of some specific attribute. One of the nice features of the ISO-11179 rules is that they prevent this mixing of data and metadata in a way that can be checked mechanically. Ignore this comment and continue heading for the edge of the cliff.

The Dewey Decimal and ICD codes are digits and have the same format—three digits, a decimal point, and more digits (usually three); the ISO-3166 Country Codes are alphabetic. Oops, we now need another CHECK constraint that will look at the "code_type" and make sure that the string is in the right format. Now the table looks something like this, if anyone attempted to do it right, which is not usually the case:

```
CREATE TABLE OTLT
(code_type CHAR(10) NOT NULL
      CHECK("code_type" IN ('DDC','ICD','ISO3166', ..),
 code_value VARCHAR(255) NOT NULL,
    CHECK
    (CASE code_type
     WHEN 'DDC'
          AND code_value
              SIMILAR TO '[0-9][0-9][0-9].[0-9][0-9][0-9]'
     THEN 1
     WHEN 'ICD'
          AND code_value
              SIMILAR TO '[0-9][0-9][0-9].[0-9][0-9][0-9]'
     THEN 1
     WHEN 'ISO3166'
          AND code_value SIMILAR TO '[A-Z][A-Z]'
     THEN 1 ELSE 0 END = 1),
code_description VARCHAR(255) NOT NULL,
PRIMARY KEY (code_value, code_type));
```

The "SIMILAR TO" predicate is the SQL-92 version of a regular expression parser based on the POSIX Standards, if you are not familiar with it. Since the typical application database can have dozens and dozens of codes in it, just keep extending this pattern for as long as required. Not very pretty, is it? In fact, there is a good chance that you might exceed the number of WHEN clauses allowed in a CASE expression in a major corporation. That is why most OTLT programmers do not bother with this absolutely vital constraint.

Now let us consider adding new rows to the OTLT.

```
INSERT INTO OTLT (code_type, code_value, code_description)
VALUES
('ICD', 259.0, 'Inadequate Genitalia after Puberty');
```

and also

```
INSERT INTO OTLT (code_type, code_value, code_description)
VALUES ('DDC', 259.0, 'Christian Pastoral Practices &
Religious Orders');
```

If you make an error in the "code_type" during insert, update, or delete, you have screwed up a totally unrelated value. If you make an error in the "code_type" during a query, the results could be interesting.

This can be really hard to find when one of the similarly structured schemes had unused codes in it.

The next thing you notice about this table is that the columns are pretty wide VARCHAR(n), or even worse, that they are NVARCHAR(n), which can store characters from a strange language. The value of (n) is most often the largest one allowed in that particular SQL product.

Since you have no idea what is going to be shoved into the table, there is no way to predict and design with a safe, reasonable maximum size. The size constraint has to be put into the WHEN clause of that second CHECK() constraint between "code_type" and "code_value". Or you can live with fixed length codes that are longer (or fatally shorter) than what they should be.

These large sizes tend to invite bad data. You give someone a VARCHAR(n) column, and you eventually get a string with a lot of white space and a small odd character sitting at the end of it. You give someone an NVARCHAR(255) column and eventually it will get a Buddhist sutra in Chinese Unicode.

Now let's consider the problems with actually using the OTLT in a query. It is always necessary to add the "code_type" as well as the value that you are trying to lookup.

```
SELECT P1.ssn, P1.lastname, .., L1.code_description
 FROM OTLT AS L1, Personnel AS P1
WHERE L1."code_type" = 'ICD'
  AND L1.code_value = P1.disease_code
  AND ..;
```

In this sample query, you need to know the "code_type" of the Personnel table disease_code column and of every other encoded column in the table. If you got a "code_type" wrong, you can still get a result.

You also need to allow for some overhead for data type conversions. It might be more natural to use numeric values instead of VARCHAR(n) for some encodings to ensure a proper sorting order. Padding a string of digits with leading zeros adds overhead and can be risky if programmers do not agree on how many zeros to use.

When you execute a query, the SQL engine has to pull in the entire lookup table, even if it only uses a few codes. If one code is at the start of the physical storage, and another is at the end of physical storage, I can do a lot of caching and paging. When I update the OTLT table, I have to lock out everyone until I am finished. It is like having to carry an encyclopedia set with you when all you needed was a magazine article.

Now consider the overhead with a two-part FOREIGN KEY in a table:

```
CREATE TABLE EmployeeAbsences
(..
 "code_type" CHAR(3) -- min length needed
   DEFAULT 'ICD' NOT NULL
   CHECK ("code_type" = 'ICD'),


code_value CHAR(7) NOT NULL, -- min length needed
 FOREIGN KEY ("code_type", code_value)
   REFERENCES OTLT ("code_type", code_value),
 ..);
```

Now I have to convert the character types for more overhead. Even worse, ICD has a natural DEFAULT value (000.000 means "undiag-nosed"), while Dewey Decimal does not. Older encoding schemes often used all 9s for "miscellaneous" so they would sort to the end of the reports in COBOL programs. Just as there is no magical universal "id," there is no magical universal DEFAULT value. I just lost one of the most important features of SQL!

I am going to venture a guess that this idea came from OO program-mers who think of it as some kind of polymorphism done in SQL. They say to themselves that a table is a class, which it is not, and therefore it ought to have polymorphic behaviors, which it does not.

4.5   Definition of a Proper Table

There are good reasons for the data modeling principle that a well-designed table is a set of things of the same kind instead of a pile of unrelated items.

At one extreme, we have the "attribute split" tables, and on the other, the extreme conglomerated tables. When I've posted in newsgroups, I've referred to a "Britney Spears, Squids, and Automobiles" procedure and table for years—attempts to make one table or procedures serve as many purposes as possible. What is funny about this that there is a "Britney Spears or Squid" website (*http://scienceblogs.com/ deepseanews/2007/02/weekend_foolishness.php*) posted after she shaved her head in 2007.

CHAPTER 5

Auxiliary Tables

AUXILIARY TABLES HOLD information that is not part of the data model but is needed by the system to work. They are used in queries rather than just providing a simple lookup, as discussed in the last chapter.

Again, the primary key of an auxiliary table is never an identifier; an identifier is unique in the schema and refers to one entity anywhere it appears. As an example of an identifier, your automobile's VIN is constant, no matter where you park the car, who owns it, what database it is in, or anything else.

An auxiliary table's primary key is a set of one or more parameters for the function it models. We will discuss this in detail in Chapter 8.

These tables are an alternative to computations and procedural code. At one end of the spectrum are simple lookup tables that translate encodings for display in the applications. At the middle level, there are complex function tables that handle the irregular nature of a hard-to-compute function. At the far end, there are complex, irregular functions that take multiple parameters or that have to be updated via feedback loops.

5.1 Sequence Table

The Sequence table is a simple list of integers from 1 to (n) that is used in place of looping constructs in a procedural language. Rather than incrementing a countervalue inside a loop, we try to work in parallel with a complete set of values.

The table can include other data related to sequential numbering, such as the ordinal and cardinal number names, repeating or nonrepeating pseudo-random numbers, prime number flags, or whatever you need for your particular enterprise.

This table has the general declaration:

```
CREATE TABLE Sequence
(seq INTEGER NOT NULL PRIMARY KEY
     CONSTRAINT non_negative_nbr
     CHECK (seq > 0),
-- cardinal_name VARCHAR(25) NOT NULL,
-- ordinal_name VARCHAR(25) NOT NULL,
 ...
 CONSTRAINT seq_is_complete
 CHECK ((SELECT COUNT(*) FROM Sequence) =
        (SELECT MAX(seq) FROM Sequence)));
```

Consider what you would have to do to write a function to convert a numeric value into English words. This is not a common function in SQL products, nor is it part of the Standards. It is a safe bet that the Standards will stay silent on this because they would have to cover all possible languages and not just English. Here is a solution by Stu Bloom. First, create a table

```
CREATE TABLE NbrWords
(seq INTEGER PRIMARY KEY,
 nbr_word VARCHAR(30) NOT NULL);
```

Then, populate it with the literal strings of all number names from 0 to 999. Assuming that your range is 1–999,999,999, use the following query; it should be obvious how to extend it for larger numbers and fractional parts.

```
CASE WHEN :num < 1000
     THEN (SELECT nbr_word FROM NbrWords
           WHERE seq = :num)
     WHEN :num < 1000000
     THEN (SELECT nbr_word FROM NbrWords
           WHERE seq = :num / 1000)
```

```
                || ' thousand '
                || (SELECT nbr_word FROM NbrWords
                       WHERE MOD(seq = :num, 1000))
        WHEN :num < 1000000000
        THEN (SELECT nbr_word FROM NbrWords
                 WHERE seq = :num / 1000000)
             || ' million '
             || (SELECT nbr_word FROM NbrWords
                    WHERE seq = MOD((:num / 1000), 1000))
             || CASE WHEN MOD((:num / 1000), 1000) > 0
                     THEN ' thousand '
                     ELSE '' END
             || (SELECT nbr_word FROM NbrWords
                    WHERE seq = MOD(:num, 1000))
END;
```

Notice that we have implicitly made a decision as to whether to convert 2,500 to "Twenty-five Hundred" or to "Two Thousand Five Hundred" by virtue of the second WHEN clause.

I have found that is it a bad idea to start with zero, though that seems more natural to computer programmers. The reason for omitting zero is that this auxiliary table is often used to provide row numbering by being CROSS JOIN-ed to another table and the zero would toss off the one-to-one mapping. I have also found that in most applications, you can establish an upper bound of a few thousand rows (most people do not work with queries that return millions of rows) and limit the Sequence table to that range. However, if you are worried about exceeding the size of the Sequence table, use a LEFT OUTER JOIN to generate NULLs that can be trapped.

5.1.1 Creating a Sequence Table

Since the Sequence table is built only once, there is no need for a fast query to stock it with values, but it is a good programming exercise to see how many different ways you can find.

The simplest and fastest way is to set up a table of the digits and multiple by powers of ten. You have to set an upper limit and to remove zero.

```
WITH Digits(i)
AS
```

```
(VALUES (0), (1), (2), (3), (4), (5), (6), (7), (8), (9))
SELECT ((D3.i *100) +(D2.i *10) + D1.i) AS seq
  FROM Digits AS D1
       CROSS JOIN Digits AS D2
       CROSS JOIN Digits AS D3
 WHERE (D3.i *100) +(D2.i *10) + D1.i)
       BETWEEN 1 AND :n;
```

A slow way using the recursive Common Table Expression (CTE) is just hiding a loop in new syntax. This will add one row for each level of recursion, which might be a problem if the upper limit for the levels of recursion in your SQL product is less than your target.

```
WITH RECURSIVE Sequence (seq)
AS
(VALUES (1)
 UNION ALL
 SELECT seq + 1
   FROM Sequence
  WHERE (seq + 1) <= :n)
 SELECT seq FROM Sequence;
```

A more direct approach with the new SQL-99 syntax is to grab a table of known size and number the rows in it.

```
SELECT seq
  FROM (SELECT ROW_NUMBER() OVER (ORDER BY key_col)
  FROM BigTable)
WHERE seq <= :n;
```

Depending on the indexing in your SQL product, this can be quite fast or very slow. I am sure that you can come up with other methods yourself.

5.1.2 Sequence Constructor

Unfortunately, SEQUENCE is a reserved word for a proposed construct in Standard SQL that builds a sequence of numbers, but handles them as if they were a list or file rather than a set. The same reserved word is found in Oracle and DB2, but not used in other products.

The syntax of the sequence looks something like this—each product's syntax will vary, but should have the same parameters.

```
CREATE SEQUENCE <seq_name> AS <data type>
START WITH <value>
INCREMENT BY <value>
[MAXVALUE <value>]
[MINVALUE <value>]
[[NO]CYCLE];
```

To get a value from it, this expression is used wherever it is a legal data type.

```
NEXT VALUE FOR <seq name>
```

If a sequence needs to be reset, you use this statement to change the optional clauses or to restart the cycle.

```
ALTER SEQUENCE <seq name>
RESTART WITH <value>; -- begin over
```

To remove the sequence, use the obvious statement:

```
DROP SEQUENCE <seq name>;
```

Even when this feature becomes widely available, it should be avoided. It is a nonrelational extension that behaves like a sequential file or procedural function rather than in a set-oriented manner. You currently find it in Oracle, DB2, Postgres, and Mimer products.

If there is a *true sequence* in the data model, such as invoice numbers, then you have to account for each sequence number—the status (issued, voided, reserved, etc.), the current state of the sequence (i.e., the last valid number issued) and validation of the numbers.

This is a lot more programming than a simple autonumbering. You need to consider audit trails, SOX compliance, and other legal requirements.

5.1.3   Replacing an Iterative Loop

You are given a quoted string that is made up of integers separated by commas and your goal is to break each of integers out as a row in a table. The proper relational solution is not to allow non-first normal form (NFNF) data into the schema. But you will see newbies using this poor programming technique, so you need to be able to defend yourself against it in your staging tables (more on that later).

The procedural solution is to write code that will loop over the input string and cut off all characters from the start up to, but not including, the first comma, cast the substring as an integer, and then iterate through the rest of the string. Think of a loaf of bread being sliced.

```
CREATE PROCEDURE ParseList (IN inputstring VARCHAR(1000))
LANGUAGE SQL
BEGIN DECLARE slicer INTEGER;
SET slicer = 1; -- iter control variable
-- add sentinel comma to end of input string
SET inputstring = TRIM (BOTH '' FROM inputstring || ',');
WHILE slicer < CHAR_LENGTH(inputstring)
   DO WHILE SUBSTRING(inputstring, slicer, 1) <> ','
      DO SET slicer = slicer + 1;
      END WHILE;
 SET outputstring = SUBSTRING(inputstring FROM 1
 FOR slicer-1);
 INSERT INTO Outputs
 VALUES (CAST (outputstring AS INTEGER));
 SET inputstring = SUBSTRING(inputstring FROM slicer+1);
 END WHILE;
END;
```

Another way to do this is with an auxiliary table of sequential numbers and this strange-looking query that is written in Core SQL-99.

```
CREATE PROCEDURE ParseList (IN inputstring VARCHAR(1000))
LANGUAGE SQL
INSERT INTO ParmList (parmeter_position, param)
 SELECT S1.comma_loc,
       CAST (SUBSTRING (('' || inputstring || ',')
                FROM (S1.comma_loc + 1)
                 FOR (S2.comma_loc - S1.comma_loc - 1))
            AS INTEGER)
 FROM Sequence AS S1(comma_loc),
     Sequence AS S2(comma_loc)
   WHERE SUBSTRING(('' || inputstring || ',')
   FROM S1.comma_loc FOR 1) = ','
    AND SUBSTRING(('' || inputstring || ',')
    FROM S2.comma_loc FOR 1) = ','
    AND S2.comma_loc
```

```
         = (SELECT MIN(S3.slicer)
               FROM Sequence AS S3(comma_loc)
               WHERE S1.comma_loc < S3. comma_loc
                 AND SUBSTRING((',' || inputstring || ',')
                         FROM S3.comma_loc FOR 1) = ',')
      AND S1.comma_loc <= S2.comma_loc
      AND S2.comma_loc < CHAR_LENGTH (inputstring + 2);
```

The trick here is to concatenate commas on the left and right sides of the `input string`. To be honest, you would probably want to trim blanks and perhaps do other tests on the `string`, such as seeing that `LOWER(:instring) = UPPER(:instring)` to avoid alphabetic characters, and so forth. That edited result `string` would be kept in a local variable and used in the `INSERT INTO` statement.

The `integer substrings` are located between the (i)th and (i+1)th comma pairs. In effect, the sequence table replaces the loop counter by marking the commas all at once instead of slicing them off the `input string`. The last two predicates are to avoid a Cartesian product with the Sequence table and to save going over the length of the `input string`.

The Sequence table has to have enough numbers to cover the entire string, but unless you really like to type in long parameter lists, this should not be a problem. As an aside, newbies who do not understand first normal form (1NF) will often use such a comma-separated list as a parameter to make SQL look like their original procedural language. This is an awful programming technique. You can easily work around it in the 4GL languages in modern SQL products, because they can handle hundreds of parameters.

```
CREATE PROCEDURE LongList
(IN p1 INTEGER, IN p2 INTEGER, .., IN pN INTEGER)
LANGUAGE SQL
BEGIN
  ..
SELECT target
  FROM Foobar
WHERE target
  IN (SELECT parm
      FROM (VALUES (p1), .., (pN)) AS ParmList(parm)
      WHERE parm IS NOT NULL);
..
END;
```

Missing values will be set to NULL and need to be trimmed out. Ideally, we would prefer to have a separate ParmList table that is loaded before being used in the procedure rather than constructed inside it.

5.2 Permutations

Mike Whiting asked for code to generate all the possible permutations of a string. This was a popular problem in the *British Computer Journal* a few decades ago. They published several Algol programs with good discussions at that time. A good reference website is *http://portal.acm. org/citatioN.cfm?id=356692*, but you can find others. But because they were written for a procedural programming language, many of the articles focus on the sequence of generation of permutations, rather than just getting the entire set.

5.2.1 Permutations via Recursion

Alex Kuznetsov replied with a recursive CTE solution that assumes an auxiliary Sequence table. Begin by setting the :input_str = 'ABCDE' and running this query:

```
WITH RECURSIVE Subsets (token, perm_nbr, iter)
AS
(SELECT CAST(SUBSTRING(input_str FROM seq FOR 1)
AS VARCHAR(5)),
       CAST('.' || CAST(seq AS CHAR(1))|| '.'
       AS VARCHAR(11)),
       1
  FROM Sequences
 WHERE seq BETWEEN 1 AND 5
UNION ALL
SELECT CAST(token || SUBSTRING(:input_str FROM seq FOR 1)
AS VARCHAR(5)),
       CAST(perm_nbr || CAST(seq AS CHAR(1))|| '.'
       AS VARCHAR(11,
       (S.iter + 1)
  FROM Subsets AS S, Sequence AS N
 WHERE S.perm_nbr NOT LIKE '%.'|| CAST(seq AS CHAR(1)) || '.%'
   AND S.iter < 5
   AND Sequence BETWEEN 1 AND 5
-- AND S.iter = (SELECT MAX (iter) FROM Subsets)
)
```

```
SELECT token, perm_nbr
  FROM Subsets
 WHERE iter = 5;

Subsets -- 120 rows created
```

```
    token        perm_nbr
======================
   'ABCDE'   '.1.2.3.4.5.'
   'ABCED'   '.1.2.3.5.4.'
   'ABDCE'   '.1.2.4.3.5.'
     ..            ..
   'EDBCA'   '.5.4.2.3.1.'
   'EDCAB'   '.5.4.3.1.2.'
   'EDCBA'   '.5.4.3.2.1.'
```

The permutation number is not really needed, but it demonstrates an ordering of the permutations that gives us a unique pattern for each one. In a procedural algorithm, each permutation can be generated by the previous one, following various rules.

5.2.2   Permutations via CROSS JOIN

The specification did not say if the permutations were with or without duplicate letters. I will assume no duplicates. Since the number of permutations is (n!), you might want to limit the size the procedure can handle. I picked 9! = 362,880, since 10! = 3,628,800 and that might be a bit larger than you want.

First, let's create a table or a view to hold the letters used.

```
CREATE TABLE Alpha
(ltr CHAR(1) PRIMARY KEY CONSTRAINT is_letter
     CHECK (ltr BETWEEN 'A' AND 'Z'));
```

We will need a table to hold the permuted strings:

```
CREATE TABLE Perm9 (p CHAR(9) NOT NULL PRIMARY KEY);
```

And a procedure to load that table:

```
CREATE PROCEDURE Permute (IN a1 CHAR(1), IN a2 CHAR(1), IN a3
CHAR(1),
```

```
                    IN a4 CHAR(1), IN a5 CHAR(1), IN a6
CHAR(1),
                    IN a7 CHAR(1), IN a8 CHAR(1), IN a9
CHAR(1)')
AS
BEGIN
--clear out working tables
DELETE FROM Alpha;
DELETE FROM Perm9;

-- load letters into alpha table
INSERT INTO Alpha
VALUES (a1), (a2), (a3),
       (a4), (a5), (a6),
       (a7), (a8), (a9);

-- cross joins to get permutations
INSERT INTO Perm9 (p)
SELECT A1.ltr || A2.ltr || A3.ltr || A4.ltr || A5.ltr ||
A6.ltr || A7.ltr || A8.ltr || A9.ltr
  FROM Alpha AS A1, Alpha AS A2, Alpha AS A3,
       Alpha AS A4, Alpha AS A5, Alpha AS A6,
       Alpha AS A7, Alpha AS A8, Alpha AS A9
 WHERE A1.ltr NOT IN (A2.ltr, A3.ltr, A4.ltr, A5.ltr,
A6.ltr, A7.ltr, A8.ltr, A9.ltr)
   AND A2.ltr NOT IN (A3.ltr, A4.ltr, A5.ltr, A6.ltr,
   A7.ltr, A8.ltr, A9.ltr)
   AND A3.ltr NOT IN (A4.ltr, A5.ltr, A6.ltr, A7.ltr,
   A8.ltr, A9.ltr)
   AND A4.ltr NOT IN (A5.ltr, A6.ltr, A7.ltr, A8.ltr,
   A9.ltr)
   AND A5.ltr NOT IN (A6.ltr, A7.ltr, A8.ltr, A9.ltr)
   AND A6.ltr NOT IN (A7.ltr, A8.ltr, A9.ltr)
   AND A7.ltr NOT IN (A8.ltr, A9.ltr)
   AND A8.ltr NOT IN (A9.ltr);
END;

EXEC Permute ('A', 'B', 'C', 'D', 'E', 'F', 'G', 'H', 'I');
```

This will probably run faster than the previous example, because recursion and string manipulation is expensive. The nice part with the CROSS JOIN is that once you have the (n = 9) table, you can keep it and create VIEWs for (n < 9) easily.

```
CREATE VIEW Perm8 (p)
AS
SELECT DISTINCT REPLACE (p, 'I', '')
  FROM Perm9;

CREATE VIEW Perm7 (p)
AS
SELECT DISTINCT REPLACE (REPLACE (p, 'H', '') 'I', '')
  FROM Perm9;
```

And if you want repetitions in the string, such as "AABBCD", just change the REPLACE() calls. Remember that SQL is a database language, not a computational language. Think sets and data, avoid sequences and procedures.

5.3 Functions

Before pocket calculators became cheap and powerful, we used lookup tables in books. Go to a used bookstore, pick up an old finance, trig, or statistics book, and look in the back. There will be tables of functions for net present value, sine and cosine, and assorted statistical tests. The most famous book was *CRC Standard Mathematical Tables and Formulae* for tables. The 31st edition was published in 1995, which gives you an idea how long it has been around. You can now get it on a CD.

The obvious question is why I would want to implement a function as a lookup table when I have fast, cheap computing power. One good reason is that if you only use a few thousand values of the function, they will fit into main storage, where they can be joined in parallel to produce results faster than recomputing those same results over and over. This is not completely true on hardware platforms as of this writing, because we are still using single-processor chips. The future belongs to multiprocessor, massively parallel architectures. Both databases and database programming are going to change in such a world.

At the time of this writing, there is an experimental SQL/PSM implementation that looks to see if a procedure has been declared DETERMINISTIC or not. If it has been declared DETERMINISTIC, then a hidden auxiliary lookup table is built and the procedural code is modified to check the hidden table first before executing the computational code. Any new values can then be added to the hidden table for the next execution.

You can code a procedure something like this by hand using this simple template:

```
CREATE FUNCTION Foobar(IN parm <data type>, ..)
RETURNS <data type>
LANGUAGE SQL
DETERMINISTIC
RETURN (CASE parm
        WHEN p1 THEN r1
        WHEN p2 THEN r2

          ..

        WHEN pN THEN rN
        ELSE (<computations>)
        END;
```

There are warnings with this template; you have to handle NULLs in an appropriate manner. In most cases in SQL, a NULL parameter will return a NULL function result, following the convention that NULLs propagate. It is a good idea to use "RETURN (CAST (NULL AS <data type>))" to ensure that the results are the right data type.

The second warning is that it will not give you the advantage of parallelism in a JOIN, but it can save you the extra computational time.

In the real world, the procedure is probably subject to a Zipfian distribution—in plain English, this means that 80% to 90% of the cases are handled by 10% to 20% of the rows in the lookup table. For example, in medicine, the rule is expressed as the maxim "Look for a horse, not a zebra" to remind doctors that the patient probably has a common disease and not an exotic one—in spite of what we see on television medical shows.

5.3.1   Functions without a Simple Formula

Not all functions are computable via some simple formula. An obvious example is calendrical calculations that involve solar and lunar cycles, such as Easter. But there are also functions that involve recursion, integrals, trig functions for longitude and latitude, or other forms of higher math that are not easily done with SQL's rather simple set of functions.

It is fairly easy to get a tool like MathLab, Maple, or Mathematica and create a lookup table in a few minutes. These packages also have the advantage of correcting for floating-point errors, which SQL typically does not do. If you have to work with floating-point numbers,

I strongly suggest that you read "What Every Computer Scientist Should Know about Floating-Point Arithmetic" by David Goldberg (*Computing Surveys*; March 1991) at *http://docs.sun.com/source/806-3568/ncg_goldberg.html*.

If you thought that NULLs in SQL were confusing, then you will hate the IEEE 754 Standard. It specifies the following special values: ± 0, denormalized numbers, $\pm \infty$ and NaNs (short for "not a number," and there are several types). The NaNs are special values that are returned from an expression rather than halting. In general, whenever a NaN participates in a floating-point operation, the result is another NaN. This is much like NULLs in SQL.

The plus and minus zeros test equal to each other, but their sign effects the sign of the results in computations.

The division 0/0 results in a NaN. A nonzero number divided by 0 returns infinity, with a sign: $1/0 = +\infty$ and $-1/0 = -\infty$. Most SQL implementations will halt on a division by zero. Likewise, most have no infinity symbol and will halt on an underflow or overflow error; but in SQL, you have to watch for NULL/0, which will result in a NULL (the rule is that NULLs propagate).

Denormalized numbers are used to handle rounding problems so that values that are "close enough" to each other can be treated as if they are equal. But it is up to the programmer to make sure that this works.

The IEEE Standard divides exceptions into five classes: overflow, underflow, division by zero, invalid operation, and inexact. There is a separate status flag for each class of exception.

Consider writing a function to compute $(x \verb|^| n)$, where (n) is an integer. When $(n > 0)$, a simple routine like this will do the job:

```
CREATE FUNCTION PositivePower (IN x FLOAT, IN n INTEGER)
RETURNS FLOAT
LANGUAGE SQL
DETERMINISTIC
 BEGIN
 WHILE MOD(n, 2) = 0 -- n is even
 DO SET x = x * x;
    SET n = n/2;
 END WHILE;
 SET u = x;
 WHILE (1 = 1)
    DO SET n = n/2;
       IF (n = 0)
       THEN RETURN (u);
```

```
                END IF;
                SET x = x * x;
                IF MOD(n, 2) = 1 -- n is odd
                THEN SET u = u * x;
                END IF;
         END WHILE;
      END;
```

If (n < 0), then a more accurate way to compute (x^n) is not to call PositivePower(1.0/x, −n) but rather 1.0/PositivePower(x, −n). The first expression accumulates a rounding error from each division inside the loop, while the second expression has a single division and therefore only one additional rounding error. Notice that I have skipped over underflow problems and trapping them.

5.4   Encryption via Tables

The DES Public Key Encryption algorithm (FIPS 42-2) is driven by tables of permutations on a 64-bit block of data. I do not want to go into the algorithms, since they typically involve low-level bit fiddling for which SQL was never intended, but encryption is a class of functions for which they try to make it hard to find an inverse function.

A very simple, but surprisingly good, encryption is to use a table of integers between 0 and 7 (or 0 and 15 for Unicode) to determine how far to circular shift an ASCII character. Circular shift is a machine-level that shifts the bits right (or left) for (n) positions as if they were in a circle, so no bits are lost. For example, RgtRotate('01110111', 3) = '11101110'.

```
CREATE TABLE Encryptor
(char_pos INTEGER NOT NULL PRIMARY KEY,
shift_distance INTEGER NOT NULL
 CHECK (shift_distance BETWEEN 0 AND 7);
```

You encode with a right rotation and decrypt with a left rotation. The nice part is that the results are always ASCII for an ASCII input because of the parity bit.

If you do not have bit-level operators in your SQL, then you can build a lookup table with 128 rows in it to map each character to its shifted version:

```
CREATE TABLE Encryptor
(ascii CHAR(1) NOT NULL PRIMARY KEY,
```

```
shift_1 CHAR(1) NOT NULL,
shift_2 CHAR(1) NOT NULL,
shift_3 CHAR(1) NOT NULL,
shift_4 CHAR(1) NOT NULL,
shift_5 CHAR(1) NOT NULL,
shift_6 CHAR(1) NOT NULL,
shift_7 CHAR(1) NOT NULL);
```

This is not an industrial-strength algorithm, but you can construct very long keys easily.

5.5   Random Numbers

Random numbers used by programmers are usually pseudo-random numbers. That is, you have a function that takes a starting value, the seed, and each call to the function returns a new result. Most of the pseudo-random-number generators (usually just called RNG) return a floating-point fraction value between 0.00 and 0.9999... at whatever precision your SQL engine has. The choice of a seed to start the generator can be a constant or a constantly changing value like the system clock—given the same seed, it will always generate the same sequence.

This is obviously "mathematical heresy," and there are RNGs that were later found not to pass statistical tests for randomness. However, a good RNG will have desirable properties, such as having a uniform distribution of values, and will be acceptable to users.

There are two kinds of random selection from a set:

1.   With replacement, which means you can get multiple copies of the same value. This is like shooting dice and how most RNGs will work in practice. Most applications are trying to get a random integer and not a floating-point number between 0.00 and 1.00. The floating-point rounding errors and truncation to an integer will lead to duplicates.

2.   Without replacement, which means you can use each value from the set only once and associate a sequence number with it. This is shuffling playing cards, and is probably more useful for an application program that wants to hide information. Sequential numbers on documents exposes the count—if I see an account #42, then I know that there is an account #41 out

there somewhere that I can try to hack. But if the accounts are numbered randomly, the odds of guessing one are greatly reduced.

Building the replacement lookup table is relatively easy.

```
CREATE TABLE RandomDice
(toss_seq INTEGER NOT NULL PRIMARY KEY,
 toss_nbr INTEGER DEFAULT 0 NOT NULL
     CHECK (toss_nbr BETWEEN 2 AND 12);
```

Since you are only going to do this once, you might as well use a cursor, loop through the table, and replace the zero values with an RNG number. Technically, you should be using something like a Geiger counter or interstellar radio noise, since these things are random at the subatomic level. There are circuit boards that will gather that information and turn it into digital formats for computers to use. They are expensive and not very popular outside of laboratories and gambling machines.

Knowing random series up to the (n)th value does not help you predict the (n+1)th value, but the series as a whole tends to converge to a particular distribution, which is usually known in advance. The dice will tend toward a bell curve, if they are fair. Knowing this lets you test how good your table is by constructing a histogram and doing some other statistical tests.

Building the nonreplacement lookup table is a little trickier. I would start with a table that has two sequentially numbered columns in it:

```
CREATE TABLE CardDeck
 (deck_seq INTEGER NOT NULL PRIMARY KEY
     CHECK (deck_seq BETWEEN 1 AND 52),
  card_nbr INTEGER DEFAULT 0 NOT NULL UNIQUE
     CHECK (card_nbr BETWEEN 1 AND 52);

INSERT INTO CardDeck (deck_seq, card_nbr)
SELECT seq AS deck_seq, seq AS card_nbr FROM Sequence
WHERE seq <= 52;
```

The reason for naming the columns in the SELECT is to avoid any duplicate name problems in the results as well as for documentation.

Now shuffle the deck by scanning down the deck of cards and swapping the current card with a random card from anywhere in the deck. Assume we have a RANDOM() function in the library that behaves well.

```
CREATE PROCEDURE ShuffleCards(IN seed FLOAT)
LANGUAGE SQL
NOT DETERMINISTIC
BEGIN
DECLARE current_card INTEGER;
DECLARE random_card INTEGER;
SET current_card = (SELECT COUNT(*) FROM CardDeck);
WHILE current_card > 0
DO SET random_card = (SELECT COUNT(*) FROM CardDeck)
                        * RANDOM(seed) + 1.0;
   UPDATE CardDeck
     SET card_nbr =
         CASE WHEN card_seq = current_card
             THEN random_card
             WHEN card_seq = random_card
             THEN current_card
             ELSE card_nbr END
   WHERE deck_seq IN (current_card, random_card);
   SET current_card = current_card- 1;
END WHILE;
END;
```

In a sampling without replacement, there is only one statistical distribution—every value will appear one time and one time only. We are really dealing with permutations in this case.

Here is an implementation of the additive congruent method of generating nonrepeating values in pseudo-random order. It is due to Roy Hann of Rational Commerce Limited, an Ingres consulting firm (see the details at: *http://www.rationalcommerce.com/resources/surrogates.htm*). It is based on a shift-register and an XOR-gate, and it has its origins in cryptography. While there are other ways to do this, this code is nice because:

1.   The algorithm can be written in C or another low-level language for speed. But math is fairly simple even in base ten.

2.   The algorithm tends to generate successive values that are (usually) "far apart," which is handy for improving the performance of tree indexes. You will tend to put data on separate physical data pages in storage.

3.   The algorithm does not cycle until it has generated every possible value, so we don't have to worry about duplicates. Just count how many calls have been made to the generator.

4.   The algorithm produces uniformly distributed values, which is a nice mathematical property to have. It also does not include zero.

Generalizing the algorithm to arbitrary binary word sizes, and therefore longer number sequences, is not as easy as you might think. Finding the "tap" positions where bits are extracted for feedback varies according to the word-size in an extremely nonobvious way.

Choosing incorrect tap positions results in an incomplete and usually very short and unusable cycle. If you want the details and tap positions for words of one to 100 bits, see E. J. Watson, "Primitive Polynomials (Mod 2)," *Mathematics of Computation*, Vol. 16, 1962, pp. 368–369. Here is code for a `31-bit integer`, which you can use:

```
UPDATE Generator31
SET seq
   = seq/2 + MOD(MOD(seq, 2) + MOD(seq/2, 2), 2) * 8;
```

Or if you prefer, the algorithm in C:

```
int Generator31 ()
{static int n = 1;
n = n >> 1 | ((n^n >> 3) & 1) << 30;
return n;
}
```

A quick Google search will locate code for random number generators. There are many very good ones that run on a PC.

In 1946, the RAND Corporation needed random numbers for Monte Carlo simulations. These had to be real random numbers and not the usual pseudo-random numbers that most of us get from a `RANDOM()` function in a software vendor math library. It took until 1955 to get a list of one million random digits and print them in a book. The New York Public Library originally indexed this book under the heading "Psychology," because nobody knew what to do with it.

This table of random numbers has become the standard reference, and it is still the largest published source of random digits and normal deviates in the world. You can still get the hard copy (ISBN 10: 0-8330-3047-7) or go on-line and download a Zip file (0.6 MB) in plain text form. There is also a file of 100,000 normal deviates zipped in plain text form.

Here are a few good books on the topic:

Randomness by Deborah Bennett, 1998, ISBN 0-674-10745-4.

What Is Random? by Edward Beltrami, 1999, ISBN 0-387-98737-1.

Exploring Randomness by Gregory J. Chaitin, 2001, ISBN 0-85233-417-7.

5.6   Interpolation

In a previous section, I mentioned that books used to have lookup tables in the back for functions. But what happens when you have a value that is not in those tables? Before pocket calculators and personal computers became cheap and powerful, we used interpolation.

This technique is a way of guessing the results of a function that lies between two known values. Let's call the two known functional values a and b, and their results from the function $f(a)$ and $f(b)$, and try to find $f(x)$, where ($a <= x <= b$), but x is not in the table. We have to make a lot of assumptions about the function. It has to be continuous over the interval [a, b] and behave in a smooth fashion. Thank goodness, polynomials and most other common functions do behave nicely.

Linear interpolation is the easiest method, and if the table has a high precision, it will work quite well for most applications. It is based on the idea that a straight line drawn between two function values $f(a)$ and $f(b)$ will approximate the function well enough that you can take a proportional increment of x relative to (a, b) and get a usable answer for $f(x)$.

The algebra looks like this:

```
f(x) ≈ f(a) + (x - a) * ((f(b) - f(a))/(b-a))
```

Figure 5.1
Linear
Interpolation

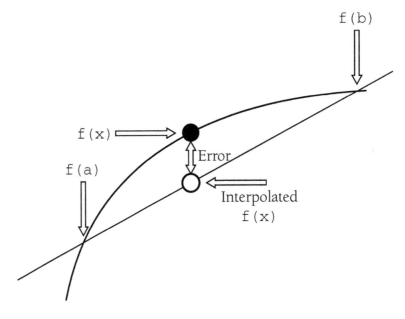

This can be translated into SQL like this, where x is my_parameter, F1
is related to the variable a, and F2 is related to the variable b:

```
SELECT :my_parameter AS my_input,
       (F1.answer + (:my_parameter - F1.param)
     * ((F2.answer - F1.answer)
         / (CASE WHEN F1.param = F2.param
                  THEN 1.00
                  ELSE F2.param - F1.param END)))
       AS answer
 FROM SomeFunction AS F1, SomeFunction AS F2
WHERE F1.param -- establish a and f(a)
  = (SELECT MAX(param)
           FROM SomeFunction
          WHERE param <= :my_parameter)
  AND F2.param -- establish b and f(b)
  = (SELECT MIN(param)
           FROM SomeFunction
          WHERE param >= :my_parameter);
```

The CASE expression in the divisor is to avoid division by zero errors
when f(x) is actually in the table.

The rules for interpolation methods are always expressible in four-function arithmetic, which is good for Standard SQL. In the old days, the function tables often gave an extra value with each parameter and result pair, called a second delta, which was based on finite differences. This was like a second derivative and could be used in a formula to improve the accuracy of the approximation.

This is not a book on numerical analysis, so you will have to go to a library to find details—or ask an old engineer. The best detailed reference is *Interpolation* by J. F. Steffensen (ISBN 10: 0-486-45009-0), which is available from Dover Publications. The book deals with methods for calculating limits on errors and is written at the college level.

CHAPTER 6

Views

A VIEW IS a virtual table defined by a query that does not exist until it is invoked by name in an SQL statement. I will get into details about what the invocation can mean in physical terms shortly. The Standard SQL syntax for the VIEW definition is

```
CREATE VIEW <table name> [(<view column list>)]
AS <query expression>
[WITH [<levels clause>] CHECK OPTION]
<levels clause> ::= CASCADED | LOCAL
```

The <levels clause> option in the WITH CHECK OPTION did not exist in SQL-89 and it is still not widely implemented. This clause has no effect on queries, but only on UPDATE, INSERT, and DELETE statements. You cannot put constraints on a VIEW, as you can with base and TEMPORARY tables. A VIEW has no existence in the database until it is invoked, while a TEMPORARY table is persistent. A derived table exists only in the query in which it is created.

The name of the VIEW must be unique within the entire database schema, like a table name. The VIEW definition cannot reference itself, since it does not exist yet. Nor can the definition reference only other VIEWs; the nesting of VIEWs must eventually resolve to underlying base tables. This only makes sense; if no base tables were involved, what would you be viewing?

6.1   Mullins VIEW Usage Rules

Craig Mullins gave the following rule to ensure that VIEWs are created in a responsible and useful manner. Simply stated, the VIEW creation strategy should be goal-oriented. VIEWs should be created only when they achieve a specific, reasonable goal. Each VIEW should have a specific application or business requirement that it fulfills before it is created. That requirement should be documented somewhere, preferably in a data dictionary.

Although this rule seems obvious, VIEWs are implemented at some shops without much thought as to how they will be used. This can cause the number of VIEWs that must be supported and maintained to continually expand until so many VIEWs exist that it is impossible to categorize their uses.

Unlike other virtual tables, a VIEW is defined in the information tables, and its definition (not its content!) is persisted. VIEWs have storage overhead, and whenever a base table used by a VIEW definition is changed, then all those VIEWs have to be recompiled and checked. Since VIEWs can be built on top of VIEWs, this can be tricky.

This also means that the creator of a VIEW must have ADMIN privileges, while other virtual tables can be created and persisted only in a single statement by a user. Unfortunately, many shops grant this privilege to too many programmers, and the results are many versions of the same or nearly the same VIEW crowding the schema.

The "nearly the same" VIEWs are a special problem. One user might have read the spec "Employees must be over 21 years of age to serve alcohol" to mean (CURRENT_DATE - INTERVAL '21' YEARS > Personnel.birth_date) while a second user saw it as (CURRENT_ DATE - INTERVAL '21' YEARS >= Personnel.birth_date) instead. If VIEW creation had been left to just the DBA, only one of these VIEWs would exist and it would have the correct business rule. The ideal design should give each user a set of VIEWs that make it look as if the schema was designed for just his or her use, without regard to the rest of the enterprise.

6.1.1   Efficient Access and Computations

VIEWs can also be used to ensure optimal access paths. By coding efficient predicates in the VIEW definition SQL, efficient access to the underlying base tables can be guaranteed and will not have to depend on the caliber of each user. This will depend on your SQL product, and you will need some knowledge of how it works with a query. This technique becomes more useful as the SQL becomes more complex.

As optimizers get better and better, this is not as true as it once was. But very often a simple programming trick can make a lot of difference. Consider a VIEW that is to remove the digits from a project identifier and just leave the alphabetic prefix. One way to do this is with a series of nested REPLACE() function calls (if your SQL supports it) and another is with procedural code in a function. The function will be slower, but much easier to invoke that typing in-line code like this:

```
CREATE VIEW ProjectPrefixes (prefix, etc.)
AS
SELECT REPLACE ('9' WITH '' IN
       REPLACE ('8' WITH '' IN
        REPLACE ('7' WITH '' IN
         REPLACE ('6' WITH '' IN
          REPLACE ('5' WITH '' IN
           REPLACE ('4' WITH '' IN
            REPLACE ('3' WITH '' IN
             REPLACE ('2' WITH '' IN
              REPLACE ('1' WITH '' IN
               REPLACE ('0' WITH '' IN proj_id)
           ))))))))), etc.
 FROM Projects
WHERE ..;
```

By putting the nested library function calls into a VIEW, we ensure that the fastest method is used. Later, when we move to an SQL with call to TRANSLATE (proj_id USING RemoveDigits), we can replace the REPLACE() calls with that and get more improvements while having to change any other code.

6.1.2 Column Renaming

You can rename columns in the header of a VIEW as well as in the SELECT clause of the body of a VIEW. This is particularly useful if a base table contains arcane or complicated column names. There are some prime examples of such names in the various vender schema information tables.

Sometimes older applications were developed without sound naming conventions. One example given by Mr. Mullins was a table where the column names are A1, A2, A3, and so forth. Using a VIEW to rename those columns into something useful would be a very good idea.

The VIEW option is worth considering because actually renaming the columns in the table would require dropping and recreating the table— with the entire change management headache that is entailed with such a change. Extending this "rule" should mention that VIEWs can be used to "rename" tables, too. If the table name is ugly, like T1 or some company internal series of characters and numbers (e.g., TR513X7), then it can make sense to create a VIEW on the table with a "better" name (Foobar_Customers).

6.1.3 Proliferation Avoidance

Mullins' second rule is the proliferation avoidance rule. It is simple to state and directly to the point: Do not needlessly create schema objects that are not necessary.

Whenever a schema object is created, additional entries are placed in the Schema Information Tables. Creating needless VIEWs (indeed, any object) causes "catalog clutter"; that is, entries in the catalog for objects that are not needed or not used.

The proliferation avoidance rule is based on common sense. Why create something that is not needed? It just takes up space that could be used for something that is needed.

6.1.4 The VIEW Synchronization Rule

The final VIEW implementation rule is the VIEW synchronization rule. The basic intention of this rule is to ensure that VIEWs are kept in sync with the base tables upon which they are based.

Whenever a change is made to a base table, all VIEWs that are dependent upon that base table should be analyzed to determine if the change impacts them. Each VIEW was created for a specific reason (the VIEW usage rule) and should remain logically pure.

The VIEW should therefore remain useful for that specific reason. This can only be accomplished by ensuring that all subsequent changes that are pertinent to a specified usage are made to all VIEWs that satisfy that usage.

For example, say a VIEW was created to satisfy an access usage, such as a PersonnelAssignments VIEW that was created to provide information about employees and their departments. If a column is added to the Personnel table specifying the employee's Social Security number, it should also be added to the PersonnelAssignments VIEW only if it is pertinent to that VIEW's specific use. Of course, the column can be added to the table immediately and to the VIEW at the earliest convenience of the development team.

The synchronization rule requires that strict change impact analysis procedures be in place. You need to inspect queries, other VIEWs built on the modified VIEW, and dynamic SQL. VIEW synchronization is needed to support the VIEW usage rule. By keeping VIEWs in sync with table changes, the original purpose of the VIEW is maintained.

This is why we do not ever use "SELECT *" in a VIEW definition in production code. You should always use the column list option in the CREATE VIEW clause. When the columns of a base table change, the definition of the "star" will also change. If you are lucky, you will get an error when the VIEW has too many or too few columns when it is invoked. If you are not so lucky, the VIEW will run and give you unexpected answers. If you are unlucky, the VIEW will run and give you wrong answers that you use.

6.2 Updatable and Read-Only VIEWs

Unlike base tables, VIEWs are either updatable or read-only, but not both. INSERT, UPDATE, and DELETE operations are allowed on updatable VIEWs and base tables, subject to any other constraints. INSERT, UPDATE, and DELETE are not allowed on read-only VIEWs, but you can change their base tables, as you would expect.

An updatable VIEW is one that can have each of its rows associated with exactly one row in an underlying base table. When the VIEW is changed, the changes pass through the VIEW to that underlying base table unambiguously. Updatable VIEWs in Standard SQL are defined only for queries that meet these criteria:

1.   Built on only one table

2.   No GROUP BY clause

3.   No HAVING clause

4.   No aggregate functions

5.   No calculated columns

6.   No UNION, INTERSECT or EXCEPT

7.   No SELECT DISTINCT clause

8.   Any columns excluded from the VIEW must be NULLable or have a DEFAULT clause in the base table, so that a whole row can be constructed for insertion

By implication, the VIEW must also contain a key of the table. In short, we are absolutely sure that each row in the VIEW maps back to one and only one row in the base table.

Some updating is handled by the CASCADE option in the referential integrity constraints on the base tables, not by the VIEW declaration.

The definition of updatability in Standard SQL is actually pretty limited, but very safe. The database system could look at information it has in the referential integrity constraints to widen the set of allowed updatable VIEWs. You will find that some implementations are now doing just that, but it is not common yet.

For example in DB2, a view cannot be defined with a query that contains any of these vendor extensions:

1.   FOR UPDATE OF

2.   ORDER BY

3.   OPTIMIZE FOR n ROWS

The major advantage of this limited definition is that it is based on syntax and not semantics. For example, these VIEWs are logically identical:

```
CREATE VIEW Foo1 (a, b, ..) -- updatable, has a key!
AS SELECT (a, b, ..)
     FROM Foobar
   WHERE x IN (1,2);

CREATE VIEW Foo2 (a, b, ..) -- not updatable!
AS SELECT (a, b, ..)
     FROM Foobar
   WHERE x = 1
 UNION ALL
 SELECT (a, b, ..)
  FROM Foobar
  WHERE x = 2;
```

But Foo1 is updatable and Foo2 is not. While I know of no formal proof, I suspect that determining whether a complex query resolves to an updatable query for allowed sets of data values possible in the table is an NP-complete problem.

Without going into details, here is a list of types of queries that can yield updatable VIEWs, as taken from "VIEW Update Is Practical" (N. Goodman, *InfoDB*, Vol. 5, No. 2, 1990):

1.   Projection from a single table (Standard SQL)

2.   Restriction/projection from a single table (Standard SQL)

3.   UNION VIEWs

4.   Set difference VIEWs

5.   One-to-one joins

6.   One-to-one outer joins

7.   One-to-many joins

8.   One-to-many outer joins

9.   Many-to-many joins

10.   Translated and coded fields

The CREATE TRIGGER mechanism for tables indicates an action to be performed BEFORE, AFTER, or INSTEAD OF a regular INSERT, UPDATE, or DELETE to that table. It is possible for a user to write INSTEAD OF triggers on VIEWs, which catch the changes and route them to the base tables that make up the VIEW. The database designer has complete control over the way VIEWs are handled.

The INSTEAD OF trigger was the Standards Committee letting the DBA decide on how to resolve the VIEW updating problem. These triggers are added to a VIEW and are executed on base tables instead of making changes directly to the VIEW itself. If you think about it, how would a program change the VIEW anyway? It does not exist.

6.3   Types of VIEWs

The type of SELECT statement and its purpose can classify VIEWs. The strong advantage of a VIEW is that it will produce the correct results when it is invoked, based on the current data. Trying to do the same sort of things with temporary tables or computed columns within a table can be subject to errors and slower to read from disk.

6.3.1   Single-Table Projection and Restriction

In practice, many VIEWs are projections or restrictions on a single base table. This is a common method for security control by removing rows or columns that a particular group of users is not allowed to see. These VIEWs are usually implemented by in-line macro expansion, since the optimizer can easily fold their code into the final query plan.

6.3.2   Calculated Columns

One common use for a VIEW is to provide summary data across a row. For example, given a table with measurements in metric units, we can construct a VIEW that hides the calculations to convert them into English units.

It is important to be sure that you have no problems with NULL values when constructing a calculated column. For example, given a Personnel table with columns for both salary and commission, you might construct this VIEW:

```
CREATE VIEW Payroll (emp_nbr, paycheck_amt)
AS
SELECT emp_nbr, (salary + COALESCE(commission), 0.00)
 FROM Personnel;
```

Office workers do not get commissions, so the value of their commission column will be NULL; we use the COALESCE() function to change the NULLs to zeros.

SQL Server introduced a computed column construct in their table declaration syntax, <expression> AS <column name>. This is proprietary and has some limitations in that it can only reference columns in the same row.

6.3.3   Translated Columns

Another common use of a VIEW is to translate codes into text or other codes by doing table lookups. This is a special case of a joined VIEW based on a FOREIGN KEY relationship between two tables. For example, an order table might use a part number that we wish to display with a part name on an order entry screen. This is done with a JOIN between the order table and the inventory table, thus:

```
CREATE VIEW Screen (part_nbr, part_name, ...)
AS SELECT Orders.part_nbr, Inventory.part_name, ...
    FROM Inventory, Orders
   WHERE Inventory.part_nbr = Orders.part_nbr;
```

The idea of JOIN VIEWs to translate codes can be expanded to show more than just one translated column. The result is often a "star" query with one table in the center, joined by FOREIGN KEY relations to many other tables to produce a result that is more readable than the original central table.

Missing values are a problem. If there is no translation for a given encoding, no row appears in the VIEW, or if an OUTER JOIN was used, a NULL will appear. The programmer should establish a referential integrity constraint to CASCADE changes between the tables to prevent loss of data.

6.3.4   Grouped VIEWs

A grouped VIEW is based on a query with a GROUP BY clause. Since each of the groups may have more than one row in the base from which it was built, these are necessarily read-only VIEWs. Such VIEWs usually have one or more aggregate functions and they are used for reporting purposes. They are also handy for working around weaknesses in SQL. Consider a VIEW that shows the largest sale in each state. The query is straightforward:

```
CREATE VIEW BigSales (state, sales_amt_total)
AS SELECT state_code, MAX(sales_amt)
    FROM Sales
   GROUP BY state_code;
```

SQL does not require that the grouping column(s) appear in the select clause, but it is a good idea in this case.

These VIEWs are also useful for "flattening out" one-to-many relationships. For example, consider a Personnel table, keyed on the employee number (emp_nbr), and a table of dependents, keyed on a combination of the employee number for each dependent's parent (emp_nbr) and the dependent's own serial number (dep_id). The goal is to produce a report of the employees by name with the number of dependents each has.

```
CREATE VIEW DepTally1 (emp_nbr, dependent_cnt)
AS SELECT emp_nbr, COUNT(*)
    FROM Dependents
   GROUP BY emp_nbr;
```

The report is simply an OUTER JOIN between this VIEW and the Personnel table.

The OUTER JOIN is needed to account for employees without dependents with a NULL value, like this:

```
SELECT emp_name, dependent_cnt
FROM Personnel AS P1
   LEFT OUTER JOIN
   DepTally1 AS D1
   ON P1.emp_nbr = D1.emp_nbr;
```

6.3.5   UNIONed VIEWs

VIEWs based on a UNION or UNION ALL operation are read-only, because there is no way to map a change onto just one row in one of the base tables. The UNION operator will remove duplicate rows from the results. Both the UNION and UNION ALL operators hide which table the rows came from. Such VIEWs must use a <view column list>, because the columns in a UNION [ALL] have no names of their own. In theory, a UNION of two disjoint tables, neither of which has duplicate rows in itself, should be updatable.

Using the problem given in Section 6.3.4 on grouped VIEWs, this could also be done with a UNION query that would assign a count of zero to employees without dependents, thus:

```
CREATE VIEW DepTally2 (emp_nbr, dependent_cnt)
AS (SELECT emp_nbr, COUNT(*)
      FROM Dependents
    GROUP BY emp_nbr)
   UNION
   (SELECT emp_nbr, 0
     FROM Personnel AS P2
    WHERE NOT EXISTS (SELECT *
                        FROM Dependents AS D2
                       WHERE D2.emp_nbr = P2.emp_nbr));
```

The report is now a simple INNER JOIN between this VIEW and the Personnel table. The zero value, instead of a NULL value, will account for employees without dependents. The report query looks like this:

```
SELECT emp_name, dependent_cnt
 FROM Personnel, DepTally2
WHERE DepTally2.emp_nbr = Personnel.emp_nbr;
```

Major DBMSs, such as Oracle and DB2, support inserts, updates, and delete from such views. Under the covers, each partition is a separate table, with a rule for its contents. One of the most common partitioning concepts is temporal, so each partition might be based on a date range. The goal is to improve query performance by allowing parallel access to each partition member.

The trade-off is a heavy overhead under the covers with the UNIONed VIEW partitioning, however. For example, DB2 attempts to insert any given row into each of the tables underlying the UNION ALL view. It then counts how many tables accepted the row. It has to process the entire view, one table at a time, and collect the results.

1.   If exactly one table accepts the row, the insert is accepted.

2.   If no table accepts the row, a "no target" error is raised.

3.   If more than one table accepts the row, an "ambiguous target" error is raised.

The use of INSTEAD OF triggers gives the user the effect of a single table, but there can still be surprises. Think about three tables; A, B, and C. Table C is disjoint from the other two. Tables A and B overlap. So I can always insert into C and may or may not be able to insert into A and B if I hit overlapping rows.

Going back to my Y2K consulting days, I ran into a version of such a partition by calendar periods. Their Table C was set up on fiscal quarters and got leap year wrong because one of the fiscal quarters ended on the last day of February.

Another approach somewhat like this is to declare explicit partitioning rules in the DDL with a proprietary syntax. The system will handle the housekeeping, and the user sees only one table. In the Oracle model, the goal is to put parts of the logical table to different physical tablespaces. Using standard data types, the Oracle syntax looks like this:

```
CREATE TABLE Sales
(invoice_nbr INTEGER NOT NULL PRIMARY KEY,
 sale_year INTEGER NOT NULL,
 sale_month INTEGER NOT NULL,
 sale_day INTEGER NOT NULL)
PARTITION BY RANGE (sale_year, sale_month, sale_day)
(PARTITION sales_q1 VALUES LESS THAN (1994, 04, 01)
 TABLESPACE tsa,
PARTITION sales_q2 VALUES LESS THAN (1994, 07, 01)
TABLESPACE tsb,
PARTITION sales_q3 VALUES LESS THAN (1994, 10, 01)
TABLESPACE tsc,
PARTITION sales_q4 VALUES LESS THAN (1995, 01, 01)
TABLESPACE tsd);
```

Again, this will depend on your product, since this has to do with the physical database and not the logical model.

6.3.6   JOINs in VIEWs

A VIEW whose query expression is a joined table is not usually updatable, even in theory.

One of the major purposes of a joined view is to "flatten out" a one-to-many or many-to-many relationship. Such relationships cannot map one row in the VIEW back to one row in the underlying tables on the "many" side of the JOIN. Perhaps the major advantage of putting complex joins into a VIEW is that everyone will use the same code. When you get to four more tables and a complex search condition, it is hard to be sure that everyone is reading and coding the specs the same way.

One of the most useful examples of this is the relational division. A query to find which projects are using all of the tools in a toolshed can be written like this:

```
SELECT DISTINCT project_id
  FROM Projects AS P1
 WHERE NOT EXISTS
       (SELECT *
          FROM Toolshed AS T
         WHERE NOT EXISTS
               (SELECT *
                  FROM Projects AS P2
                 WHERE (P1.project_id = P2.project_id)
                   AND (P2.tool_id = T.tool_id)));
```

This query uses correlated subselects to return a list of all projects in the Projects table that require every tool in the toolshed table. By coding this SQL into a VIEW called, say, "Tool_Usage," the end user will need only to issue the following simple SELECT statement instead of the more complicated query:

```
SELECT project_nbr, ..
  FROM Tool_Usage;
```

Now is that not a lot simpler?

6.3.7   Nested VIEWs

A point that is often missed, even by experienced SQL programmers, is that a VIEW can be built on other VIEWs. The only restrictions are that circular references within the query expressions of the VIEWs are illegal and that a VIEW must ultimately be built on base tables. One problem with nested VIEWs is that different updatable VIEWs can reference the same base table at the same time. If these VIEWs then appear in another VIEW, it becomes hard to determine what has happened when the highest-level VIEW is changed. As an example, consider a table with two keys:

```
CREATE TABLE CanadianDictionary
(english_id INTEGER UNIQUE,
french_id INTEGER UNIQUE,
eng_word CHAR(30),
french_word CHAR(30)j
CHECK (COALESCE (english_id, french_id) IS NOT NULL);
```

The table declaration is a bit strange. It allows an English-only or French-only word to appear in the table. But the CHECK() constraint requires that a word must fall into one or both type codes.

```
INSERT INTO CanadianDictionary
VALUES (1, 2, 'muffins', 'croissants'),
       (2, 1, 'bait', 'escargots');
```

```
CREATE VIEW EnglishWords
AS SELECT english_id, eng_word
    FROM CanadianDictionary
   WHERE eng_word IS NOT NULL;
```

```
CREATE VIEW FrenchWords
AS SELECT french_id, french_word
    FROM CanadianDictionary
   WHERE french_word IS NOT NULL);
```

We have now tried the escargots and decided that we wish to change our opinion of them:

```
UPDATE EnglishWords
   SET eng_word = 'appetizer'
 WHERE english_id = 2;
```

Our French user has just tried haggis and decided to insert a new row for his experience:

```
UPDATE FrenchWords
   SET french_word = 'Le swill'
 WHERE french_id = 3;
```

The row that is created is (NULL, 3, NULL, 'Le swill'), since there is no way for VIEW FrenchWords to get to the VIEW EnglishWords columns. Likewise, the English VIEW user can construct a row to record his translation, (3, NULL, 'Haggis', NULL). But neither of them can consolidate the two rows into a meaningful piece of data.

To delete a row is also to destroy data; the French speaker who drops "croissants" from the table also drops "muffins" from VIEW EnglishWords.

6.4   Modeling Classes with Tables

Many years ago, the ANSI X3H2 Database Standards Committee (now the INCITS H2 Database Standards Committee) had a meeting in Rapid City, South Dakota. We had Mount Rushmore and Bjarne Stroustrup as special attractions. Mr. Stroustrup did his slide show about Bell Labs inventing C++ and OO programming for us, and we got to ask questions.

One of the questions was how we should put OO stuff into SQL. His answer was that Bells Labs, with all their talent, had tried four different approaches to this problem and had come the conclusion that you should not do it. OO was great for programming but deadly for data.

I have watched people try to force OO models into SQL and it falls apart in about a year. Every typo becomes a new attribute or class, queries that would have been so easy in a relational model are now multitable monster outer joins, redundancy grows at an exponential rates, constraints are virtually impossible to write so you can kiss data integrity goodbye, and so forth.

Having said all that, here are some suggestions for modeling classes with tables. There are products that will do this sort of mapping for you, but you should know what is actually happening and be able to maintain control of your schema.

6.4.1   Class Hierarchies in SQL

The classic scenario calls for a root class with all the common attributes and then put specialized subclasses under it. As an example, let's take the class of Publications and use Global Trade Identification Numbers (GTIN) as our standard and add two mutually exclusive subclasses, 'Book' and 'Disk' media.

```
CREATE TABLE Publications
(gtin CHAR(15) NOT NULL PRIMARY KEY,
```

```
media_type CHAR(4) NOT NULL
   CHECK(media_type IN ('Book', 'Disk')),
UNIQUE (gtin, media_type),
publication_title VARCHAR(75) NOT NULL,
..);
```

I then use a compound key (gtin, media_type) and a constraint in each subclass table to ensure that the media_type is locked and agrees with the Publications table. Add some DRI actions and you are done:

```
CREATE TABLE Books
(gtin CHAR(15) NOT NULL PRIMARY KEY,
media_type CHAR(4) DEFAULT 'Book' NOT NULL
   CHECK (media_type = 'Book'),
UNIQUE (gtin, media_type),
FOREIGN KEY (gtin, media_type)
 REFERENCES Publications (gtin, media_type)
 ON UPDATE CASCADE
 ON DELETE CASCADE,
book_size CHAR(10) NOT NULL
   CHECK (book_size IN ('folio', 'quarto', 'sexto',
        'octavo', 'duodecimo', 'sextodecimo', ..),
   ..);
```

```
CREATE TABLE Disks
(gtin CHAR(15) NOT NULL PRIMARY KEY,
media_type CHAR(4) DEFAULT 'Disk' NOT NULL
   CHECK (media_type = 'Disk'),
UNIQUE (gtin, media_type),
FOREIGN KEY (gtin, media_type)
 REFERENCES Publications (gtin, media_type)
 ON UPDATE CASCADE
 ON DELETE CASCADE,
..);
```

I can continue to build a hierarchy like this. For example, if I had the Disks class that broke down into CDs and DVDs, I could create a schema like this:

```
CREATE TABLE Disks
(gtin CHAR(15) NOT NULL PRIMARY KEY,
 media_type CHAR(4) DEFAULT 'Disk' NOT NULL
   CHECK(media_type IN ('CD', 'DVD', 'Disk')),
```

```
UNIQUE (gtin, media_type),
FOREIGN KEY (gtin, media_type)
 REFERENCES Publications (gtin, media_type)
 ON UPDATE CASCADE
 ON DELETE CASCADE,
..);

CREATE TABLE CompactDisks
(gtin CHAR(15) NOT NULL PRIMARY KEY,
 media_type CHAR(4) DEFAULT 'CD' NOT NULL
   CONSTRAINT cd_only
   CHECK(media_type = 'CD'),
UNIQUE (gtin, media_type),
FOREIGN KEY (gtin, media_type)
 REFERENCES Disks (gtin, media_type)
 ON UPDATE CASCADE
 ON DELETE CASCADE,
track_cnt INTEGER NOT NULL,
 ..);

CREATE TABLE DigitalVideoDisks
(gtin CHAR(15) NOT NULL PRIMARY KEY,
 media_type CHAR(4) DEFAULT 'DVD' NOT NULL
   CONSTRAINT dvd_only
   CHECK(media_type = 'DVD'),
UNIQUE (gtin, media_type),
FOREIGN KEY (gtin, media_type)
 REFERENCES Disks (gtin, media_type)
 ON UPDATE CASCADE
 ON DELETE CASCADE,
 studio_name CHAR(15) NOT NULL,
..);
```

The idea is to build a chain of identifiers and types in a UNIQUE()
constraint that go up the tree when you use a REFERENCES constraint.
Obviously, you can do variants of this trick to get different class
structures.

If an entity does not have to be exclusively one subtype, you play
with the root of the class hierarchy:

```
CREATE TABLE Publications
(gtin CHAR(15) NOT NULL,
```

```
media_type CHAR(4) NOT NULL
  CHECK(media_type IN ('Book', 'Disk')),
PRIMARY KEY (gtin, media_type),
..);
```

Now start hiding all this stuff in VIEWs immediately, and add an INSTEAD OF trigger to those VIEWs. Otherwise, the queries, updates, and inserts will quickly become too complex for the average programmer to maintain.

6.4.2   Subclasses via ASSERTIONs and TRIGGERs

Another approach to keeping the subclasses disjoint is due to David Portas. If you have a full implementation of SQL-92, then you can use this construct:

```
CREATE ASSERTION ProductTypesAreDisjoint
CHECK (UNIQUE (SELECT gtin FROM Books
                UNION ALL
                SELECT gtin FROM CDs
                UNION ALL
                SELECT gtin FROM DVDs));
```

An ASSERTION is a CHECK() constraint that applies to the entire schema rather than being attached to any particular table. This lets me reference several tables in one constraint and enforce relationships among them. Because of ASSERTIONs, CHECK() constraint names have to be globally unique in Standard SQL. They also get around the problem that all table constraints are TRUE when the table is empty, so that you cannot easily check for an empty table.

This same constraint can be put into TRIGGERs on the three tables shown here, but then the optimizer will not get any help from the declarative code.

6.5   How VIEWs Are Handled in the Database System

Standard SQL requires a system schema table with the text of the VIEW declarations in it. What would be handy, but is not easily done in all SQL implementations, is to trace the VIEWs down to their base tables by printing out a tree diagram of the nested structure. You should check your user library and see if it has such a utility program (for example, FINDVIEW in the SPARC library for SQL/DS). There are several ways to handle VIEWs, and systems will often use a mixture of them. The major categories of algorithms are materialization and in-line text expansion.

6.5.1   VIEW Column List

The <view column list> is optional; when it is not given, the VIEW will inherit the column names from the query. The number of column names in the <view column list> has to be the same as the degree of the query expression. If any two columns in the query have the same column name, you must have a <view column list> to resolve the ambiguity. The same column name cannot be specified more than once in the <view column list>.

6.5.2   VIEW Materialization

Materialization means that whenever you use the name of the VIEW, the database engine finds its definition in the schema information tables and creates a working table with that name that has the appropriate column names with the appropriate data types. Finally, this new table is filled with the results of the SELECT statement in the body of the VIEW definition.

The decision to materialize a VIEW as an actual physical table is implementation-defined in Standard SQL, but the VIEW must act as if it were materialized when accessed for a query. If the VIEW is not updatable, this approach automatically protects the base tables from any improper changes and is guaranteed to be correct. It uses existing internal procedures in the database engine (create table, insert from query), so this is easy for the database to do.

The downside of this approach is that it is not very fast for large VIEWs, it uses extra storage space, it cannot take advantage of indexes already existing on the base tables, it usually cannot create indexes on the new table, and it cannot be optimized as easily as other approaches.

However, materialization is the best approach for certain VIEWs. A VIEW whose construction has a hidden sort is usually materialized. Queries with SELECT DISTINCT, UNION, GROUP BY, and HAVING clauses are usually implemented by sorting to remove duplicate rows or to build groups. As each row of the VIEW is built, it has to be saved to compare it to the other rows, so it makes sense to materialize it.

Another reason to materialize a VIEW is to share it with other queries. A database has a scheduler that looks at the waiting jobs and decides in which order to execute them. If there are summary VIEWs for a reporting period, and lots of reports will be run against them at the same time, it makes more sense to materialize one result as a physical table than to make a local copy for each of the queries using it.

Some products also give you the option of controlling the materializations yourself. The vendor terms vary. A "snapshot" means materializing a table that also includes a timestamp. A "result set" is a materialized table that is passed to a front-end application program for display. Check your particular product.

6.6   In-Line Text Expansion

Another approach is to store the text of the CREATE VIEW statement and work it into the parse tree of the SELECT, INSERT, UPDATE, or DELETE statements that use it. This allows the optimizer to blend the VIEW definition into the final query plan. For example, you can create a VIEW based on a particular department, thus:

```
CREATE VIEW SalesDept (dept_name, city_name, ...)
AS SELECT 'Sales', city_name, ...
     FROM Departments
    WHERE dept_name = 'Sales';
```

and then use it as a query, thus:

```
SELECT *
  FROM SalesDept
 WHERE city_name = 'New York';
```

The parser expands the VIEW into text (or an intermediate tokenized form) within the FROM clause. The query would become, in effect,

```
SELECT *
  FROM (SELECT 'Sales', city_name, ...
          FROM Departments
         WHERE dept_name = 'Sales')
        AS SalesDept (dept_name, city_name, ...)
 WHERE city_name = 'New York';
```

and the query optimizer would then "flatten it out" into:

```
SELECT *
  FROM Departments
 WHERE (dept_name = 'Sales')
   AND (city_name = 'New York');
```

Since we know that the short identification number is a key, we can use this VIEW:

```
CREATE VIEW Shorty (short_id, amt1, amt2, ...)
AS SELECT DISTINCT SUBSTRING(long_id FROM 1 TO 6),
amt1, amt2, ...
     FROM TableA;
```

Then the report query is:

```
SELECT short_id, SUM(amt1), SUM(amt2), ...
  FROM Shorty
 GROUP BY short_id;
```

Note that VIEWs cannot have their own indexes. However, VIEWs can inherit the indexing on their base tables when they are used as in-line code. The materialized VIEWs generally cannot do that.

6.7   WITH CHECK OPTION Clause

If WITH CHECK OPTION is specified, the viewed table has to be updatable. This is actually a fast way to check how your particular SQL implementation handles updatable VIEWs. Try to create a version of the VIEW in question using the WITH CHECK OPTION and see if your product will allow you to create it. The WITH CHECK OPTION is part of the SQL-89 standard, which was extended in Standard SQL by adding an optional <levels clause>. CASCADED is implicit if an explicit LEVEL clause is not given. Consider a VIEW defined as

```
CREATE VIEW V1
AS SELECT *
     FROM Foobar
   WHERE col1 = 'A';
```

and now UPDATE it with

```
UPDATE V1 SET col1 = 'B';
```

The UPDATE will take place without any trouble, but the rows that were previously seen now disappear when we use V1 again. They no longer meet the WHERE clause condition! Likewise, an INSERT INTO statement with VALUES (col1 = 'B') would insert just fine, but its rows would never be seen again in this VIEW. VIEWs created this way will always have all the rows that meet the criteria, and that can be handy. For example, you can set up a VIEW of rows with a status code of "to be done", work on them, and change a status code to "finished", and they will disappear from your view. The important point is that the WHERE clause condition was checked only at the time when the VIEW was invoked.

The WITH CHECK OPTION makes the system check the WHERE clause condition upon insertion or UPDATE. If the new or changed row fails the test, the change is rejected and the VIEW remains the same. Thus, the previous UPDATE statement would get an error message and you could not change certain columns in certain ways. For example, consider a VIEW of salaries under $30,000 defined with a WITH CHECK OPTION to prevent anyone from giving a raise above that ceiling.

The WITH CHECK OPTION clause does not work like a CHECK constraint.

```
CREATE TABLE Foobar (col_a INTEGER);

CREATE VIEW TestView (col_a)
AS
SELECT col_a FROM Foobar WHERE col_a > 0
WITH CHECK OPTION;

INSERT INTO TestView VALUES (NULL); — This fails!

CREATE TABLE Foobar_2 (col_a INTEGER CHECK (col_a > 0));
INSERT INTO Foobar_2(col_a)
VALUES (NULL); -- This succeeds!
```

The WITH CHECK OPTION must be TRUE while the CHECK constraint can be either TRUE or UNKNOWN. Once more, you need to watch out for NULLs.

Standard SQL has introduced an optional <levels clause>, which can be either CASCADED or LOCAL. If no <levels clause> is given, a <levels clause> of CASCADED is implicit. The idea of a CASCADED check is that the system checks all the underlying levels that built the VIEW, as well as the WHERE clause condition in the VIEW itself. If anything causes a row to disappear from the VIEW, the UPDATE is rejected. The idea of a WITH LOCAL check option is that only the local WHERE clause is checked. The underlying VIEWs or tables from which this VIEW is built might also be affected, but we do not test for those effects. Consider two VIEWs built on each other from the salary table:

```
CREATE VIEW Lowpay
AS SELECT *
     FROM Personnel
    WHERE salary <= 250;

CREATE VIEW Mediumpay
AS SELECT *
     FROM Lowpay
    WHERE salary >= 100;
```

If neither VIEW has a WITH CHECK OPTION, the effect of updating Mediumpay by increasing every salary by $1,000 will be passed without any check to Lowpay. Lowpay will pass the changes to the underlying Personnel table. The next time Mediumpay is used, Lowpay will be rebuilt in its own right and Mediumpay rebuilt from it, and all the employees will disappear from Mediumpay.

If only Mediumpay has a WITH CASCADED CHECK OPTION on it, the UPDATE will fail. Mediumpay has no problem with such a large salary, but it would cause a row in Lowpay to disappear, so Mediumpay will reject it. However, if only Mediumpay has a WITH LOCAL CHECK OPTION on it, the UPDATE will succeed. Mediumpay has no problem with such a large salary, so it passes the change along to Lowpay. Lowpay, in turn, passes the change to the Personnel table and the UPDATE occurs. If both VIEWs have a WITH CASCADED CHECK OPTION, the effect is a set of conditions, all of which have to be met. The Personnel table can accept UPDATEs or INSERTs only where the salary is between $100 and $250.

This can become very complex. Consider an example from an ANSI X3H2 paper by Nelson Mattos of IBM (Celko 1993). Let us build a five-layer set of VIEWs, using xx and yy as placeholders for CASCADED or LOCAL, on a base table T1 with columns c1, c2, c3, c4, and c5, all set to a value of 10, thus:

```
CREATE VIEW V1 AS SELECT * FROM T1 WHERE (c1 > 5);

CREATE VIEW V2 AS SELECT * FROM V1 WHERE (c2 > 5)
        WITH xx CHECK OPTION;

CREATE VIEW V3 AS SELECT * FROM V2 WHERE (c3 > 5);
```

```
CREATE VIEW V4 AS SELECT * FROM V3 WHERE (c4 > 5)
      WITH yy CHECK OPTION;

CREATE VIEW V5 AS SELECT * FROM V4 WHERE (c5 > 5);
```

When we set each one of the columns to zero, we get different results, which can be shown in this chart, where S means success and F means failure:

```
xx/yy                  c1   c2   c3   c4   c5
=========================================
cascade/cascade    F    F    F    F    S
local/cascade      F    F    F    F    S
local/local        S    F    S    F    S
cascade/local      F    F    S    F    S
```

To understand the chart, look at the last line. If xx = CASCADED and yy = LOCAL, updating column c1 to zero via V5 will fail, whereas updating c5 will succeed. Remember that a successful UPDATE means the row(s) disappear from V5.

Follow the action for UPDATE V5 SET c1 = 0; VIEW V5 has no with check options, so the changed rows are immediately sent to V4 without any testing. VIEW V4 does have a WITH LOCAL CHECK OPTION, but column c1 is not involved, so V4 passes the rows to V3. VIEW V3 has no with check options, so the changed rows are immediately sent to V2. VIEW V2 does have a WITH CASCADED CHECK OPTION, so V2 passes the rows to V1 and awaits results. VIEW V1 is built on the original base table and has the condition c1 > 5, which is violated by this UPDATE. VIEW V1 then rejects the UPDATE to the base table, so the rows remain in V5 when it is rebuilt. Now the action for

```
UPDATE V5 SET c3 = 0;
```

VIEW V5 has no with check options, so the changed rows are immediately sent to V4, as before. VIEW V4 does have a WITH LOCAL CHECK OPTION, but column c3 is not involved, so V4 passes the rows to V3 without awaiting the results. VIEW V3 is involved with column c3 and has no with check options, so the rows can be changed and passed down to V2 and V1, where they UPDATE the base table. The rows are not seen again when V5 is invoked, because they will fail to get past VIEW V3. The real problem comes with UPDATE statements that change more than one column at a time. For example,

```
UPDATE V5 SET c1 = 0, c2 = 0, c3 = 0, c4 = 0, c5 = 0;
```

will fail for all possible combinations of `<levels clause>`s in the example schema.

Standard SQL defines the idea of a set of conditions that are inherited by the levels of nesting. In our sample schema, these implied tests would be added to each `VIEW` definition:

```
local/local
V1 = none
V2 = (c2 > 5)
V3 = (c2 > 5)
V4 = (c2 > 5) AND (c4 > 5)
V5 = (c2 > 5) AND (c4 > 5)

cascade/cascade
V1 = none
V2 = (c1 > 5) AND (c2 > 5)
V3 = (c1 > 5) AND (c2 > 5)
V4 = (c1 > 5) AND (c2 > 5) AND (c3 > 5) AND (c4 > 5)
V5 = (c1 > 5) AND (c2 > 5) AND (c3 > 5) AND (c4 > 5)

local/cascade
V1 = none
V2 = (c2 > 5)
V3 = (c2 > 5)
V4 = (c1 > 5) AND (c2 > 5) AND (c4 > 5)
V5 = (c1 > 5) AND (c2 > 5) AND (c4 > 5)

cascade/local
V1 = none
V2 = (c1 > 5) AND (c2 > 5)
V3 = (c1 > 5) AND (c2 > 5)
V4 = (c1 > 5) AND (c2 > 5) AND (c4 > 5)
V5 = (c1 > 5) AND (c2 > 5) AND (c4 > 5)
```

6.7.1   WITH CHECK OPTION as CHECK() clause

Lothar Flatz, an instructor for Oracle Software Switzerland, made the observation that while Oracle cannot put subqueries into `CHECK()` constraints, and triggers would not be possible because of the mutating table problem, you can use a `VIEW` that has a `WITH CHECK OPTION` to enforce subquery constraints.

For example, consider a hotel registry that needs to have a rule that you cannot add a guest to a room that another is or will be occupying. Instead of writing the constraint directly, like this:

```
CREATE TABLE Hotel
(room_nbr INTEGER NOT NULL,
arrival_date DATE NOT NULL,
departure_date DATE NOT NULL,
guest_name CHAR(30) NOT NULL,
CONSTRAINT schedule_right
CHECK (H1.arrival_date <= H1.departure_date),
CONSTRAINT no_overlaps
CHECK (NOT EXISTS
     (SELECT *
        FROM Hotel AS H1, Hotel AS H2
      WHERE H1.room_nbr = H2.room_nbr
        AND H2.arrival_date < H1.arrival_date
        AND H1.arrival_date < H2.departure_date)));
```

The schedule_right constraint is fine, since it has no subquery, but many products will choke on the no_overlaps constraint. Leaving the no_overlaps constraint off the table, we can construct a VIEW on all the rows and columns of the Hotel base table and add a WHERE clause that will be enforced by the WITH CHECK OPTION.

```
CREATE VIEW Hotel_V (room_nbr, arrival_date,
departure_date, guest_name)
AS SELECT H1.room_nbr, H1.arrival_date, H1.departure_date,
H1.guest_name
     FROM Hotel AS H1
   WHERE NOT EXISTS
       (SELECT *
        FROM Hotel AS H2
       WHERE H1.room_nbr = H2.room_nbr
         AND H2.arrival_date < H1.arrival_date
         AND H1.arrival_date < H2.departure_date)
     AND H1.arrival_date <= H1.departure_date
  WITH CHECK OPTION;
```

For example,

```
INSERT INTO Hotel_V
VALUES (1, '2006-01-01', '2006-01-03', 'Ron Coe');
```

```
COMMIT;
INSERT INTO Hotel_V
VALUES (1, '2006-01-03', '2006-01-05', 'John Doe');
```

will give a WITH CHECK OPTION clause violation on the second
INSERT INTO statement, as we wanted.

6.8   Dropping VIEWs

VIEWs, like tables, can be dropped from the schema. The Standard SQL
syntax for the statement is:

```
DROP VIEW <table name> <drop behavior>

<drop behavior> ::= [CASCADE | RESTRICT]
```

The <drop behavior> clause did not exist in SQL-86, so vendors
had different behaviors in their implementation. The usual way of
storing VIEWs was in a schema-level table with the VIEW name, the
text of the VIEW, and other information. When you dropped a VIEW,
the engine usually removed the appropriate row from the schema
tables. You found out about dependencies when you tried to use VIEWs
built on other VIEWs that no longer existed. Likewise, dropping a base
table could cause the same problem when the VIEW was accessed.

The CASCADE option will find all other VIEWs that use the dropped
VIEW and remove them as well. If RESTRICT is specified, the VIEW
cannot be dropped if there is anything that is dependent on it. This
implies a structure for the schema tables that is different from just a
simple single table.

The bad news is that some older products will let you drop the
table(s) from which the view is built, but not drop the view itself.

```
CREATE TABLE Foobar (col_a INTEGER);
CREATE VIEW TestView
AS SELECT col_a
     FROM Foobar;

DROP TABLE Foobar; -- drop the base table
```

Unless you also cascaded the DROP TABLE statement, the text of
the view definition was still in the system. Thus, when you reuse the
table and column names, they are resolved at run-time with the view
definition.

```
CREATE TABLE Foobar
(foo_key CHAR(5) NOT NULL PRIMARY KEY,
col_a REAL NOT NULL);
INSERT INTO Foobar VALUES ('Celko', 3.14159);
```

This is a potential security flaw and a violation of the SQL Standard, but be aware that it exists. Notice that the data type of `TestView.col_a` changed from `INTEGER` to `REAL` along with the new version of the table. This is where vendors will have further restrictions based on their dialect.

6.9   Outdated Uses for VIEWs

Over the years, `VIEW`s have been used for other purposes that made sense at the time, but have been rendered obsolete with the advent of new DBMS functionality. You no longer need to program this way, but you might run into it in some old schemas. Each SQL product's programmers tended to use some of these tricks more than other products, so finding them is more of a local dialect problem than an exact science.

Two of these `VIEW` usages are to simulate domain support and to implement queries that access both summary and detail information in a single row. Let me elaborate on both and tell you why these usages are outdated.

6.9.1   Domain Support

It is a sad fact of life that most relational database management systems do not support `CREATE DOMAIN` statements. Domains are an instrumental component of the relational model and were in Dr. Codd's original relational model. In Dr. Codd's model, domains included operators, rules for comparisons of values within a domain so joins could be defined and rules for casting one domain to another.

In SQL, the `CREATE DOMAIN` statement is really global shorthand for a column definition, which can include a data type, default, and `CHECK()` constraints. Some of the functionality of domains used to be implemented using `VIEW`s and the `WITH CHECK OPTION` clause. This was a DB2 idiom more than any other SQL.

The `WITH CHECK OPTION` clause will guarantee that all data inserted or updated using the `VIEW` will adhere to the `VIEW` specification. We have already discussed the `WITH CHECK OPTION` in detail in another section.

6.9.2   Table Expression VIEWs

Another past usage for VIEWs was to do the work of CTEs and/or
scalar table expressions. Early SQL products were not as orthogonal
as the current ones. Instead of putting the table expression in-line, the
programmers created VIEWs, and then used them. This is why many
shops allowed programmers to have ADMIN privileges. This was a
Sybase/SQL Server idiom more than any other SQL products, because
their Transact-SQL dialect allows programmers the ability to create
temporary tables and do other ADMIN functions. It is a short step from
loading a temp table and putting the query into a VIEW.

6.9.3   VIEWs for Table Level CHECK() Constraints

Table Level CHECK() constraints are still not widely implemented, so
this is still a valid trick in many products. In full SQL-92 and higher,
a CHECK() constraint can apply to a single column, as in "CHECK
(order_qty > 0)"; apply to more than one column in the table, as
in "CHECK (order_qty = shipped_qty + backorder_qty)";
apply to the whole table at an aggregate level, as in "CHECK ((SELECT
SUM(order_qty) FROM CustomerOrders) <= (SELECT
SUM(shiped_qty) FROM CustomerOrders))"; or apply to multiple
tables in the schema, as in "CHECK ((SELECT SUM(order_qty)
FROM CustomerOrders) <= (SELECT SUM(onhand_qty) FROM
Inventory))". All of these options can be faked using the WITH
CHECK OPTION, such as this:

```
CREATE VIEW X (..)
AS
SELECT ..
  FROM CustomerOrders
 WHERE ..
   AND NOT EXISTS
       ((SELECT SUM(order_qty) FROM CustomerOrders)
 >= (SELECT SUM(onhand_qty) FROM Inventory))
WITH CHECK OPTION;
```

This technique has problems in that such a VIEW was not updatable
until we had INSTEAD OF triggers. But any product advanced enough
to have such triggers probably also has good support for CHECK()
constraints, DRI actions, and so forth.

6.9.4 One VIEW per Base Table

Oftentimes the dubious recommendation is made to create one VIEW for each base table in a DB2 application system. Craig Mullins calls this "The Big VIEW Myth" in his writings. The reasoning behind this myth was the desire to insulate application programs from database changes. All programs were to be written against VIEWs instead of base tables. When a change is made to the base table, the programs would not need to be modified because they access a VIEW—not the base table.

There is no adequate rationale for enforcing a strict rule of one VIEW per base table for DB2 application systems. In fact, the evidence supports not using VIEWs in this manner.

Although this sounds like a good idea in principle, indiscriminate VIEW creation should be avoided. The implementation of database changes requires scrupulous analysis regardless of whether VIEWs or base tables are used by your applications. Consider the simplest type of database change—adding a column to a table. If you do not add the column to the VIEW, no programs can access that column unless another VIEW is created that contains that column. But if you create a new VIEW every time you add a new column it will not take long for your environment to be swamped with VIEWs. Even more troublesome is the question of which VIEW should be used by which program. Similar arguments can be made for any structural change to the tables.

In general, if you follow good SQL programming practices, you will usually not encounter situations where the usage of VIEWs initially would have helped program/data isolation anyway. By dispelling The Big VIEW Myth, you will decrease the administrative burden of creating and maintaining an avalanche of base table VIEWs.

CHAPTER 7

Virtual Tables

TABLES ARE NOT anything like files. Traditional procedural programmers have to make a "leap of abstraction (faith)" in SQL that does not exist in their model of data. Imagine that you are working with nothing but punch cards and magnetic tapes. Every step in your processing will result in the creation of a physical file. A master tape file was merged with punch card or tape transaction files to produce a new master file. Most of the machine time was spent doing sorts and merges on such files. Electronic data processing (EDP, as we called it back in those days) depended on sequential access to data so that computations could be done in relatively small primary storage devices. You could not put an entire file into primary storage, so you materialized it on scratch tapes. Even later, when disk drives became available, they were used as "faster scratch tapes" rather than as random access devices.

In SQL, tables do not have to have a physical existence on secondary storage. However, if you go to any Internet SQL newsgroup, you can find postings asking for help updating one table from the contents of another in exactly the way we did tape file merges over 40 years ago. Even worse, you will often find a newbie who is using a cursor to mimic an old COBOL or AutoCoder program rather than using a set-oriented UPDATE statement.

7.1　Derived Tables

A derived table is a table expression embedded in a containing statement. It has to be placed inside parentheses. It can optionally be given a correlation name, and its columns can also optionally be given names.

```
(<table expression>)[[AS] <correlation name>
[(<derived column list>)]]
```

The derived table will act as if it is materialized during the duration of the statement that uses it. Notice the phrase "act as if" in that last sentence. The optimizer is free to rearrange the statement in any way that it wishes, so long as the results are the same as the original statement.

Materialization is not an easy choice. If one statement is using a derived table, it might be better to integrate it into that statement. But if many statements are using the same derived table, it might be better to materialize it once, put it in primary or secondary storage, and share. This is the same decision the SQL engine had to make with VIEWs. But the derived tables are not in the schema where the optimizer can find them and keep statistics about them. It takes a pretty smart optimizer to filter them out for materialization.

This is why it is better to put a derived table definition into a VIEW when it is reused often.

7.1.1　Column Naming Rules

Derived tables should follow the same naming rules as the base tables. A table is a table.

The keyword "AS" is not required, but it is a good programming practice, and so is naming the columns. If you do not provide names, then the SQL engine will attempt to do it for you. The table name will not be accessible to you since it will be a temporary internal reference in the schema information table. The SQL engine will use scoping rules to qualify the references in the statement—and what you said might not be what you meant. Likewise, columns in a derived table inherit their names from the defining table expression, but only if the defining table expression creates such names. For example, the columns in a UNION statement have no names unless you use the AS clause.

When you have multiple copies of the same table expression in a statement, you need to tell them apart with different correlation names.

For example, given a table of sports players, we want to show a team captain and team cocaptain.

```
SELECT T1.team_name,
       T1.last_name AS captain,
       T2.last_name AS cocaptain
  FROM Teams AS T1, Teams AS T2
 WHERE T1.team_name = T2.team_name
   AND T1.team_position = 'captain'
   AND T2.team_position = 'cocaptain';
```

I have found that using a short abbreviation and a sequence of integers for correlation names works very well. This also illustrates another naming rule. The player's last name is used in two different roles in this query, so you need to rename the column to the role name (if it stands by itself without qualification) or use the role name as a prefix (e.g., use "`boss_emp_id`" and "`worker_emp_id`" to qualify each employee's role in this table).

7.1.2   Scoping Rules

A derived table can be complete in itself and without a scoping problem at all. For example, consider this query:

```
SELECT O.order_nbr, B.box_size
  FROM Orders AS O,
       (SELECT box_size, packing_qty) FROM Boxes)
       AS B(box_size, packing_qty)
 WHERE O.ship_qty <= B.packing_qty;
```

The derived table "B" has no outer references and it can be retrieved immediately while another parallel processor works on the rest of the

Figure 7.1
SQL Scoping
Rules

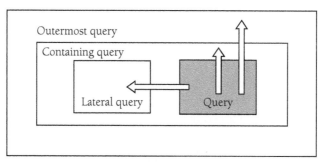

query. Another form of this kind of derived table is a simple scalar subquery:

```
SELECT O.order_nbr AS over_sized_order
  FROM Orders AS O
 WHERE O.ship_qty > (SELECT MAX(packing_qty) FROM Boxes);
```

The scalar subquery is computed; the one-row, one-column result table is converted into a unique scalar value, and the WHERE clause is tested. If the scalar subquery returns an empty result set, it is converted into a NULL. Watch out for that last case, since NULLs have a data type in SQL, and in some weird situations you can get casting errors.

When a table expression references correlation names in which they are contained, you have to be careful. The rules are not that much different from any block structured programming language. You work your way from the inside out.

Chris Date's version of relational division is a popular example of correlation name scoping. The idea is that a divisor table is used to partition a dividend table and produce a quotient or results table. The quotient table is made up of those values of one column for which a second column had all of the values in the divisor.

This is easier to explain with an example. We have a table of pilots and the planes they can fly (dividend); we have a table of planes in the hangar (divisor); we want the names of the pilots who can fly every plane (quotient) in the hangar.

```
SELECT DISTINCT pilot_name
  FROM PilotSkills AS PS1
 WHERE NOT EXISTS
       (SELECT *
          FROM Hangar AS H
         WHERE NOT EXISTS
               (SELECT *
                  FROM PilotSkills AS PS2
                 WHERE PS1.pilot_name = PS2.pilot_name
                   AND PS2.plane_name = H.plane_name));
```

The quickest way to explain what is happening in this query is to imagine a World War II movie where a cocky pilot has just walked into the hangar, looked over the fleet, and announced, "There ain't no plane in this hangar that I can't fly!", which is bad English but good logic.

Notice that PilotSkills appears twice in the query, as PS1 and as PS2. Go to the innermost "SELECT.. FROM.." construct. We have a local

copy of PilotSkills as `PS2` and outer references to tables `H` and `PS1`.
We find that `H` is a copy of the Hangar table one level above us. We find
that `PS1` is a copy of the PilotSkills table two levels above us.

If we had written "`WHERE pilot_name = PS2.pilot_name`"
in the innermost `SELECT`, the scoping rules would have looked for a
local reference first and found it. The search condition would be the
equivalent of "`WHERE PS2.pilot_name = PS2.pilot_name`",
which is always `TRUE` since we cannot have a `NULL` pilot name. Oops,
not what we meant!

It is a good idea to always qualify the column references with a
correlation name. Hangar did not actually need a correlation name
since it appears only once in the statement. But do it anyway. It makes
the code a little easier to understand for the people that have to maintain it—consistent style is always good. It protects your code from
changes in the tables. Imagine several levels of nesting in which an
intermediate table gets a column that had previously been an outer
reference.

7.1.3 Exposed Table Names

The nesting in SQL has the concept of an "exposed name" within a
level. An exposed name is a correlation name, a table name that is not
followed by a correlation name, or a view name that is not followed by
a correlation name. The exposed names must be unique. Here are some
examples to demonstrate scoping rules.

```
SELECT ..
  FROM (SELECT * FROM A WHERE A.x = 1)
       INNER JOIN
       (SELECT * FROM B WHERE B.x = 2)
 WHERE .. ;
```

Tables A and B can be referenced in the outer `WHERE` clause. These are
both exposed names.

```
SELECT ..
  FROM (SELECT * FROM A WHERE A.x = 1)
       INNER JOIN
       (SELECT * FROM B WHERE B.x = 2) AS X(..)
 WHERE .. ;
```

Tables A and X can be referenced in the outer `WHERE` clause. The
correlation name X is now an exposed name.

```
SELECT ..
  FROM ((SELECT * FROM A WHERE A.x = 1)
          INNER JOIN
          (SELECT * FROM B WHERE B.x = 2)) AS X(..)
 WHERE .. ;
```

Only Table X can be referenced in the WHERE clause. The correlation name X is now the only exposed name.

```
SELECT ..
  FROM (SELECT *
          FROM A
         WHERE A.x
             = (SELECT MAX(xx) FROM C))
         INNER JOIN
         (SELECT * FROM B WHERE B.x = 2)
 WHERE .. ;
```

Table C is not exposed to any other SELECT statement.

7.1.4   LATERAL() Clause

Usually an outer reference to a table expression has to be at a higher nesting level. The reason for this restriction is that the table expressions in the FROM clause at the same level are supposed to be created "all at once," and the optimizer is free to decide on the order of creation.

It is possible in SQL-99 to create an outer reference among tables at the same nesting level with the LATERAL() clause in the FROM clause. But the cost is that you can use outer references only to tables that precede the lateral derived table in the FROM clause. This forces a certain order of creation of the table expressions.

If you have worked with procedural languages, you will understand the concept of a "Forward Reference" in many of them. The idea is that you cannot use something before it is created in the module unless you signal the compiler. The most common example is a set of coroutines in which Routine A calls Routine B, then Routine B calls Routine A, and so forth. If Routine A is declared first, it then calls to B have to have an additional declaration that tells the compiler Routine B will be declared later in the module.

The following example is valid:

```
SELECT D1.dept_nbr, D1.dept_name, E.sal_avg, E.emp_cnt
  FROM Departments AS D1,
```

```
(SELECT AVG(E.salary), COUNT(*)
   FROM Personnel AS P
  WHERE P.dept_nbr
        = (SELECT D2.dept_nbr
             FROM Departments AS D2
            WHERE D2.dept_nbr = P.workdept)
) AS E (sal_avg, emp_cnt);
```

Notice that the Departments table appears as D1 and D2 at two levels—D1 is at level one and D2 is a level three.

The following example is not valid because the reference to D.dept_nbr in the WHERE clause of the nested table expression references the Personnel table via P.dept_nbr that is in the same FROM clause—Error, Personnel, and Departments are on the same level.

```
SELECT D.dept_nbr, D.dept_name, E.sal_avg, E.emp_cnt
  FROM Departments AS D,
  (SELECT AVG(P.salary), COUNT(*)
     FROM Personnel AS P
   WHERE P.dept_nbr = D.dept_nbr) AS E(sal_avg, emp_cnt);
```

To make the query valid, we need to add a LATERAL clause in front of the subquery. Notice the order of Personnel and Departments with a LATERAL clause:

```
SELECT D.dept_nbr, D.dept_name, E.sal_avg, E.emp_cnt
  FROM Departments AS D,

 LATERAL (SELECT AVG(P.salary), COUNT(*)
 FROM Personnel AS P
 WHERE P.dept_nbr = D.dept_nbr) AS E(sal_avg, emp_cnt);
```

If your SQL product also has procedures or other syntax that return tables, you might be able to use a LATERAL clause with them.

```
SELECT * FROM A, LATERAL (ProcedureName(A.x)) AS LT;
```

Another syntax for the same concept:

```
SELECT T.c1, X.c5
  FROM T, TABLE (TF(T.c2)) AS X
 WHERE T.c3 = X.c4;
```

I would strongly recommend that you give the results a name, so that multiple calls to the procedure can be identified. I would also recommend that they be avoided for reasons of portability and replaced with VIEWs if needed.

```
SELECT T.c1, X.c5
  FROM T, TABLE(TF (T.c2)) AS X
 WHERE T.c3 = X.c4;
```

Another consideration is that UNION, EXCEPT, and INTERSECT table expressions do not inherit column names. You must use an AS clause to provide column names.

```
SELECT X.a, X.b, X.c, ..
 FROM (X1
       UNION
       X2
       INTERSECT
       X3
       EXCEPT
       X4) AS X (a, b, c, ..)
WHERE ..;
```

It is important to remember that the FROM clause will be executed in left-to-right order unless you use parentheses. There is no operator precedence in SQL. You will also find that many dialects require that the tables have exactly the same data types in corresponding columns; they will not CAST() them for you.

7.2 Common Table Expressions

SQL-99 added the common table expression, or CTE. It is also a query expression that is given a name, just like a derived table. The difference is that they appear before the SELECT statement to which they belong.

7.2.1 Nonrecursive CTEs

The syntax is fairly straightforward for the simple CTE.

```
WITH <cte list> <select stmt>;
<cte list> ::= <cte expr> [, <cte expr>]..
<cte exp> ::= <cte name> [(<column name list>)]
AS (<select stmt>)
```

The query or other statement begins with the keyword WITH, followed by a comma-separated list of CTEs. Each CTE has a unique name within the statement, an optional list of column names, and the keyword AS (it is required) followed by the defining query. In short, the same elements we have in a VIEW or derived table, but in a different order.

The CTE can now be referenced inside the statement to which it is attached in the FROM clause. The reason this is handy is that in Standard SQL, a user cannot create schema objects. That is an administrative power. The CTE acts like a VIEW and can be invoked many times in the same statement, but it does not require storage in the Schema Information Tables like a VIEW.

```
WITH FloobInventory (product_name, unit_price)
AS
(SELECT I.product_name, I.unit_price
   FROM Inventory AS I
  WHERE I.product_category = 'Floob')
SELECT product_name
  FROM FloobInventory
 WHERE unit_price BETWEEN 10.00 AND 50.00;
```

This example is a bit silly, since the whole query could be done without it. The real power starts to show up with multiple CTEs or with self-joins.

For example, the following query uses two CTEs. The subsequent SELECT query THEN uses an INNER JOIN to match together the records FROM the two CTEs:

```
WITH FloobInventory (product_name, unit_price)
AS
(SELECT I.product_name, I.unit_price
   FROM Inventory AS I
  WHERE I.product_category = 'Floob'),
 --next CTE
MailCustomers (cust_name, product_name)
AS
(SELECT cust_name, COUNT(*)
   FROM Orders AS O
  WHERE shipment_method = 'Mail'
 GROUP BY cust_name
 HAVING COUNT(*) > 5)
SELECT M.cust_name, O.product_name
  FROM FloobInventory AS F, MailCustomers AS M
 WHERE O.product_name = N.product_name;
```

Again, this could be done with a single query and derived tables. The advantage is that the more complex query to find customers who want to get their Floobs in the mail is contained in one block of code. I have actually seen this style carried to an extreme in a single 15-page query in DB2.

Assume that we have a Personnel table that uses a nested sets model, and we want to find how deep the hierarchy is in the accounting department.

```
WITH AccountingPersonnel (emp_name, lft, rgt)
AS
(SELECT emp_name, lft, rgt
   FROM Personnel AS P1
  WHERE P1.dept_name = 'Accounting')
SELECT AP2.emp_name,
       COUNT(AP1.emp_name)-1) AS lvl
  FROM AccountingPersonnel AS AP1,
       AccountingPersonnel AS AP2
 GROUP BY AP2.emp_name;
```

Without the CTE, the code for the AccountingPersonnel would have to have been repeated as derived tables. We would then have to hope that the optimizer is smart enough to factor out the common table expressions and decide if it should materialize them or not.

Another advantage is that if the criteria for the query used in the self-join changes, you need only fix it in one place, one time.

7.2.2   Recursive CTEs

Unless you are a programmer in Lisp, Algol, Pascal, or other recursive languages, you probably do not remember much about recursion. A recursive process or structure has three steps:

1. *Initialization.* This is where the process starts.

2. *Recursion.* The process is first repeated on the initial data and then on the results of the prior step.

3. *Termination.* The process gets to some predefined state and stops. The results are now ready. One of the most common errors is messing up the termination step and going into an endless recursive cycle.

The SQL model starts with a SELECT statement and puts that result set into a working table. The working table is then UNION ALLed with the second SELECT statement results.

That result becomes the new working table. This process is repeated until the second SELECT statement returns an empty set or a termination state. The working table is now the result set.

Just as Factorial is the standard example used for recursive functions, the standard example used for recursive CTEs is an adjacency list model of an organizational chart.

```
CREATE TABLE OrgChart
(dept_id INTEGER NOT NULL,
 dept_name VARCHAR(20) NOT NULL,
 emp_count INTEGER NOT NULL,
 super_dept_id INTEGER);
```

To retrieve the number of employees of a given department, including all their subordinate organizational units:

```
WITH RECURSIVE CTE_1(dept_id, emp_count, super_dept_id) AS
(SELECT O1.dept_id, O1.emp_count, O1.super_dept_id
   FROM OrgChart AS O1
  WHERE O1.dept_name = 'Accounting'
UNION ALL
  SELECT O2.dept_id, O2.emp_count, O2.super_dept_id
    FROM OrgChart AS O2, CTE_1 AS O3
   WHERE O2.super_dept_id = O3.dept_id)
SELECT 'Accounting' AS dept_name, SUM(emp_count) FROM CTE_1;
```

This will work as long as there are no loops in the organizational hierarchy. If the recursive query definition returns the same department id for both the subordinate and the superior departments, you get an infinite loop.

You might want to see if your SQL product has a proprietary way to limit the number of recursion levels allowed for a specific statement.

Options and performance for the recursive CTEs will vary from product to product, but as a rule they are slow. It is hard to optimize repeated queries of unknown depth or to even discover if they terminate for the general case. The intermediate result set has to be materialized so it can be stored and used by the following steps.

7.3 Temporary Tables

The SQL engine has always been free to create temporary working tables to hold intermediate results. The user will never see these constructs, nor should he or she wish to do so. However, in the early versions of the SQL Standards and vendor products, users were given access to such tables in various ways.

7.3.1 ANSI/ISO Standards

The ANSI/ISO Standards have a clear strong separation of user and admin privileges. In 30 words or less, a USER can INSERT, UPDATE, DELETE, and query the schema. An ADMIN has those privileges plus the ability to change the schema structure with CREATE, ALTER, and DROP statements.

Tables in Standard SQL can be defined as persistent base tables, local temporary tables, or global temporary tables. The complete syntax is

```
<table definition> ::=
  CREATE [{GLOBAL | LOCAL} TEMPORARY] TABLE <table name>
    <table element list>
    [ON COMMIT {DELETE | PRESERVE} ROWS]
```

A local temporary table belongs to a single user. A global temporary table is shared by more than one user and can be used to pass data among them. When a session using a temporary table is over and the work is COMMITted, the table can be either emptied or saved for the next transaction in the user's session. This is a way of giving users working storage without giving them CREATE TABLE (and therefore DROP TABLE and ALTER TABLE) administrative privileges.

7.3.2 Vendors Models

Vendor products that predate the ANSI/ISO Standards have allowed a programmer to create temporary tables on the fly. The mechanism had to exist for the SQL engine, so it was easy to expose. These tables may or may not persist after a user session.

The temporary tables are actual materialized tables with unique system-generated names to keep them local to their creator; they take up physical storage space. If a hundred users call the same procedure, it can allocate tables for a hundred copies of the same data and bring performance down to nothing.

The real problem is that an SQL procedure quickly becomes a sequential file-processing program with the temporary working tapes replaced by temporary working tables. This is particularly true among SQL Server and Sybase programmers.

A better programming technique is to avoid temporary tables altogether. Derived tables and VIEWs allow the optimizer to decide to materialize the data or not, how to share among users, and how to do other optimizations. Such code will be much more portable than a proprietary implementation of temporary tables.

7.4 The Information Schema

The Standards define an information schema that is supposed to be universally implemented in all SQL products. This schema provides VIEWs that are defined in terms of base tables that hold metadata about the other schemas. The only purpose of the definition schema is to provide a data model to support the information schema and to assist understanding. An implementation need do no more than simulate the existence of the definition schema, as seen through the information schema VIEWs.

We start with the INFORMATION_SCHEMA, which allows us to access these VIEWs in the same way we would access any other tables in any other schema. SELECT on all of these VIEWs is granted to PUBLIC WITH GRANT OPTION, so that they can be queried by any user and so that SELECT privilege can be further granted on VIEWs that reference these information schema VIEWs. No other privilege is granted on them, so they cannot be updated.

The information schema also contains a small number of domains and ASSERTIONs that it uses internally. USAGE on all these domains is granted to PUBLIC WITH GRANT OPTION, so that they can be used by any user.

An implementation can put more objects into the INFORMATION_SCHEMA and also add columns to its tables. The base tables are defined as being in a schema named DEFINITION_SCHEMA. The definition schema cannot be accessed in an SQL statement, because its name is protected.

Some older SQL products allowed a clever hacker to get into the local equivalent of INFORMATION_SCHEMA and DEFINITION_SCHEMA and destroy the entire database. This is an insanely dangerous way to program, but there were "cowboy coders" who would do it in the name of speed and efficient programming.

The Standards state that information schema tables should be represented in the definition schema in the same way as any other tables and are hence self-describing. This is SQL describing itself.

7.4.1   The INFORMATION_SCHEMA Declarations

Things begin with the declaration:

```
CREATE SCHEMA INFORMATION_SCHEMA;
AUTHORIZATION INFORMATION_SCHEMA;

CREATE TABLE INFORMATION_SCHEMA_CATALOG_NAME
(CATALOG_NAME SQL_IDENTIFIER,
CONSTRAINT INFORMATION_SCHEMA_CATALOG_NAME_PRIMARY_KEY
PRIMARY KEY (CATALOG_NAME));
```

The value of CATALOG_NAME is the name of the catalog in which this information schema resides. The INFORMATION_SCHEMA_CATALOG_ NAME_CARDINALITY assertion ensures that there is exactly one row in the INFORMATION_SCHEMA_CATALOG_NAME table.

```
CREATE ASSERTION INFORMATION_SCHEMA_CATALOG_NAME_CARDINALITY
CHECK (1 = (SELECT COUNT(*)
FROM INFORMATION_SCHEMA_CATALOG_NAME));
```

From this point, a set of VIEWs is declared to hold commonly used information about the schemas. For example, the user and the schemas that he or she owns appear in this VIEW.

7.4.2   A Quick List of VIEWS and Their Purposes

SCHEMATA = Locates the schemas, their names, catalogs, default character set, and so forth.

DOMAINS = Identifies the domains defined in this catalog that are accessible to a given user.

DOMAIN_CONSTRAINTS = Identifies the domain constraints of domains in this catalog that are accessible to a given user.

TABLES = Identifies the tables defined in this catalog that are accessible to a given user.

VIEWS = Identifies the viewed tables defined in this catalog that are accessible to a given user.

COLUMNS = Identifies the columns of tables defined in this catalog that are accessible to a given user.

TABLE_PRIVILEGES = Identifies the privileges on tables defined in this catalog that are available to or granted by a given user.

COLUMN_PRIVILEGES = Identifies the privileges on columns of tables defined in this catalog that are available to or granted by a given user.

USAGE_PRIVILEGES = Identifies the USAGE privileges on objects defined in this catalog that are available to or granted by a given user. Newbies often think only in terms of privileges on TABLEs and VIEWs, but a schema also contains Stored Procedures, TRIGGERs, COLLATIONs, and many other things.

TABLE_CONSTRAINTS = Identifies the table constraints defined in this catalog that are owned by a given user.

REFERENTIAL_CONSTRAINTS = Identifies the referential constraints defined in this catalog that are owned by a given user.

CHECK_CONSTRAINTS = Identifies the check constraints defined in this catalog that are owned by a given user.

KEY_COLUMN_USAGE = Identifies the columns defined in this catalog that are constrained as keys by a given user.

ASSERTIONS = Identifies the assertions defined in this catalog that are owned by a given user.

CHARACTER_SETS = Identifies the character sets defined in this catalog that are accessible to a given user.

COLLATIONS = Identifies the character collations defined in this catalog that are accessible to a given user.

TRANSLATIONS = Identifies the character translations defined in this catalog that are accessible to a given user.

VIEW_TABLE_USAGE = Identifies the tables on which viewed tables defined in this catalog and owned by a given user are dependent.

VIEW_COLUMN_USAGE = Identifies the columns on which viewed tables defined in this catalog and owned by a given user are dependent.

CONSTRAINT_TABLE_USAGE = Identifies the tables that are used by referential constraints, unique constraints, check constraints, and assertions defined in this catalog and owned by a given user.

CONSTRAINT_COLUMN_USAGE = Identifies the columns used by referential constraints, unique constraints, check constraints, and assertions defined in this catalog and owned by a given user.

COLUMN_DOMAIN_USAGE = Identifies the columns defined in this catalog that are dependent on a domain defined in this catalog and owned by a user.

SQL_LANGUAGES = Identifies the conformance levels, options, and dialects supported by the SQL-implementation processing data defined in this catalog. What you will find in the ANSI/ISO Standards are the so-called "X3J Languages" that were defined in documents from the ANSI X3 group. They are important because the INCITS H2 Database standards define embeddings and data type conversions for them. They also happen to be the major language in actual use, such as COBOL, FORTRAN, PL/I, Pascal, C, and so forth.

7.4.3 DOMAIN Declarations

These exist simply to make the VIEWs and other schema information tables easier to write. They pretty much explain themselves, but the idea is that when a new SQL Standard comes out, the domains can be ALTERed and the results will cascade through the schema.

SQL_IDENTIFIER = Defines a domain that contains all valid identifiers. They are variable-length character values that conform to the rules for an SQL identifier and default character set. This is a fiction to make defining the VIEWs easier; in practice, they are validated by a parser, not by a table lookup.

The maximum length of <identifier> is implementation-defined. The SQL-92 Standard used 18 characters (an old COBOL standard), and SQL:1999 boosted that to 128.

CHARACTER_DATA = Defines a domain that contains any character data. Again, this is a fiction to make defining the VIEWs easier; in practice, they are validated by a parser, not by a table lookup. Again, the maximum length of a string is implementation-defined.

CARDINAL_NUMBER = Defines a domain that contains any nonnegative number that is less than the implementation-defined maximum for INTEGER (i.e., the implementation-defined value of NUMERIC_PRECISION_RADIX raised to the power of implementation-defined NUMERIC_PRECISION).

The real purpose is to make the VIEWs easier to declare without having to constantly add "CHECK (x >= 0)" on the columns of the base tables.

7.4.4 Definition Schema

The base tables are all defined in a <schema definition> for the schema named DEFINITION_SCHEMA. The table definitions are as complete as the definitional power of SQL allows, so some things might have to be done with other features of the SQL engine.

The specification provides only a model of the base tables that are required and their functionality; it is not an implementation plan.

DEFINITION_SCHEMA Schema

This is where we have the base tables that were used to build the VIEWs we just discussed.

```
CREATE SCHEMA DEFINITION_SCHEMA
AUTHORIZATION DEFINITION_SCHEMA;
```

USERS = The USERS base table has one row for each <authorization identifier> referenced in the information schema of the catalog. These are all those <authorization identifier>s that may grant or receive privileges as well as those that may create a schema, or currently own a schema created through a <schema definition>.

SCHEMATA = The SCHEMATA table has one row for each schema.

DATA_TYPE_DESCRIPTOR = The DATA_TYPE_DESCRIPTOR base table has one row for each domain and one row for each column (in each table) that is defined as having a data type rather than a domain. It effectively contains a representation of the data type descriptors.

DOMAINS = The DOMAINS base table has one row for each domain. DOMAIN_CONSTRAINTS base table

DOMAIN_CONSTRAINTS = This base table has one row for each domain constraint associated with a domain.

TABLES = The TABLES base table contains one row for each table, including VIEWs. This where you can find out if a table is a base table, a global or local temporary table, or a VIEW.

VIEWS = The VIEWs table contains one row for each row in the TABLES table with a TABLE_TYPE of 'VIEW'. Each row describes the query expression that defines a view.

This varies a lot in practice. Some products store the VIEW definition exactly as it was written, others clean it up a bit, and some also store a parsed version that can be immediately used in query parse tree.

The standard requires that any implicit <column reference>s that were contained in the <query expression> used in the <view definition> are replaced by explicit <column reference>s in VIEW_DEFINITION.

COLUMNS = The COLUMNS base table has one row for each column. It simply describes the properties of each column in each table, giving its default, data type, length and so forth.

VIEW_TABLE_USAGE = This is the first of two base tables that allow VIEWs to be treated as tables.

VIEW_COLUMN_USAGE = The VIEW_COLUMN_USAGE base table has one row for each column referenced by a view.

TABLE_CONSTRAINTS = The TABLE_CONSTRAINTS table has one row for each table constraint associated with a table. This is where you see the FOREIGN KEY, PRIMARY KEY, and CHECK constraints described. It also holds information about the deferability of these constraints.

KEY_COLUMN_USAGE = The KEY_COLUMN_USAGE base table has one or more rows for each row in the TABLE_CONSTRAINTS table that has a CONSTRAINT_TYPE of "UNIQUE", "PRIMARY KEY", or "FOREIGN KEY" where it lists the columns that constitute each unique constraint, and the referencing columns in each foreign key constraint.

REFERENTIAL_CONSTRAINTS = The REFERENTIAL_CONSTRAINTS base table has one row for each row in the TABLE_CONSTRAINTS table that has a CONSTRAINT_TYPE of "FOREIGN KEY" and their associated DRI actions.

CHECK_CONSTRAINTS = The CHECK_CONSTRAINTS base table has one row for each domain constraint, table check constraint, and assertion. Those are all the places that CHECK() can be used.

The implicit <column reference>s that were contained in the <search condition> associated with a <check constraint definition> or an <assertion definition> are replaced by explicit <column reference>s in CHECK_CONSTRAINTS.

CHECK_TABLE_USAGE = The CHECK_TABLE_USAGE base table has one row for each table referenced by the <search condition> of a check constraint, domain constraint, or assertion.

CHECK_COLUMN_USAGE = The CHECK_COLUMN_USAGE base table has one row for each column referenced by the <search condition> of a check constraint, domain constraint, or assertion. As you can see, there is a pattern of having a table-related base table followed by a matching column-related base table.

TABLE_PRIVILEGES = The TABLE_PRIVILEGES table has one row for each table privilege descriptor. This table is constantly used by the Data Control Language (DCL) to verify the GRANTOR and GRANTEE of the user for the tables and views.

The basic user privileges are SELECT, DELETE, INSERT, UPDATE, and REFERENCES. There is also a flag, IS_GRANTABLE, which tells us if the privilege being described was granted WITH GRANT OPTION and is thus grantable.

COLUMN_PRIVILEGES = Once more, you see the table and column pattern. The COLUMN_PRIVILEGES base table has one row for each column privilege descriptor.

USAGE_PRIVILEGES = The USAGE_PRIVILEGES base table has one row for each usage privilege descriptor. Usage applies to schema objects that are not tables or views. These include DOMAINs, CHARACTER SETs, COLLATIONs, TRANSLATIONs, and usually stored procedures.

CHARACTER_SETS = The CHARACTER_SETS base table has one row for each character set descriptor. These days, that means Unicode Standards, not vendor-defined sets any more.

COLLATIONS = The COLLATIONS base table has one row for each character collation descriptor. Besides the Unicode information, the table also has padding/no padding with spaces.

A row always exists in this table for the collation SQL_TEXT. This is the one used to write your SQL code and these base tables.

TRANSLATIONS = The TRANSLATIONS base table has one row for each character translation descriptor. Translation is underused, and you can do some tricky programming easily with it.

SQL_LANGUAGES = The SQL_LANGUAGES base table has one row for each ISO and implementation-defined programming language binding claimed by this SQL product. The ANSI X3J languages appear in the Standard, of course. They are identified by the name of the language and the year of the Standard. There are also codes for "DIRECT" and "EMBEDDED" and "MODULE" language binding styles.

7.4.5   INFORMATION_SCHEMA Assertions

Since all table constraints are true on an empty table, we need to use CREATE ASSERTION statements to add global constraints to the information schema.

UNIQUE_CONSTRAINT_NAME = The UNIQUE_CONSTRAINT_NAME assertion ensures that the same combination of <schema name> and <constraint name> is not used by more than one constraint. Because an ASSERTION applies to the whole schema, you cannot have local constraint names.

EQUAL_KEY_DEGREES = The assertion EQUAL_KEY_DEGREES ensures that every foreign key is of the same degree as the corresponding unique constraint. Again, this has to be done at the global level.

KEY_DEGREE_GREATER_THAN_OR_EQUAL_TO_1 = The assertion KEY_DEGREE_GREATER_THAN_OR_EQUAL_TO_1 ensures that every UNIQUE or PRIMARY KEY constraint has at least one unique column and that every referential constraint has at least one referencing column.

Complicated Functions via Tables

AS WE MENTIONED in Section 5.3, before pocket calculators became cheap and powerful, we used printed lookup tables. They were in the appendices of finance, trig, or statistics textbooks, or added to the back of exam papers. Today, the teacher assumes that the students have a pocket calculator and puts some restrictions on just how "smart" the calculators are allowed to be (e.g., can you hide "cheat sheets" in the memory?).

The reasons for a return to auxiliary lookup tables depend on the improvements in hardware and parallel software. A table with a few thousand values of the function will fit into main storage, where the values can be joined in parallel in queries and shared among multiple users to produce results faster than recomputing those same results over and over, even with parallel processors.

8.1 Functions without a Simple Formula

Not all functions are computable via some simple formula. An obvious example is calendrical calculations that involve solar and lunar cycles, such as Easter. For a detailed discussion of the 14-step algorithm used by the Catholic Church to approximate Easter, I suggest reading *The Calendar* by David Ewing Duncan (ISBN-10: 1-85702-979-8).

But there are also functions that involve recursion, integrals, or other forms of higher math that are even harder to do with SQL's rather simple set of functions. And even if you can write them, most SQL products do not correct for floating-point errors.

Lookup tables make the database code easier to maintain. The tricky functions are computed in an external tool or imported from a trusted source once. Changes to the vendor's function library will not change the table the way they might change a computation. Computing a value to the highest precision available can be costly—a few more cycles in an iteration or recursion to make a calculation more accurate can be expensive.

Finally, such tables are sharable with applications. You do not have multiple copies of the same algorithm written in different programming languages. Multiple code bases have consistency problems from language to language (Does Pascal compute the MOD() function the same way as FORTRAN? Does COBOL even have a MOD() function?). With a lookup table, a change in the database will be shared with the Pascal, FORTRAN, COBOL, and whatever happens to be the "application language du jour" programs, thus reducing their maintenance needs.

8.1.1   Encryption via Tables

The DES Public Key Encryption algorithm (FIPS 42-2) is driven by tables of permutations on 64-bit blocks of data. The AES algorithm (Advanced Encryption Standard or Rijndaelor FIPS. 127 standard) uses 24-byte and 32-byte block sizes. I do not want to go into the algorithms, since they typically involve low-level bit fiddling for which SQL was never intended, but encryption is a class of functions that try to be hard.

A very simple, but surprisingly good, encryption is to use a table of integers between 0 and 7 (or 0 and 15 for Unicode) to determine how far to circular shift an ASCII character. Circular shift is a machine-level that shifts the bits right (or left) for (n) positions as if they were in a circle, so no bits are lost. For example,

```
RgtRotate('01110111', 3) = '11101110'.
CREATE TABLE Encryptor
(char_pos INTEGER NOT NULL PRIMARY KEY,
 shift_distance INTEGER NOT NULL
  CHECK (shift_distance BETWEEN 0 AND 7);
```

You encode with a right rotation and decrypt with a left rotation. The nice part is that the results are always ASCII for an ASCII input because of the parity bit.

If you do not have bit-level operators in your SQL, then you can build a lookup table with 128 rows in it to map each character to its shifted version:

```
CREATE TABLE Encryptor
(ascii CHAR(1) NOT NULL PRIMARY KEY,
shift_1 CHAR(1) NOT NULL,
shift_2 CHAR(1) NOT NULL,
shift_3 CHAR(1) NOT NULL,
shift_4 CHAR(1) NOT NULL,
shift_5 CHAR(1) NOT NULL,
shift_6 CHAR(1) NOT NULL,
shift_7 CHAR(1) NOT NULL);
```

This is not an industrial-strength algorithm, but you can construct very long keys easily.

8.2 Check Digits via Tables

You can find a discussion of check digits at *http://www.academic.marist. edu/mwa/idsn.htm*. The idea is that by making an encoded value a little longer, you can validate it at input time and not have to do an edit in the database. The application program can perform a relatively simple operation and spot invalid inputs. You do this by inspection when you reject a date like 2007-02-31 or a ZIP code like 78727 with a State code of NY instead of TX in the mailing address.

8.2.1 Check Digits Defined

Charles Babbage, the father of the computer, observed in the mid-1800s that an inseparable part of the cost of obtaining data is the cost of verifying its accuracy. The best situation is to exclude bad data on entry so that it is never in the system.

This situation implies that the data can verify itself in some way at entry time without having to go to the database. That is the idea of a check digit. By applying a formula or procedure to a numeric code, we want to be able to tell if that code is valid or not. Statistics classifies errors as either Type I or Type II. A Type I error rejects truth and a Type II error accepts a falsehood. In a database, a Type I error would be a failure to get valid data into the schema. This is usually a physical failure of some kind, and the hardware tells you your transaction failed.

But a Type II error is harder to detect. Some of these errors do require that the data get to the database to be checked against other internal data ("Mr. Celko, your checking account is overdrawn!") or even checked against external data ("Mr. Celko, there is a warrant for your arrest from the FBI!").

But most of the time, the Type II error is a keying error that can be detected at input time. F. J. Damerau (Damerau 1964) reported that four common input errors cause 80% of the total spelling errors:

1.   A single missing character

2.   A single extra character

3.   A single erroneous character

4.   Pairwise-transposed characters

The single erroneous, missing, or extra character explained 60% to 95% of all errors in his sample of 12,000 errors; pairwise transposes accounted for 10% to 20% of the total.

The first three categories can be expanded to more than a single character, but the single-character cases are by far the most common. In the last category, pairwise transposes ("ab" becomes "ba") are far more common than jump transposes (transposes of pairs with one or more characters between them, as when "abc" becomes "cba"). This is because we use keyboards for data entry and your fingers can get ahead of each other.

If a human is doing the data entry from verbal input, you might wish to include a special case for phonetic errors, which are language-dependent (e.g., 30 and 13 sound alike in English). Verhoeff gave more details in his study, *Error-Detecting Decimal Codes* (Verhoeff 1969).

8.2.2   Error Detection versus Error Correction

The distinction between error-detecting and error-correcting codes is worth mentioning. The error-detecting code will find that an encoding is wrong, but gives no help in finding the error itself. An error-correcting code will try to repair the problem. Error-correcting schemes for binary numbers play an important part in highly reliable computers, but require several extra digits on each computer word to work. If you would like to do research on error-correction codes, some of the algorithms are:

■ Hamming codes

■ Fire codes

- Bose-Chandhuri-Hocquenghem (BCH) codes

- Reed-Solomon (RS) codes

- Goppa codes

On the other hand, error detection can be done with only one extra digit, and it is important to people who design codes for a database because they keep the data clean without triggers or procedures by simply excluding bad data. The algorithms can often be written in CHECK() clauses, too.

8.3   Classes of Algorithms

The most common check digit procedures come in a few broad classes. One class takes the individual digits, multiplies them by a constant value (called a weight) for each position, sums the results, divides the sum by another constant, and uses the remainder as the check digit. These are called weighted-sum algorithms.

Another approach is to use functions based on group theory, a branch of abstract algebra; these are called algebraic algorithms. A discussion of group theory is a little too complex to take up here, so I will do a little hand-waving when I get to the mathematics. Finally, you can use lookup tables for check digit functions that cannot be easily calculated.

The lookup tables can be almost anything, including functions that are tuned for the data in a particular application.

8.3.1   Weighted-Sum Algorithms

Weighted-sum algorithms are probably the most common class of check digit. They have the advantages of being easy to compute by hand, since they require no tables or complex arithmetic, so they were first used in manual systems.

To calculate a weighted-sum check digit:

1.   Multiply each of the digits in the encoding by a weight. A weight is a positive integer value.

2.   Add the products of the above multiplications to get a sum, s.

3.   Take that sum s and apply a function to it. The function is usually MOD(s, n) where (n is a prime number and n <= 10), but it can be more complicated. An exception in this step is to allow the letter X (Roman numeral ten) as the

result of a MOD(s, 11) function. This is a very strong check digit and was used in the old International Standard Book Number (ISBN).

4.   The check digit is concatenated to the encoding.

This is one of the most popular check digit procedures. It is easy to implement in hardware or software. It will detect most of the single-character and pairwise transpose errors. However, it is not perfect.

Consider the bank check digit, whose weights are 3, 7, and 1, repeated as needed from left to right with a MOD(s, 10) function. This is used in the United States on personal checks, where the bank processing numbers have eight information digits. Look at the lower left-hand corner of your checkbook in the magnetic ink character recognition (MICR) numbers for your bank's code. The formula uses the check digit itself in the formula, so that the result should be a constant zero for correct numbers. Otherwise, you could use "10 - MOD(total, 10) = check digit" for your formula.

This scheme fails when the digits of a pairwise transpose differ by 5. For example, imagine that we wanted to validate the number 1621, but we typed 6121 instead, swapping the first two digits.

Since $(6-1) = 5$, this algorithm cannot detect the problem. Here is the arithmetic:

```
  1 * 3 = 3
+ 6 * 7 = 42
+ 2 * 1 = 2
+ 1 * 3 = 3
==================
  total 50
MOD(50, 10) = 0

  6 * 3 = 18
+ 1 * 7 = 7
+ 2 * 1 = 2
+ 1 * 3 = 3
==================
  total 30
MOD(30, 10) = 0
```

A better scheme is the IBM Check, whose weights alternate between 1 and f(x), where f(x) is defined by the lookup table given below or

by the formula `f(x) = IF (x < 9) THEN MOD((x + x), 9)`
`ELSE 9`, where x is the position of the digit in the code.

```
f(1) = 2
f(2) = 4
f(3) = 6
f(4) = 8
f(5) = 1
f(6) = 3
f(7) = 5
f(8) = 7
f(9) = 9
```

```
CREATE TABLE Weights
(digit_position INTEGER NOT NULL PRIMARY KEY,
wgt INTEGER NOT NULL);
```

The lookup table is usually faster than doing the arithmetic, since it is small and can take advantage of indexing and parallel processing. Obviously, the lookup table needs to have as many rows as digits in the encoding.

```
SELECT foo_code,
         MOD(SUM(CAST(SUBSTRING(foo_code FROM seq FOR 1)
                  AS INTEGER) * W.wgt), 10) AS
         check_digit
  FROM Weights AS W,
       Foobar AS F,
       Sequence AS S
WHERE S.seq <= 4 -- length of encoding -1
  AND W.digit_position = S.seq
GROUP BY foo_code;
```

DB2 has a special optimization that detects Star schemas by looking for a large fact table with many smaller dimension tables referenced by it. This works nicely with this kind of query.

Another popular version of the weighted-sum check digit are the Bull codes, which use the sum of two alternating sums, each with a modulus less than 10. The modulus pair has to be relatively prime. The most popular pairs, in order of increasing error detection ability, are (4, 5), (4, 7), (3, 7), (3, 5), (5, 6) and (3, 8).

For example, using the pair (4, 5) and modulus 7, we could check the code 2345-1 with these calculations: $((2*4)+ (3*5) + (4*4) + (5*5)) = 64$ MOD $7 = 1$.

8.3.2   Power-Sum Check Digits

The weights can be defined as variable powers of a fixed base number; then apply a modulus to get the remainder. A prime number is the best modulus, but 10 is very common. The most common schemes use a base of 2 or 3 with a modulus of 7, 10, or 11. The combination of 2 and 11 with a separate symbol for a remainder of 10 is one of these types of check digit. For example, we could check the code 2350 with these calculations:

```
(2^2) + (2^3) + (2^5) = 44
MOD (44, 11) = 0
```

You can prove that any pair of weights, a and b, for which it is true that b = a + 2n and n is an integer, suffer from the fault that they do not detect transpose errors that differ by five.

Let x = digit

```
y = following digit
y = x + 5
```

Let a = weight of x

```
b = weight of y
b = a + 2n
```

Compute the check digit for

```
  a*x + b*y
= a*x + (a + 2n) * (x + 5)
= a*x + a*x + 5*a + 2*n*x + 10*n
= 2*a*x + 5*a + 2*n*x + 10*n
```

Compute the check digit for

```
  a*y + b*x =
= a*(x + 5) + (a + 2*n)*x =
= a*x + 5*a + a*x + 2*n*x =
= 2*a*x + 5*a + 2*n*x
```

The difference between the two is (10*n), thus they have the same remainder when dividing by 10.

8.3.3   Luhn Algorithm

The Luhn formula is also known as "double-add-double" check-digit, or "mod ten" method. It was patented by IBM scientist Hans Peter Luhn in 1960 and is widely used today.

Step 1: Double the value of alternate digits, beginning with the first right-hand digit (low order).

Step 2: Add the individual digits comprising the products obtained in step one to each of the unaffected digits in the original number.

Step 3: Subtract the total obtained in step 2 from the next higher number ending in 0. This in the equivalent of calculating the "tens complement" of the low-order digit (unit digit) of the total. If the total obtained in step 2 is a number ending in zero (30, 40, etc.), the check digit is 0.

Example:
Account number without check digit: 4992 73 9871

```
4   9   9   2   7   3   9   8   7   1   original number
1   2   1   2   1   2   1   2   1   2   * weights
-----------------------------------
4  18   9   4   7   6   9  16   7   2 = 64 total

70 - 64 = 6
```

Account number with check digit is 4992-73-9871-6. The weakness is that it fails on a transposition of 09 and 90 in the input.

A lookup table for this is very short:

```
CREATE TABLE Luhn
(digit INTEGER NOT NULL PRIMARY KEY,
twice INTEGER NOT NULL);

INSERT INTO Luhn
VALUES (0, 0), (1, 2), (2, 4), (3, 6), (4, 8),
       (5, 1), (6, 3), (7, 5), (8, 7), (9, 9);

SELECT F.foo_code,
```

```
     MOD (SUM(CASE WHEN MOD(seq, 2) = 0
                    THEN L.twice
                    ELSE L.digit END), 10)
        AS checkdigit
  FROM Foobar AS F, Sequence AS S, Luhn AS L
 WHERE L.digit = SUBSTRING(foo_code FROM seq FOR 1)
   AND S.seq < CHARLENGTH(foo_code)
 GROUP BY F.foo_code;
```

8.3.4 Dihedral Five Check Digit

A very good, but somewhat complicated, scheme was proposed by
J. Verhoeff in a tract from the Mathematical Centre in Amsterdam,
Netherlands (Verhoeff 1969). It is based on the properties of multi-
plication in an algebraic structure known as the dihedral five group.

Though some of the calculations could be done with arithmetic
formulas, the easiest and fastest way is to build lookup tables for
functions. The lookup tables involved are a multiplication lookup
table, an inverse lookup table, and a permutation table. This makes the
programs look larger, but the superior ability of this scheme to detect
errors more than makes up for the very slight increase in size.

This is the multiplication table for the dihedral five group. The
important thing to notice is that D5 multiplication (shown by ¤) does
not always commute, for example (8 ¤ 9) = 4 and (9 ¤ 8) = 1. This property is what lets it detect transposition errors that other methods miss.

(i ¤ j)

j \ i	0	1	2	3	4	5	6	7	8	9
0	0	1	2	3	4	5	6	7	8	9
1	1	2	3	4	0	6	7	8	9	5
2	2	3	4	0	1	7	8	9	5	6
3	3	4	0	1	2	8	0	5	6	7
4	4	0	1	2	3	9	5	6	7	8
5	5	9	8	7	6	0	4	3	2	1
6	6	5	9	8	7	1	0	4	3	2
7	7	6	5	9	8	2	1	0	4	3
8	8	7	6	5	9	3	2	1	0	4
9	9	8	7	6	5	4	3	2	1	0

This is a permutation based on the position of a digit in the input string. The positions of the digits are counted from right to left, starting with zero. This repeats after eight rows.

	0	1	2	3	4	5	6	7	8	9
0	0	1	2	3	4	5	6	7	8	9
1	1	5	7	6	2	8	3	0	9	4
2	5	8	0	3	7	9	6	1	4	2
3	8	9	1	6	0	4	3	5	2	7
4	9	4	5	3	1	2	6	8	7	0
5	4	2	8	6	5	7	3	9	0	1
6	2	7	9	3	8	0	6	4	1	5
7	7	0	4	6	9	1	3	2	5	6

The third table is the multiplicative inverse (i.e., (k ¤ inv(j)) = 0.

	0	1	2	3	4	5	6	7	8	9
i	0	4	3	2	1	5	6	7	8	9

Using an example from *http://www.augustana.ab.ca/~mohrj/algorithms/ checkdigit.html*, given the encoding 1428570, validate the check digit.

Step 1. Compute P(digit, position number) from the second table. Remember that we count from right to left starting at zero.

```
P(0, 0) = 0
P(7, 1) = 0
P(5, 2) = 9
P(8, 3) = 2
P(2, 4) = 5
P(4, 5) = 5
P(1, 6) = 7
```

Step 2. Add these digits together using the ¤ operator in order:

```
((((((0 ¤ 0) ¤ 9) ¤ 2) ¤ 5) ¤ 5) ¤ 7) = 0
```

This is a little easier to see written out in a tabular, step-by-step format.

Position	Digit	P(pos, digit)	Previous Sum in D5	Sum = prev sum P(pos,digit))
0 = check digit	0	0	0	0
1	7	0	0	0
2	5	9	0	9
3	8	2	9	7
4	2	5	7	2
5	4	5	2	7
6	1	7	7	0

When the final cumulative sum is zero, then we have a valid check digit. The idea is that position zero is set to the inverse of the cumulative dihedral five total of positions one to (n) and sets the final results to zero.

8.4   Declarations, Not Functions, Not Procedures

After I have given all of these algorithms, you should not use them in procedural code in your schema. Convert them to constraints instead. This is an example of thinking in sets and not procedures. In a posting on *www.swug.org*, a regular contributor posted a Transact-SQL function that calculates the checksum digit of a standard, 13-digit bar code. The rules are simple:

1.   Sum each digit in an odd position to get S1.

2.   Sum each digit in an even position to get S2.

The formula is ABS(MOD(S1-S2), 10) for the bar code checksum digit. Here is the author's suggested function code, translated from T-SQL into Standard SQL/PSM:

```
CREATE FUNCTION BarcodeCheckSum(IN my_barcode CHAR(12))
RETURNS INTEGER
LANGUAGE SQL
DETERMINISTIC
 BEGIN
 DECLARE barcode_checkers INTEGER;
 DECLARE idx INTEGER;
```

```
DECLARE sgn INTEGER;
SET barcode_checkers = 0;
-- check if given barcode is numeric
IF IsNumeric(my_barcode) = 0
THEN RETURN -1;
END IF;
-- check barcode length
IF CHAR_LENGTH(TRIM(BOTH ' ' FROM my_barcode)) <> 12
THEN RETURN -2;
END IF;
-- compute barcode checksum algorithm
SET idx = 1;
WHILE idx <= 12
DO — Calculate sign of digit
 IF MOD(idx, 2) = 0
 THEN SET sgn = -1;
 ELSE SET sgn = +1;
 END IF;
 SET barcode_checkers = barcode_checkers +
   CAST(SUBSTRING(my_barcode FROM idx FOR 1) AS INTEGER)
       * sgn;
 SET idx = idx + 1;
END WHILE;

-- check digit
RETURN ABS(MOD(barcode_checkers, 10));
END;
```

Let's see how it works:

```
barcode_checkSum('283723281122')
= ABS (MOD(2-8 + 3-7 + 2-3 + 2-8 + 1-1 + 2-2), 10))
= ABS (MOD(-6 -4 -1 -6 + 0 + 0), 10)
= ABS (MOD(-17, 10))
= ABS(-7) = 7
```

Okay, where to begin? Notice the creation of unneeded local variables, the assumption of an IsNumeric() function taken from T-SQL dialect, and the fact that the check digit is supposed to be a character in the bar code and not an integer separated from the bar code. We have three IF statements and a WHILE loop in the code. This is about as procedural as you can get.

In fairness, SQL/PSM does not handle errors by returning negative numbers, but I don't want to get into a lesson on the mechanism used, which is quite different from the one used in T-SQL dialect.

Why use all that procedural code? Most of it can be replaced by declarative expressions. Let's start with the usual Sequence auxiliary table in place of the loop, nest function calls, and use CASE expressions to remove IF statements.

The rough pseudo-formula for conversion is:

1. A procedural loop becomes a sequence set:

```
FOR seq FROM 1 TO n DO f(x);
=> SELECT seq FROM Sequence WHERE seq <= n;
```

2. A procedural selection becomes a CASE expression:

```
IF.. THEN .. ELSE
=> CASE WHEN.. THEN .. ELSE.. END;
```

3. A series of assignments and function calls become a single nested set of function calls:

```
DECLARE x <type>;
SET x = f(y, ..);
SET y = g(x);
..;
=> f(g(x), ..)
```

Here is a translation of those guidelines into a first shot at a rewrite:

```
CREATE FUNCTION Barcode_CheckSum(IN my_barcode CHAR(12))
RETURNS INTEGER
BEGIN
 IF barcode NOT SIMILAR TO '%[^0-9]%'
 THEN RETURN -1;
 ELSE RETURN
 (SELECT ABS(SUM((CAST (SUBSTRING(barcode
                          FROM S.seq FOR 1) AS INTEGER)
        * CASE MOD(S.seq, 2) WHEN 0 THEN 1 ELSE -1 END)))
   FROM Sequence AS S
  WHERE S.seq <= 12);
END IF;
END;
```

The SIMILAR TO regular expression predicate is a cute trick worth mentioning. It is a double negative that ensures the input string is all digits in all 12 positions. Remember that an oversized string will not fit into the parameter and will give you an overflow error, while a short string will be padded with blanks.

But wait! We can do better:

```
CREATE FUNCTION Barcode_CheckSum(IN my_barcode CHAR(12))
RETURNS INTEGER
RETURN
 (SELECT ABS(SUM((CAST (SUBSTRING(barcode
                               FROM S.seq FOR 1) AS INTEGER)
       * CASE MOD(S.seq, 2)WHEN 0 THEN 1 ELSE -1 END)))
  FROM Sequence AS S
 WHERE S.seq <= 12
   AND barcode NOT SIMILAR TO '%[^0-9]%');
```

This will return a NULL if there is an improper bar code. It is only one SQL statement, so we are doing pretty well. There are some minor tweaks, like this:

```
CREATE FUNCTION Barcode_CheckSum(IN my_barcode CHAR(12))
RETURNS INTEGER
RETURN
 (SELECT ABS(SUM(CAST(SUBSTRING(barcode
        FROM Weights.seq FOR 1) AS INTEGER)
        * Weights.wgt))
   FROM (VALUES (CAST(1 AS INTEGER), CAST(-1 AS INTEGER)),
(2, +1), (3, -1), (4, +1), (5, -1),
        (6, +1), (7, -1), (8, +1), (9, -1), (10, +1),
(11,-1), (12, +1)) AS Weights(seq, wgt)
WHERE barcode NOT SIMILAR TO '%[^0-9]%');
```

Another cute trick in Standard SQL is to construct a table constant with a VALUES() expression. The first row in the table expression establishes the data types of the columns by explicit casting.

What is the best solution? The real answer is none of the above. The point of this exercise was to come up with a set-oriented, declarative answer. We have been writing functions to check a condition. What we want is a CHECK() constraint for the bar code. Try this instead.

```
CREATE TABLE Products
(..
barcode CHAR(13) NOT NULL
```

```
CONSTRAINT all_numeric_checkdigit
CHECK (barcode NOT SIMILAR TO '%[^0-9]%')
CONSTRAINT valid_checkdigit
CHECK (
       (SELECT ABS(SUM(CAST(SUBSTRING(barcode
                    FROM Weights.seq FOR 1) AS INTEGER)
          * Weights.wgt))
    FROM (VALUES (CAST(1 AS INTEGER), CAST(-1 AS INTEGER)),
(2, +1), (3, -1), (4, +1), (5, -1),
       (6, +1), (7, -1), (8, +1), (9, -1), (10, +1),
(11, -1), (12, +1)) AS weights(seq, wgt)
 = CAST(SUBSTRING(barcode FROM 13 FOR 1) AS INTEGER)),
 .. );
```

This will keep bad data out of the schema. The reason for splitting
the code into two constraints is to provide better error messages.
That is how we think in SQL. Avoid procedural code in favor of
declarative code.

8.5   Data Mining for Auxiliary Tables

We do not always know what values we want to add to a lookup table.
Very often, we need to do some data mining in our historical data to
discover rules we did not know.

If you watch the Food Channel on cable or just like Memphis-style
barbeque, you know the name Corky's. The chain was started in 1984
in Memphis by Don Pelts and has grown by franchise at a steady rate
ever since. They sell a small menu of 25 items by mail order or from
their website (*www.corkysbbq.com*) and ship the merchandise in special
boxes, sometimes using dry ice. Most of the year, their staff can handle
the orders. But at Christmastime, they have the problem of success.

Their packing operation consists of two lines. At the start of the line,
someone pulls a box of the right size, and puts the pick list in it. As it
goes down the line, packers put in the items, and when it gets to the end
of the line, it is ready for shipment. This is a standard business operation
in lots of industries. Their people know what boxes to use for the standard gift packs and can pretty accurately judge any odd-sized orders.

At Christmastime, however, mail-order business is so good that they
have to get outside temporary help. The temporary help does not have
the experience to judge the box sizes by looking at a pick list. If a box
that is too small starts down the line, it will jam up things at some point.
The supervisor has to get it off the line, and repack the order by hand.

If a box that is too large goes down the line, it is a waste of money and creates extra shipping costs.

Mark Tutt (On The Mark Solutions, LLC) has been consulting with Corky's for years and set up a new order system for them on a Sybase platform. One of the goals of the new system is print the pick list and shipping labels with all of the calculations done, including what box size the order requires.

Following the rule that you do not reinvent the wheel, Mr. Tutt went to the newsgroups to find out if anyone had already discovered a solution. The suggestions tended to be along the lines of getting the weights and shapes of the items and using a 3D Tetris program to figure out the box size and packing.

Programmers seem to love to face every new problem as if nobody has ever done it before and nobody will ever do it again. The "Code first, research later!" mentality is hard to overcome.

The answer was not in complicated 3D math, but in the past four or five years of orders in the database. Human beings with years of experience had been packing orders and leaving a record of their work to be mined. Obviously, the standard gift packs are easy to spot. But most of the orders tend to be something that had occurred before, too. Here are the answers, if you will bother to dig them out.

First, Mr. Tutt found all of the unique configurations in the orders, how often they occurred, and the boxes used to pack them. If the same configuration had two or more boxes, then you should go with the smaller size. As it turned out, there were about 4,995 unique configurations in the custom orders that covered about 99.5% of the cases.

Next, this table of configurations was put into a stored procedure that did a slightly modified exact relational division to obtain the box size required. In the 0.5% of the orders that were not found, the box size was put into a custom packing job stack for an experienced employee to handle. If new products are added or old ones removed, the table can be regenerated overnight from the most recent data.

CHAPTER 9

Temporal Tables

SQL IS THE first programming language to have temporal data types in it. If COBOL had done this, we would never have had the "Y2K Crisis" in IT. However, each SQL product has its own version of temporal data types and functions, in spite of ANSI/ISO Standards. In 2007, the United States decided to change when Daylight Saving Time (DST) would start. The result was a "mini-crisis" because the Windows operating system had the old rule built into it and not everyone made the switchover. In Standard SQL, the entire schema is supposed to be on Universal Coordinated Time (UTC) and then converted to local lawful time—that means time zones and DST conversions for display purposes.

9.1 The Nature of Time

Time is not a simple thing. Most data processing is done with data that is discrete by its nature. An account number is or is not equal to a value. A measurement has a value to so many decimal places. But time is a continuum, which means that given any two values on the time line, you can find an infinite number of points between them. Then we have the problem of which kind of infinite. Most nonmath majors do not even know that some transfinite numbers are bigger than others!

Do not panic. For purposes of a database the rule we need to remember is that "Nothing happens instantaneously" in the real world. Einstein declared that duration in time is the fourth dimension that everything must have to exist. But before Einstein, the Greek philosopher Zeno of Elea (circa 490 to 430 BCE) wrote several paradoxes, but the one that will illustrate the point about a continuum versus a discrete set of points is the Arrow Paradox.

Aristotle stated the Arrow Paradox this way in his Physics VI:9: "If everything when it occupies an equal space is at rest, and if that which is in locomotion is always occupying such a space at any moment, the flying arrow is therefore motionless."

More informally, imagine you shoot an arrow into the air. It moves continuously from your bow to the target in some finite amount of time. Look at any *instant* in that period of time. The arrow cannot be moving during that instant because an instant has no duration amd your arrow cannot be in two different places at the same time. Therefore, at every instant in time the arrow is motionless. If this is true for all instants of time, then the arrow is motionless during the entire interval. The fallacy is that there is no such thing as an instant in time. But the Greeks only had geometry, and the ideas of the continuum had to wait for calculus. If you want more details on the topic, get a copy of *A Tour of the Calculus* by David Berlinski (ISBN-10: 0-679-74788-5), which traces the historical development of calculus from Zeno (about 450 BCE) to Cauchy in the 19th century.

9.1.1   Durations, Not Chronons

A chronon is a proposed "quantum of time" that first showed up in quantum mechanics in the 1980s with a very exact definition based on subatomic physics. The term got picked up by a small group of temporal database researchers for models of time that used some discrete "step size" so that durations could be modeled as finite sets of chronons.

The reason they were proposed was to get temporal data back to the more familiar world of discrete values. Unfortunately, it did not work very well. When the chronon was proposed by Caldirola, one chronon corresponded to about 2×10^{-23} seconds. This is not a granularity that most computer hardware can achieve. And even if they did achieve such a representation, what would it mean in a data model?

Let's assume that we have a unit of one day and express durations as a finite set of days [di:dj], in which i and j are integers such that $(i <= j)$; the notation is understood to include all the days between these end points. A single chronon is shown as [dk:dk] in this notation. Since this is a set of points, the usual set operations apply.

Determining whether intervals overlap or abut each other is also easy. You must extend operators in your SQL or use another language altogether.

Such pairs are neither scalar nor atomic, so there are some First Normal Form issues. If one database is using a week chronon and another is using a day chronon, how do they share data? Even better, what if one database uses a week starting on Mondays and another uses weeks starting on Sundays?

That last problem is the theme of Philip José Farmer's *Dayworld* trilogy of science fiction novels. The premise is that a future dystopia allows people to live only one day of the week and keeps them in suspended animation for the other six days. The novels focus on a "daybreaker" who lives more than one day a week under different identities.

Another problem is that a set of discrete chronons cannot have gaps in the series. Thus the chronon set [d1:d4] is a short hand for {d1, d2, d3, d4} and cannot mean {d1, d2, d4} or any other subset. But sets of discrete elements are not supposed to have an ordering, and any subset of such a set is itself a set. So we are not dealing with proper sets, which is what we wanted in the relational model.

This is the basis for the classic fantasy short story *Yesterday Was Monday* by Theodore Sturgeon. The hero Harry Wright wakes up to go to work: "This was a daily occurrence, and the only thing that made it remarkable at all was that he did it on a Wednesday morning, and— Yesterday was Monday." (Excerpt from "Yesterday Was Monday" by Theodore Sturgeon, *http://www.randomhouse.com/catalog/display.pperl? isbn=9780345481900 & view=excerpt.*)

Perhaps the strangest result of the chronon model is that the same operators for temporal series could be applied to any data type that is modeled this way. Assume we model parts this way via a sequential part number. Does this make any sense? No; parts are clearly not a continuum. But let that slide for now. Given a table with parts and delivery dates, both in chronon columns, how many equivalent tables can you have from the same data?

In the relational model, each (`part_nbr`, `delivery_date`) pair would be in one row to record one fact, in one place, in one way with scalar values. In the chronon model, you can group by ranges of dates, then by parts within each of the date groupings. Or you can group by ranges of part numbers, then by delivery dates within each of the part groupings. Diagram this data on a two-dimensional grid, with parts on one axis and dates on the other and shade in the cells that have a delivery of the corresponding part and date. Now the problem would be how many ways you could cut the shaded areas into rectangles, either with or without OVERLAPS ( ). That can be a large number, and it only gets worse when you add more chronon columns to a table.

The flaws in the chronon model provide themes for classic science fiction and fantasy novels, but this does not seem to be a good approach for modeling temporal data in a relational database.

9.1.2   Granularity

While we cannot put an uncountable number of temporal points into a finite computer, nor can we store a single temporal value to infinite precision, we can "muddle through" with what we have. The FIPS-127 Standards required at least five decimal places of precision in seconds in a temporal data type. This is well within the power of modern computers.

Generally speaking, there are two approaches to representing time internally in SQL products. The most direct one is the COBOL method, where each part of temporal value gets a field of its own. This is traditionally how it was done in COBOL, which did not have temporal data types. The other approach is the UNIX method, which counts hardware clock ticks after a base point, then converts that number into a timestamp (e.g., date and time in ISO-8601 format) for the user. This is how UNIX and other operating system represented time.

For example, you will find that Microsoft's SQL Server is still using an internal representation that uses a floating-point number by putting the date into the mantissa (also called the coefficient or significand) and the time into the exponent. This means that it does not properly round off in the third decimal place of the seconds, because the floating-point number is based on 3-millisecond clock ticks since a starting date.

The trade-off was supposed to be that the UNIX method made temporal math easier at the expense of more complicated display. Unfortunately, that has not applied for decades. The lack of precision and the limited range of timestamps in this method are more of a handicap than a help.

Working with the COBOL-style fields is not a problem for hardware running in nanoseconds the way it was for hardware running in milliseconds. The advantage of unlimited date ranges and precision outweighs the complexity of the internal system routines.

Perhaps one of the more interesting attempts to change from the traditional second was Swatch Internet Time, proposed by the Swatch Company of Biel, Switzerland. The system was announced on October 23, 1998 by Nicolas G. Hayek (president and CEO of the Swatch Group), G. N. Hayek (president of Swatch Ltd.), and Nicholas Negroponte (founder and then-director of the MIT Media Lab). The Swatch Company produced some timepieces that displayed Swatch Internet Time and Standard time; a few websites (such as *CNN.com*) and some video gaming products picked it for awhile to try to make intercontinental coordination easier.

The system replaced hours and minutes with a unit called a ".beat" (note the dot in front of the name; 1 .beat = 86.4 seconds, 1,000 .beats = 24 hours or 1 day). If you are a history buff, you might recognize this as the decimal minute introduced after the French Revolution.

Instead of having 24 time zones, the clock is anchored at Biel Mean Time (BMT), which is equivalent to Central European Time or UTC+1. There is no Daylight Saving Time. This means that Internet time is the same throughout the world. But this is true for the UTC standard. There are no units smaller than one .beat in the specifications; you can extend it using the usual metric prefixes and decimal divisions. The system fails to deal with leap seconds.

The notation has a period in front of the word .beat and it uses the @ sign followed by an integer, such as @200 for two hundred beats after 00:00:00 on a given date. In early 1999, Swatch had a marketing campaign for a set of Internet Time watches when they launched their Beatnik satellite.

9.2 The ISO Half-Open Interval Model

The display formats for temporal data are defined by the ISO-8601 Standard. The display formats are important, of course, but even more important is the underlying model of durations. They are considered to be half-open intervals. That means that we have an exact point in time when an event starts, but we can only approach the end of it as a limit. To make that clearer, consider the date 2006-12-31 as a shorthand for the interval (2006-12-31 00:00:00 through 2006-12-31 23:59:59.999…). There is no such time as "2006-12-31 24:00:00" in this model; technically, the hour does not exist, and you meant to say "2007:01-01 00:00:00" instead.

DB2 and other SQL products allow a timestamp whose time part is 24:00:00.000000. In Craig Mullen's opinion, this is bad design on IBM's part, because adding '00:00' to a TIMESTAMP whose time part is 24:00:00.000000 converts it to 00:00:00.000000 unexpectedly.

This is important, since one of the Standard SQL operators is EXTRACT (<datetime field> FROM <datetime value expression>), which would return the wrong year, month, or day from that false TIMESTAMP.

MySQL has an interesting version of this concept. This product allows the use of "00" for months and days in those ranges. That is, the notation 2008-10-00 means the range of dates from 2008-10-01 through 2008-10-31, or the entire month of October in 2008. Likewise, the notation 2008-00-00 means the range of dates from 2008-01-01 through 2008-12-31, or the entire year 2008.

The real advantage of the half-open interval model is that simple temporal math done with half-open intervals is closed. Using a solid dot to show that a point is in the time line and a hollow dot to show that a point is not in the time line, you can see what happens in the following diagrams. Again, this is not yet Standard SQL.

1.   Two overlapping half-open intervals produce a half-open interval.

2.   If you remove a half-open interval from another half-open interval, you get one or two half-open intervals.

3.   Two contiguous half-open intervals produce a half-open interval. But there is a problem here. Since we are dealing with limits, the open end technically never touches the open end of the next interval. The convention you need to establish is that when the two intervals are separated by less than some value, delta, they are considered to be the same point.

This concept should not surprise programmers who have worked with floating-point numbers in depth, since they also have a delta. Floating-point numbers attempt to model the other common continuum, the real number line. In calculations and predicates, this delta is handled by complex rules that attempt to correct rounding and comparison errors.

Figure 9.1
Overlapping
Half-Open Intervals

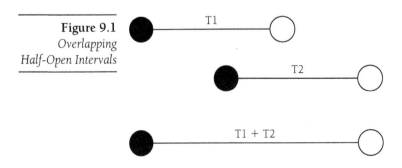

Figure 9.2
Contiguous
Half-Open Intervals

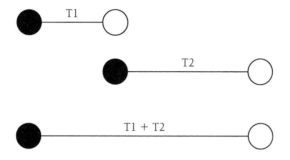

The value of temporal delta is going to vary with your particular SQL implementation and temporal data model. In a commercial application for timecards, the delta might be a five-minute increment. Another application might be fine putting data into the same day or even the same week without worry about any unit of time finer than that. For safety, however, a delta of a fraction of a second is probably a better choice in commercial applications that are shown in minutes.

9.2.1 Use of NULL for "Eternity"

The temporal model in SQL does not have a symbol for "eternity in the future" or "eternity in the past," so you have to work around it for some applications. The IEEE floating-point standard does have both a "-inf" and "+inf" symbol to handle this problem in that continuum model. In fact, the ISO model has limitations on it in that it can "only" represent timestamps in the range of years from 9999 BCE up to 9999 CE by using plus and minus signs in front of the year. The terms CE and BCE stand for Common Era and Before Common Era; they are what used to be called A.D and B.C. in the old days. Usually this range is good enough for most applications outside of archeology.

For example, when someone checks into a hotel, we know their arrival data, but we not know their departure date (an expected departure date is not the same thing as an actual one). All we know for certain is that it has to be after their arrival date. A NULL will act as a "place holder" until we get the actual departure date. The skeleton DDL for such a table would look like this:

```
CREATE TABLE HotelRegister
(patron_id INTEGER NOT NULL
```

```
    REFERENCES Patrons (patron_id),
 arrival_date TIMESTAMP DEFAULT CURRENT_TIMESTAMP NOT NULL,
 departure_date TIMESTAMP, -- null means guest still here
 CONSTRAINT arrive_before_depart
   CHECK (arrival_date <= departure_date),
 ..);
```

When getting reports, you will need to use the current timestamp in place of the NULL to accurately report the facts.

```
SELECT patron_id, arrival_date,
       COALESCE (CURRENT_TIMESTAMP, departure_date)
       AS departure_date
 FROM HotelRegister
WHERE ..;
```

9.2.2   Single Timestamp Tables

In 2007, Kevin Mellon posted a typical newbie question in a newsgroup after seeing the (start_time, finish_time) pair model for temporal data in *Developing Time-Oriented Database Applications in SQL* by Richard T. Snodgrass (a PDF file of the book can be downloaded for free at *http://www.cs.arizona.edu/people/rts/publications.html*).

Assume that an entity, a gym membership, always has a status such as "active", "dormant", "cancelled", or "banned" in the table. I would like to keep a history of my membership status. Assume I join a gym on 2008-01-01, becoming an active member on that date, and then I break some equipment on 2008-02-01. I am banned for the rest of the month and return to active status on 2008-03-01.

```
MemberHistory
```

member_status	from_date	to_date
'Active'	'2008-01-01'	'2008-02-01'
'Banned'	'2008-02-01'	'2008-03-01'
'Active'	'2008-03-01'	NULL

The question is: Given that I must always have a status, why store the "to_date" at all?

The answer is that it is the proper model of time, because it puts a complete fact in one row. If you put just the "`member_status`" and "`from_date`" in the table, you have to do a self-join to discover that Mr. X was active in January 2008. You have split duration information, and durations are atomic. As another example of atomic data that is in two scalar columns, consider (longitude, latitude) pairs—they only have meaning together; same thing with the (lft, rgt) pairs in the nested sets model of hierarchies, or (x, y, z) coordinates in three-dimensional space.

Kevin's example is the simplest version of this problem. A more typical one is the timecard table in its many forms. This table mimics a time-clock punch card that used to be part of offices and construction sites. Hence we have the expression "punching the clock" in American slang. The first time clock was invented in 1888 by Willard Bundy, and they continued to be used into the early 1950s. It is no wonder that this mental model stayed around so long.

In more recent times, the mechanical time clocks have been replaced with magnetic fobs that are read electronically. One example of this kind of product is the JobClock (*http://www.exaktime.com/*) from Exactime. The units are weatherproof, battery-powered, portable time clocks that are kept at each jobsite to collect time and attendance 24 hours a day. The employees each carry Keytabs, which are small fobs that can fit on a key ring. They touch these fobs to the JobClock when they arrive and depart from the jobsite. The fobs are color-coded so that green is for arrival and red is for departure; the user can assign more fobs of different colors for various billable tasks (i.e., the purple fob might be for plumbing, yellow for electrical work, etc.)

The JobClock records all of the time and attendance records—even if employees travel between jobsites each day.

Before running payroll, the time records are collected from each JobClock using a PalmPilot and brought back to the office. The data can be scrubbed and used to print attendance reports with labor costs, job codes, and other payroll data.

The raw data table looks something like this:

```
CREATE TABLE Timecards
(emp_id INTEGER NOT NULL
  REFERENCES Personnel (emp_id),
```

```
project_id INTEGER NOT NULL
 REFERENCES Projects (project_id)
clock_time TIMESTAMP NOT NULL,
fob_color CHAR(10) DEFAULT 'green' NOT NULL
  CHECK (fob_color IN ('red', 'green', 'purple',
  'yellow'...));
```

The trick with this data is to take blocks bracketed by green and red events and then examine the colors between them. Filling in missing data can be a problem. People will double scan a fob if they are not sure that it was read correctly, or they will miss a scan.

9.2.3   Overlapping Intervals

The OVERLAPS() predicate is a feature still not available in most SQL implementations, because it requires more of the Standard SQL temporal data features than most implementations have. You can "fake it" in many products with the BETWEEN predicate and careful use of constraints.

In ANSI/ISO Standard SQL, an INTERVAL is a measure of temporal duration, expressed in units such as days, hours, minutes, and so forth. This is how you add or subtract days to or from a date, hours and minutes to or from a time, and so forth. The OVERLAPS() predicate compares two time periods. These time periods are defined as row values with two columns. The first column (the starting time) of the pair is always a <datetime> data type and the second column (the termination time) is a <datetime> data type that can be used to compute a <datetime> value. If the starting and termination times are the same, this is an instantaneous event.

The result of the <OVERLAPS predicate> is formally defined as the result of the following expression:

```
   (S1 > S2 AND NOT (S1 >= T2 AND T1 >= T2))
OR (S2 > S1 AND NOT (S2 >= T1 AND T2 >= T1))
OR (S1 = S2 AND (T1 <> T2 OR T1 = T2))
```

where S1 and S2 are the starting times of the two time periods and T1 and T2 are their termination times. The rules for the OVERLAPS()

predicate sound like they should be intuitive, but they are not. The principles that we wanted in the Standard were:

1. A time period includes its starting point, but does not include its end point. We have already discussed this model and its closure properties.

2. If the time periods are not "instantaneous," they overlap when they share a common time period.

3. If the first term of the predicate is an INTERVAL and the second term is an instantaneous event (a <datetime> data type), they overlap when the second term is in the time period (but is not the end point of the time period). That follows the half-open model.

4. If the first and second terms are both instantaneous events, they overlap only when they are equal.

5. If the starting time is NULL and the finishing time is a <datetime> value, the finishing time becomes the starting time and we have an event. If the starting time is NULL and the finishing time is an INTERVAL value, then both the finishing and starting times are NULL.

Please consider how your intuition reacts to these results, when the granularity is at the YEAR-MONTH-DAY level. Remember that a day begins at 00:00 Hrs.

```
(today, today) OVERLAPS (today, today) = TRUE
(today, tomorrow) OVERLAPS (today, today) = TRUE
(today, tomorrow) OVERLAPS (tomorrow, tomorrow) = FALSE
(yesterday, today) OVERLAPS (today, tomorrow) = FALSE
```

Since the OVERLAPS() predicate is not yet common in SQL products, let's see what we have to do to handle overlapping times. Consider a table of hotel guests with the days of their stays based on whole days and not on a checkout time. The tables might look like this:

```
CREATE TABLE GuestRegister -- ANSI SQL
(guest_name VARCHAR (35) NOT NULL PRIMARY KEY,
 arrival_date DATE NOT NULL,
 depart_date DATE NOT NULL,
 CHECK (arrival_date <= depart_date),
 ...);
```

```
GuestRegister -- ANSI SQL

  guest_name         arrival_date    depart_date
=================================================
  'Dorothy Gale'     '2009-02-01'    '2009-11-01'
  'Indiana Jones'    '2009-02-01'    '2009-02-01'
  'Don Quixote'      '2009-01-01'    '2009-10-01'
  'James T. Kirk'    '2009-02-01'    '2009-02-28'
  'Santa Claus'      '2009-12-01'    '2009-12-25'
```

To find out who was in the hotel on a certain date is easy with a BETWEEN predicate in a product with a DATE data type. Remember that BETWEEN includes the end points of the range.

```
SELECT guest_name
  FROM GuestRegister
 WHERE DATE '2009-02-03'
       BETWEEN arrival_date AND depart_date;

RESULTS

  guest_name
================
  'Dorothy Gale'
  'Don Quixote'
  'James T. Kirk'
```

However, if you are using SQL Server or Sybase, which has only the TIMESTAMP data type (confusingly called DATETIME in their dialect for historical reasons), the dates without a time part are converted to 00:00 hrs. In effect, the table looks like this:

Figure 9.3
Simultaneous Events

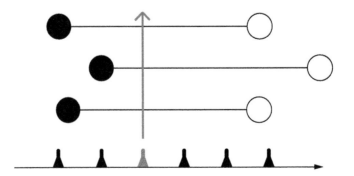

```
GuestRegister -- Sybase/SQL Server
```

guest_name	arrival_datetime	depart_datetime
===	===	===
'Dorothy Gale'	'2009-02-01 00:00'	'2009-11-01 00:00'
'Indiana Jones'	'2009-02-01 00:00'	'2009-02-01 00:00'
'Don Quixote'	'2009-01-01 00:00'	'2009-10-01 00:00'
'James T. Kirk'	'2009-02-01 00:00'	'2009-02-28 00:00'
'Santa Claus'	'2009-12-01 00:00'	'2009-12-25 00:00'

The BETWEEN predicate will fail when a guest checks out at 12:00 Hrs and the timestamp given was '2009-02-01 13:00', so we should have forced a half-open interval into the table by getting as close to the end of the departure date as we can, something like this:

```
CREATE TABLE GuestRegister -- timestamps only
(guest_name VARCHAR (35) NOT NULL PRIMARY KEY,
 arrival_time TIMESTAMP NOT NULL
    CHECK (CAST (arrival_time AS DATE) = arrival_time),
 depart_time TIMESTAMP NOT NULL
    CHECK (depart_time + INTERVAL '0.0001' SECONDS = CAST
(depart_time AS DATE) + INTERVAL '1' DAY),
CHECK (arrival_time <= depart_time),
 ...);
```

```
GuestRegister
```

guest_name	arrival_datetime	depart_datetime
===	===	===
'Dorothy Gale'	'2009-02-01 00:00'	'2009-11-01 23:59:59.9999'
'Indiana Jones'	'2009-02-01 00:00'	'2009-02-01 23:59:59.9999'
'Don Quixote'	'2009-01-01 00:00'	'2009-10-01 23:59:59.9999'
'James T. Kirk'	'2009-02-01 00:00'	'2009-02-28 23:59:59.9999'
'Santa Claus'	'2009-12-01 00:00'	'2009-12-25 23:59:59.9999'

The BETWEEN operator will work just fine with single dates that fall between the arrival and departure times. Mimicking the OVERLAP() predicate can be done by simply copying the definition into your query. But first, we need a table of Celebrations that were held at our imaginary hotel.

```
CREATE TABLE Celebrations
(event_name CHARACTER(30) PRIMARY KEY,
 start_date DATE NOT NULL,
 finish_date DATE NOT NULL,
 ...);
```

Celebrations

event_name	start_date	finish_date
===	===	===
'Apple Month'	'2009-02-01'	'2009-02-28'
'Christmas Season'	'2009-12-01'	'2009-12-25'
'Garlic Festival'	'2009-01-15'	'2009-02-15'
'National Pear Week'	'2009-01-01'	'2009-01-07'
'New Years Day'	'2009-01-01'	'2009-01-01'
'St. Freds Day'	'2009-02-24'	'2009-02-24'
'Year of the Prune'	'2009-01-01'	'2009-12-31'

Finding which guests arrived or departed during an event has already been discussed. A better question is who was at the hotel during an event, and what do we mean by "during" in this case—for the entire event or just part of it?

Instead of trying to write predicates for all possible arrangements of the durations involved, ask the question in the negative: What would the predicate be if two durations did not overlap? Disjoint durations could mean that the event was over before the guest arrived or that the event started after they departed, then negate that predicate.

```
SELECT G.guest_name, C.event_name
  FROM Guests AS G, Celebrations AS C
WHERE NOT ((G.depart_date < C.start_date)
OR (G.arrival_date > C.finish_date));
```

RESULTS

guest_name	event_name
===	===
'Dorothy Gale'	'Apple Month'
'Dorothy Gale'	'Garlic Festival'
'Dorothy Gale'	'St. Freds Day'
'Dorothy Gale'	'Year of the Prune'

```
'Indiana Jones'     'Apple Month'
'Indiana Jones'     'Garlic Festival'
'Indiana Jones'     'Year of the Prune'
'Don Quixote'       'Apple Month'
'Don Quixote'       'Garlic Festival'
'Don Quixote'       'National Pear Week'
'Don Quixote'       'New Years Day'
'Don Quixote'       'St. Freds Day'
'Don Quixote'       'Year of the Prune'
'James T. Kirk'     'Apple Month'
'James T. Kirk'     'Garlic Festival'
'James T. Kirk'     'St. Freds Day'
'James T. Kirk'     'Year of the Prune'
'Santa Claus'       'Christmas Season'
'Santa Claus'       'Year of the Prune'
```

The reason for using the NOT in the WHERE clause is so that you can add or remove it to reverse the sense of the query. For example, to find out how many celebrations each guest could have seen, you would write

```
CREATE VIEW GuestCelebrations (guest_name, event_name)
AS SELECT guest_name, event_name
     FROM Guests, Celebrations
    WHERE NOT ((depart_date < start_date) OR
    (arrival_date > finish_date));

SELECT guest_name, COUNT(*) AS celeb_count
  FROM GuestCelebrations
GROUP BY guest_name;
```

Results

```
  guest_name                  celeb_count
====================================
  'Dorothy Gale'                  4
  'Indiana Jones'                 3
  'Don Quixote'                   6
  'James T. Kirk'                 4
  'Santa Claus'                   2
```

and then to find out how many guests were at the hotel during each celebration, you would write

```
SELECT event_name, COUNT(*) AS guest_tally
 FROM GuestCelebrations
GROUP BY event_name;
```

Result

```
  event_name                    guestcount
==================================
  'Apple Month'              4
  'Christmas Season'         1
  'Garlic Festival'          4
  'National Pear Week'       1
  'New Years Day'            1
  'St. Freds Day'            3
  'Year of the Prune'        5
```

This last query is only part of the story. What the hotel management really wants to know is how many room nights were sold for a celebration. A little algebra tells you that the length of an event is (`Event.finish_date` - `Event.start_date` + `INTERVAL '1'` `DAY`) and that the length of a guest's stay is (`Guest.depart_date` - `Guest.arrival_date` + `INTERVAL '1' DAY`).

Guests 1 and 2 spent only part of their time at the celebration; Guest 3 spent all of his time at the celebration, and Guest 4 stayed even longer than the celebration. That interval is defined by the two points (`GREATEST(arrival_date, start_date)`, `LEAST(depart_date, finish_date)`).

Instead, you can use the aggregate functions in SQL to build a `VIEW` on a `VIEW`, like this:

```
CREATE VIEW Working (guest_name, event_name, entry_date,
exit_date)
AS SELECT GE.guest_name, GE.event_name, start_date,
finish_date
    FROM GuestCelebrations AS GE, Celebrations AS E1
   WHERE E1.event_name = GE.event_name
UNION
```

```
SELECT GE.guest_name, GE.event_name, arrival_date,
depart_date
   FROM GuestCelebrations AS GE, Guests AS G1
   WHERE G1.guest_name = GE.guest_name;
```

VIEW Working

guest_name	event_name	entry_date	exit_date
===	===	===	===
'Dorothy Gale'	'Apple Month'	'2009-02-01'	'2009-02-28'
'Dorothy Gale'	'Apple Month'	'2009-02-01'	'2009-11-01'
'Dorothy Gale'	'Garlic Festival'	'2009-02-01'	'2009-11-01'
'Dorothy Gale'	'Garlic Festival'	'2009-01-15'	'2009-02-15'
'Dorothy Gale'	'St. Freds Day'	'2009-02-01'	'2009-11-01'
'Dorothy Gale'	'St. Freds Day'	'2009-02-24'	'2009-02-24'
'Dorothy Gale'	'Year of the Prune'	'2009-02-01'	'2009-11-01'
'Dorothy Gale'	'Year of the Prune'	'2009-01-01'	'2009-12-31'
'Indiana Jones'	'Apple Month'	'2009-02-01'	'2009-02-01'
'Indiana Jones'	'Apple Month'	'2009-02-01'	'2009-02-28'
'Indiana Jones'	'Garlic Festival'	'2009-02-01'	'2009-02-01'
'Indiana Jones'	'Garlic Festival'	'2009-01-15'	'2009-02-15'
'Indiana Jones'	'Year of the Prune'	'2009-02-01'	'2009-02-01'
'Indiana Jones'	'Year of the Prune'	'2009-01-01'	'2009-12-31'
'Don Quixote'	'Apple Month'	'2009-02-01'	'2009-02-28'
'Don Quixote'	'Apple Month'	'2009-01-01'	'2009-10-01'
'Don Quixote'	'Garlic Festival'	'2009-01-01'	'2009-10-01'
'Don Quixote'	'Garlic Festival'	'2009-01-15'	'2009-02-15'
'Don Quixote'	'National Pear Week'	'2009-01-01'	'2009-01-07'
'Don Quixote'	'National Pear Week'	'2009-01-01'	'2009-10-01'
'Don Quixote'	'New Years Day'	'2009-01-01'	'2009-01-01'
'Don Quixote'	'New Years Day'	'2009-01-01'	'2009-10-01'
'Don Quixote'	'St. Freds Day'	'2009-02-24'	'2009-02-24'
'Don Quixote'	'St. Freds Day'	'2009-01-01'	'2009-10-01'
'Don Quixote'	'Year of the Prune'	'2009-01-01'	'2009-12-31'
'Don Quixote'	'Year of the Prune'	'2009-01-01'	'2009-10-01'
'James T. Kirk'	'Apple Month'	'2009-02-01'	'2009-02-28'

(continued)

```
guest_name              event_name              entry_date          exit_date
==============================================================================
  'James T. Kirk'       'Garlic Festival'       '2009-02-01'        '2009-02-28'
  'James T. Kirk'       'Garlic Festival'       '2009-01-15'        '2009-02-15'
  'James T. Kirk'       'St. Freds Day'         '2009-02-01'        '2009-02-28'
  'James T. Kirk'       'St. Freds Day'         '2009-02-24'        '2009-02-24'
  'James T. Kirk'       'Year of the Prune'     '2009-02-01'        '2009-02-28'
  'James T. Kirk'       'Year of the Prune'     '2009-01-01'        '2009-12-31'
  'Santa Claus'         'Christmas Season'      '2009-12-01'        '2009-12-25'
  'Santa Claus'         'Year of the Prune'     '2009-12-01'        '2009-12-25'
  'Santa Claus'         'Year of the Prune'     '2009-01-01'        '2009-12-31'
```

This will put the earliest and latest points in both intervals into one column. Now we can construct a VIEW like this:

```
CREATE VIEW Attendees (guest_name, event_name, entry_date,
exit_date)
AS SELECT guest_name, event_name, MAX(entry_date),
MIN(exit_date)
       FROM Working
     GROUP BY guest_name, event_name;
```

VIEW Attendees

```
guest_name              event_name              entry_date          exit_date
==============================================================================
  'Dorothy Gale'        'Apple Month'           '2009-02-01'        '2009-02-28'
  'Dorothy Gale'        'Garlic Festival'       '2009-02-01'        '2009-02-15'
  'Dorothy Gale'        'St. Freds Day'         '2009-02-24'        '2009-02-24'
  'Dorothy Gale'        'Year of the Prune'     '2009-02-01'        '2009-11-01'
  'Indiana Jones'       'Apple Month'           '2009-02-01'        '2009-02-01'
  'Indiana Jones'       'Garlic Festival'       '2009-02-01'        '2009-02-01'
  'Indiana Jones'       'Year of the Prune'     '2009-02-01'        '2009-02-01'
  'Don Quixote'         'Apple Month'           '2009-02-01'        '2009-02-28'
  'Don Quixote'         'Garlic Festival'       '2009-01-15'        '2009-02-15'
  'Don Quixote'         'National Pear Week'    '2009-01-01'        '2009-01-07'
  'Don Quixote'         'New Years Day'         '2009-01-01'        '2009-01-01'
  'Don Quixote'         'St. Freds Day'         '2009-02-24'        '2009-02-24'
```

```
'Don Quixote'      'Year of the Prune'    '2009-01-01'    '2009-10-01'
'James T. Kirk'    'Apple Month'          '2009-02-01'    '2009-02-28'
'James T. Kirk'    'Garlic Festival'      '2009-02-01'    '2009-02-15'
'James T. Kirk'    'St. Freds Day'        '2009-02-24'    '2009-02-24'
'James T. Kirk'    'Year of the Prune'    '2009-02-01'    '2009-02-28'
'Santa Claus'      'Christmas Season'     '2009-12-01'    '2009-12-25'
'Santa Claus'      'Year of the Prune'    '2009-12-01'    '2009-12-25'
```

The Attendees VIEW can be used to compute the total number of
room days for each celebration. Assume that the difference of two dates
will return an integer that is the number of days between them:

```
SELECT event_name,
       SUM(exit_date - entry_date + INTERVAL '1' DAY) AS
       room_days
  FROM Attendees
 GROUP BY event_name;
```

```
Result
```

```
    event_name                  roomdays
====================================
    'Apple Month'               85
    'Christmas Season'          25
    'Garlic Festival'           63
    'National Pear Week'        7
    'New Years Day'             1
    'St. Freds Day'             3
    'Year of the Prune'         602
```

If you would like to get a count of the room days sold in the month
of January, you could use this query, which avoids a BETWEEN or
OVERLAPS() predicate completely.

```
SELECT SUM(CASE WHEN depart > DATE '2009-01-31'
                THEN DATE '2009-01-31'
                ELSE depart END
         - CASE WHEN arrival_date < DATE '2009-01-01'
                THEN DATE '2009-01-01'
```

```
                ELSE arrival_date END + INTERVAL '1' DAY)
        AS room_days
    FROM Guests
  WHERE depart > DATE '2009-01-01'
    AND arrival_date <= DATE '2009-01-31';
```

9.3   State Transition Tables

When most newbies think of constraints, they know only static column constraints, such as NOT NULL, DEFAULT, and CHECK() clauses. A little bit later, they will learn about simple declarative referential integrity (DRI) constraints. That means simple PRIMARY KEY and REFERENCES clauses with some simple actions to bring the database to a state consistent with business rules.

The bad news is that there are not enough SQL constructs for all business rules. A transition constraint says that an entity can be updated only in certain ways. These constraints are often modeled as a state transition diagram. There is an initial state, flow lines that show what the next legal state(s) are, and one or more termination states.

The initial and terminal states are handy, but not required. In theory, an entity could come into existence in any state and then never cease to exist. But that a rare situation.

As a very simple example, we want to model marital status. In this example, we have only one initial state, birth, and one termination state, death. Let's start with a table skeleton and try to be careful about the possible states of our personnel.

Figure 9.4
Marital Status
State Transition
Graph

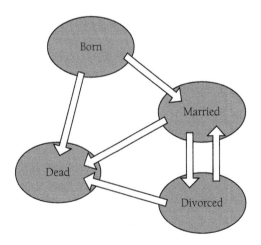

```
CREATE TABLE Personnel
( ..
martial_status VARCHAR(10)
    DEFAULT 'Birth'
    NOT NULL
  CHECK (martial_status
      IN ('Birth', 'Single', 'Married', 'Divorced',
          'Death')),
..);
```

We are being good programmers using a DEFAULT and a CHECK()
constraint. But this does not prevent us from turning death directly
to birth, and it does not enforce other rules. For example, there is
usually a legal age for getting married. Do we want to leave someone
in the 'Birth' state or immediately move them to a 'Single' status?
That is, 'Single' could mean "alive and able to marry" and 'Birth'
could mean "alive but underage" depending on the business rules.
Likewise, does a person stay in the 'Divorce' status for a while until
the paperwork is final?

One solution is to add a trigger to the table. The problem with
triggers is that while there is SQL-99 syntax for triggers, every SQL
product has a proprietary syntax and often a non-ANSI model. Here is
a SQL-99 version that can probably be improved, but it demonstrates
the idea.

```
CREATE TRIGGER MartialTransitions
AFTER UPDATE ON Personnel
REFERENCING OLD AS O1 NEW AS N1
IF EXISTS
  (SELECT *
     FROM O1, N1
    WHERE NOT (
        (prev_martial_status = 'Birth'
         AND curr_martial_status IN ('Birth', 'Single'))
       OR (prev_martial_status = 'Single'
         AND curr_martial_status IN ('Death', 'Married'))
       OR (prev_martial_status = 'Married'
         AND curr_martial_status IN ('Death', 'Divorce'))
       OR (prev_martial_status = 'Divorced'
         AND curr_martial_status IN ('Death', 'Single'))
       OR (prev_martial_status = 'Death'
         AND curr_martial_status ='Death')));
```

```
THEN ROLLBACK;
END IF;
```

This is a bit messy, but can be mechanically generated. I am assuming that the ways to succeed outnumber violations, so a negation will be easier to maintain and read. You can get the (previous—current) pairs directly from the state transition diagram.

This is often the first approach that newbies take once they get to a certain point in their SQL. They still feel more comfortable with procedural code, so triggers give them comfort. The problem is that triggers do not pass information to the optimizer, will not port and run slower than nonprocedural code.

You can actually use CHECK() constraints, but you have to store the current and previous states in a table with a previous and current state column pair. This is basically the same code as the trigger put into a CHECK() constraint.

```
CREATE TABLE Personnel
( ...
prev_martial_status VARCHAR(10) NOT NULL,
curr_martial_status VARCHAR(10) DEFAULT 'Birth' NOT NULL,
CHECK (NOT (
        (prev_martial_status = 'Birth'
         AND curr_martial_status IN ('Birth', 'Single'))
      OR (prev_martial_status = 'Single'
         AND curr_martial_status IN ('Death', 'Married'))
      OR (prev_martial_status = 'Married'
         AND curr_martial_status IN ('Death', 'Divorce'))
      OR (prev_martial_status = 'Divorced'
         AND curr_martial_status IN ('Death', 'Single'))
      OR (prev_martial_status = 'Death'
         AND curr_martial_status ='Death'))
));
```

In effect, the transition table is converted into predicates. The advantages are that it will pass information to the optimizer, will port, and will usually run faster than procedural code.

Let's generalize the CHECK() constraint. A declarative way to enforce transition constraints is put the state transitions into a table of their own and then reference the legal transitions. This requires that the target table have both the previous and the current state in two columns as before.

```
CREATE TABLE MartialTransitions
(prev_martial_status VARCHAR(10) NOT NULL,
curr_martial_status VARCHAR(10) NOT NULL,
PRIMARY KEY (prev_martial_status, curr_martial_status));

INSERT INTO MartialTransitions
VALUES ('Birth', 'Birth'), -- initial state
       ('Birth', 'Single'),
       ('Single', 'Married'),
       ('Married', 'Divorced'),
       ('Married', 'Death'),
       ('Divorced', 'Single'),
       ('Divorced', 'Death'),
       ('Death', 'Death'); -- terminal state
```

The target table looks like this:

```
CREATE TABLE Personnel
( ..
prev_martial_status VARCHAR(10) NOT NULL,
curr_martial_status VARCHAR(10) DEFAULT 'Birth' NOT NULL,
FOREIGN KEY (prev_martial_status, curr_martial_status)
  REFERENCES StateChanges (prev_martial_status,
  curr_martial_status)
  ON UPDATE CASCADE,
martial_status_time TIMESTAMP DEFAULT CURRENT_TIMESTAMP
NOT NULL,
..);
```

If you want to hide this from the users, then you can use an updatable view that shows only the current state of the entities.

The immediate advantages here are that this will pass information to the optimizer and will port, and since the rules are separated from the table declaration you can maintain them easily.

A not-so-obvious advantage is that a state transitions table can contain other data and conditions, such as temporal change data. A person has to wait (n) years from birth to become married; a person has to wait (n) days from filing to change from married to divorced; and so forth. In the skeleton table, there is a martial_status_time that will get the current timestamp when a new row is inserted. This will let you compute how long someone has been in a particular status, and perhaps automatically update it via procedures.

9.4   Consolidating Intervals

Given different data sources, you will get incomplete data about an event that you need to convert into a minimal representation. To make the problem more concrete, let's assume a simple table that looks a lot like a clipboard:

```
CREATE TABLE Events
(event_id VARCHAR(25) NOT NULL,
start_date DATE NOT NULL,
end_date DATE NOT NULL,
CHECK (start_date < end_date),
PRIMARY KEY (event_id, start_date, end_date));

INSERT INTO Events
VALUES ('Pie Eating', '2009-01-01', '2009-01-02'),
       ('Pie Eating', '2009-01-03', '2009-01-05'),
       ('Pie Eating', '2009-01-04', '2009-01-07'),
       ('Pie Eating', '2009-02-01', '2009-02-07');
```

The goal is to reduce these three rows into fewer rows that show how many days we were eating pies.

```
       ('Pie Eating', '2009-01-01', '2009-01-07')
```

The first and second rows in the INSERT INTO statement touch each other and can be replaced with

```
       ('Pie Eating', '2009-01-01', '2009-01-05')
```

The third row will overlap with this new row and can be consolidated with it, as shown before. However, the fourth row has data that occurs a month after the first three and it is disjoint from all the other rows.

Once the consolidated row is inserted, the original rows will be subsets of it and can then be removed.

An approach due to Erik Lennart is to calculate a calendar (assuming that you do not have one persisted in your schema) and then generate the gaps. Each complete interval must exist in the minimum gaps around its endpoints.

```
WITH
Cal(cal_date)
AS (SELECT MIN(start_date) - INTERVAL '1' DAY
```

```
           FROM Events
       UNION ALL
       SELECT cal_date + INTERVAL '1' DAY
         FROM Cal
        WHERE cal_date
              < (SELECT MAX(end_date) + INTERVAL '1' DAY
                   FROM Events)),
Gaps (cal_date)
AS (SELECT cal_date
      FROM Cal AS C
     WHERE NOT EXISTS
           (SELECT *
             FROM Events
            WHERE C.cal_date BETWEEN start_date AND
            end_date)), Durations (event_id, start_date,
            lower_bound, end_date, upper_bound)
AS (SELECT E.event_id, E.start_date,
           MAX(G1.d) + INTERVAL '1' DAY,
           E.end_date,
           MIN(g2.d) - INTERVAL '1' DAY
      FROM Gaps AS G1, Gaps AS G2, Events AS E
     WHERE G1.d < E.start_date
       AND G2.d > E.end_date
    GROUP BY E.event_id, E.start_date, end_date)

SELECT DISTINCT event_id, lower_bound, upper_bound
FROM Durations;
```

You can derive the gaps without the Calendar table by enumerating the dates:

```
SELECT DISTINCT
E.event_id,
(SELECT MAX(start_date))
 FROM Events AS E2
 WHERE E2.start_date <= E.start_date
   AND NOT EXISTS
     (SELECT * FROM Events AS E3
      WHERE E2.start_date - INTERVAL '1' DAY
            BETWEEN E3.start_date AND E3.end_date)),
(SELECT MIN(end_date)
   FROM Events AS E4
  WHERE E4.end_date >= E.end_date
```

```
AND NOT EXISTS
    (SELECT *
        FROM Events AS E5
      WHERE E4.end_date + INTERVAL '1' DAY
          BETWEEN E5.start_date AND E5.end_date))
FROM Events AS E;
```

9.4.1   Cursors and Triggers

A simple way to consolidate intervals is to declare a cursor with two columns, like this:

```
DECLARE EventList CURSOR FOR
SELECT DISTINCT E.event_id, C.cal_date
  FROM Events AS E, Calendar AS C
WHERE C.cal_date BETWEEN E.start_date AND E.end_date
ORDER BY E.event_id, C.cal_date ASC
FOR READ ONLY;
```

We now have a list of each day in an event.

1.   Fetch the first row and put it into local storage, making the end_date = start_date.

2.   Fetch the next row.

3.   If this current row is in the same event and INTERVAL '1' DAY after the local end_date, update the end_date with it.

4.   If the current row is not in the same event or > INTERVAL '1' DAY after the local end_date, then:

   4.1 Insert the local storage into a working table as a row.

   4.2 Overwrite the local storage with the current row, making the end_date = start_date.

5.   Loop until the end of the cursor.

6.   The working table is the desired answer.

You can also set a trigger that will catch attempts to insert overlapping time periods and force a ROLLBACK along with an error message about needing to do an UPDATE instead. Simply check for a Calendar date that appears in the query we just used for the cursor.

9.4.2   OLAP Function Solution

Another approach due to Erik Lennart uses the OLAP functions from SQL-2003.

```
SELECT event_id, min_start_date, MAX(end_date)
FROM (SELECT event_id, start_date, end_date,
             MAX(CASE WHEN start_date
                              <= max_end_date + INTERVAL '1' DAY
                      THEN NULL ELSE start_date END)
             OVER (PARTITION BY event_id
                   ORDER BY event_id, start_date, end_date
                   ROWS UNBOUNDED PRECEDING)
      FROM (SELECT event_id, start_date, end_date,
                   MAX(end_date)
                   OVER (PARTITION BY event_id
                         ORDER BY event_id, start_date,
                         end_date
                           ROWS BETWEEN UNBOUNDED PRECEDING
                                        AND 1 PRECEDING)
            FROM Events
           ) AS T1 (event_id, start_date, end_date,
             max_end_date)
        ) AS T2 (event_id, start_date, end_date,
          min_start_date)
GROUP BY event_id, min_start_date;
```

9.4.3   CTE Solution

This solution is due to Sylvester Lewandowski. It has a little bit of everything in it—CTEs with multiple UNION ALL clauses and set operators in the main body.

```
WITH EventsCTE
AS
(SELECT E1.event_id, E1.start_date, E1.end_date
   FROM Events AS E1

UNION ALL
 SELECT E.event_id, E.start_date, CTE.end_date
   FROM EventsCTE AS CTE, Events AS E
 WHERE E.event_id = CTE.event_id
```

```
          AND (CTE.start_date = E.end_date + INTERVAL '1' DAY
               OR E.end_date BETWEEN CTE.start_date AND
               CTE.end_date)
          AND E.start_date < CTE.start_date

UNION ALL
SELECT E.event_id, CTE.start_date, E.end_date
   FROM EventsCTE AS CTE, Events as E
WHERE E.event_id = CTE.event_id
   AND (CTE.end_date = E.start_date - INTERVAL '1' DAY
         OR E.start_date BETWEEN CTE.start_date AND
         CTE.end_date)
   AND E.end_date > CTE.end_date

UNION ALL
SELECT E.event_id, E.start_date, E.end_date
   FROM EventsCTE AS CTE, Events AS E
WHERE E.event_id = CTE.event_id
   AND CTE.start_date > E.start_date
   AND CTE.end_date < E.end_date)


SELECT event_id, start_date, end_date
   FROM EventsCTE
EXCEPT
SELECT event_id, start_date, end_date
   FROM EventsCTE AS C1
WHERE EXISTS
      (SELECT *
         FROM EventsCTE AS C2
        WHERE C1.event_id = C2.event_id)
          AND ((C1.start_date = C2.start_date
              AND C1.end_date < C2.end_date)
            OR (C1.start_date > C2.start_date
                AND C1.end_date < C2.end_date)
            OR (C1.start_date > C2.start_date
                AND C1.end_date = C2.end_date));
```

9.5   Calendar Tables

Calendar tables are necessary because the current calendar is so
irregular that you cannot reasonably compute events. Yes, there is a
19-year cycle (the Metonic cycle, named after the fifth-century Greek
astronomer, Meton) in which the days of the week will repeat and you

could use this to create a self-updating view if you need to use the days of the week. But it is just as easy to have a 100-year calendar in a single short table and use it.

9.5.1 Day of Week via Tables

The classic method for computing the day of the week in the Common Era calendar is a bit complicated. Here is the algorithm:

1. Take the last two digits of the year. In our example, this is 82.

2. Do integer division by 4 on the decade (two digits of the year).

3. Add the day of the month.

4. Add the month's key value, from the following table:

```
month_name          month_value
================================
   Jan                   1
   Feb                   4
   Mar                   4
   Apr                   0
   May                   2
   Jun                   5
   Jul                   0
   Aug                   3
   Sep                   6
   Oct                   1
   Nov                   4
   Dec                   6
```

5. If your date is in January or February of a leap year, subtract 1.

6. Add the century code from the following table. (These codes are for the Common Era calendar. The rule is slightly simpler for Julian dates.)

```
year_start     year_end     year_value
=======================================
   1700          1799           4
   1800          1899           2
   1900          1999           0
   2000          2099           6
```

The Common Era calendar repeats every four hundred years, so you can extend this table if you need to go further back or forward in time.

7.   Add the last two digits of the year.

8.   Perform a MOD 7 on the sum to get the answer: 1 = Sunday, 2 = Monday, and so forth.

It is a good little exercise to actually write this formula out as a SELECT or SET clause. The leap year test can be done as a CASE expression:

```
CASE WHEN MOD(my_year, 400) = 0
THEN 1
WHEN MOD(my_year, 100) = 0
THEN 0
ELSE CASE WHEN MOD(my_year, 4) = 0
          THEN 1 ELSE 0 END
END
```

Compare that computation to simply updating a column in a table with a day of the week digit derived from taking the MOD (Julian date number, 7). Putting this in a calendar table is so much easier.

9.5.2   Holiday Lists

Holidays are very irregular. A holiday can be done by decree without any repetition pattern. They can be moved to a Friday or Monday if they fall on a weekend in many countries. Asian holidays are based on the Chinese Lunar calendar. Muslim holidays are based on the Arabic solar-lunar calendar. Orthodox holidays are based on the old Julian solar calendar.

In short, you have no choice but table lookup and a calendar table. You can get a list of holidays by country at these websites:

http://en.wikipedia.org/wiki/List_of_holidays_by_country
http://www.qppstudio.net/worldholidays.htm
http://www.nationalholidaydates.com/HolidayDates/default.aspx

Note that you will need to update them on a daily basis if you are doing serious international work.

The worst way to construct a Calendar table was illustrated in the July 2007 edition of *SQL Server Magazine* in an article on how to find the number of business days between two given dates. The code was highly proprietary, even when Standard options exist in SQL Server.

For example, the product can be set to accept ISO-8601 formatted temporal input, but that was not used. *SQL Server* violates the same ISO Standard that the days of the week start with Monday =1 and begins on Sunday instead. The way that weeks are numbered in a year in *SQL Server* is also wrong. The proprietary temporal function syntax makes the code difficult to read, much less maintain.

The author creates temporary tables on the fly with more proprietary syntax using table valued functions and needless IDENTITY columns (an autoincrement feature in this dialect). The table is filled with a count of weekdays, using a "day of the week" function, and then holidays are removed from the count by using a second table of holidays. Without comment, here is some of the code used to build temporary tables on the fly each time; I leave it to you to figure it out:

```
CREATE FUNCTION Business_Age (@limit_days INTEGER)
-- T-SQL dialect
RETURNS TABLE
AS RETURN
(SELECT record_num, day1, day2, bus_age
    FROM (SELECT record_num, day1, day2,
                 DATEDIFF(day, day1, day2)
                  -2 * DATEDIFF(WK, day1, day2)
                  - (SELECT COUNT(*)
                       FROM TmpHolidays
                      WHERE hol_date BETWEEN day1 AND day2
                        AND DATEPART (DW, hol_date) NOT IN
                        (1, 7))
                  + (CASE WHEN DATEPART (DW, day1) = 7 THEN 1
                     ELSE 0 END)
                  - (CASE WHEN DATEPART (DW, day2) = 7 THEN 1
                     ELSE 0 END)
                  AS bus_age
          FROM TmpTable) AS D
      WHERE bus_age > @limit_days);
```

The simple way to do this is with a calendar table that has a Julianized business day column:

```
CREATE TABLE Calendar
(cal_date DATETIME NOT NULL PRIMARY KEY,
bus_juldate INTEGER NOT NULL,
...);
```

Ignoring the other enterprise temporal data that should go into such a table, consider these few rows at a company that takes Good Friday off:

```
INSERT INTO Calendar VALUES ('2007-04-04', 2078);
INSERT INTO Calendar VALUES ('2007-04-05', 2079);
INSERT INTO Calendar VALUES ('2007-04-06', 2079);
-- Good Friday
INSERT INTO Calendar VALUES ('2007-04-07', 2079);
INSERT INTO Calendar VALUES ('2007-04-08', 2079);
-- Easter Sunday
INSERT INTO Calendar VALUES ('2007-04-09', 2080);
INSERT INTO Calendar VALUES ('2007-04-10', 2081);
```

The query is now reduced to simple math:

```
SELECT :my_date_1, :my_date_2,
(C2.bus_juldate - C1.bus_juldate + 1) AS lapsed_days
  FROM Calendar AS C1, Calendar AS C2
WHERE C1.cal_date = :my_date_1
  AND C2.cal_date = :my_date_2;
```

The Calendar can be set up for 100 years without any trouble, altered decades in advance if a new holiday occurs or an old one moves (remember Washington's and Lincoln's birthdays versus President's Day?).

The REAL problem is that the author is not really writing SQL yet. She is still thinking in procedural code and not in data.

9.5.3   Report Periods

These tables all have the same format, namely a report period name, starting dates, ending dates, and other information that applies to that reporting period. The periods can overlap so that "Mauve Bikini Monday" can occur during "Bikini Sales Madness Week"; the extra data might be special discounts that apply on Monday in addition to or instead of the other discounts.

9.5.4   Self-Updating Views

While it is easy to keep a Calendar table for several decades with a granularity of days, it is not a good idea to retain one at the level of minutes or seconds. But such tables can be useful for reporting events at a finer granularity, such as tracking a manufacturing process in 1 minute or smaller steps for a single day. You would have 1,440 minutes and 86,400 seconds per day.

The trick is to create a VIEW that updates itself for you. First, create and populate a table of "clock ticks" at the level you desire.

```
CREATE TABLE ClockTicks
(start_tick INTERVAL MINUTE TO SECOND PRIMARY KEY,
end_tick INTERVAL MINUTE TO SECOND,
CHECK (start_tick < end_tick));

INSERT INTO ClockTicks (start_tick, end_tick)
VALUES ('00:00', '00:59.999'),
       ('01:00', '01:59.999'), etc.
```

Then use this to build a VIEW:

```
CREATE VIEW DailyTicks (start_time, end_time)
AS
SELECT CAST (CURRENT_DATE + start_tick AS TIMESTAMP),
       CAST (CURRENT_DATE + end_tick AS TIMESTAMP)
  FROM ClockTicks;
```

The VIEW will refresh itself every day and be small enough that it should fit into main storage on any modern SQL platform.

You can also use a slightly different version of this idea with named reporting periods. Imagine a table of financial periods in the format "yyyy-mm" (i.e., "2007-01" would be the first period of the year 2007).

```
CREATE TABLE Financial_Periods
(period_id CHAR(7) NOT NULL PRIMARY KEY
  CHECK (period_id LIKE '[12][0-9][0-9][0-9]-[01][0-9]'),
current_period_nbr INTEGER NOT NULL,
period_start_date DATETIME NOT NULL,
period_end_date DATETIME NOT NULL,
 CHECK (period_start_date < period_end_date),
Etc.);
```

Notice that this table holds columns that give both the current and prior periods and one that Julianizes the current period. These are tricks to make computations easier.

To keep things as simple as possible, assume we have a table of Customer Activity with the date of each activity. What we want is a list of customers who have had no activity in the previous three periods.

The first step is to find the current period's Julian number. We can do that with a CTE. Using that number, we can look back for three periods:

```
WITH X (current_period_nbr)
AS(SELECT current_period_nbr
     FROM Financial_Periods
   WHERE CURRENT_TIMESTAMP
         BETWEEN period_start_date and period_end_date)

SELECT C.customer_id
  FROM CustomerActivity AS C
       LEFT OUTER JOIN
       Financial_Periods AS P
       ON P.current_period_nbr
          IN (X.current_period_nbr,
              X.current_period_nbr-1,
              X.current_period_nbr-2)
WHERE C.activity_date BETWEEN P.start_date AND P.end_date
GROUP BY C.customer_id
HAVING COUNT (C.activity_date) = 0;
```

The idea of keeping a self-updating VIEW can also use any of the other system-level values. For example, the CURRENT_USER value can be used for security.

9.6   History Tables

The start and stop times are what you should have been catching in the first place and not the computed hours. Think raw data and single facts when designing a table. Let me use a history table for price changes. The fact to store is that a price had duration:

```
CREATE TABLE PriceHistory
(sku CHAR(13) NOT NULL
  REFERENCES Inventory(sku),
start_date DATE NOT NULL,
end_date DATE, -- null means current
CHECK(start_date < end_date),
PRIMARY KEY (sku, start_date),
item_price DECIMAL (12,4) NOT NULL
```

```
CHECK (item_price > 0.0000),
etc.);
```

You actually need more checks to assure that the start date is at 00:00 Hrs if you cannot work with whole days in your SQL engine. This is the case with MS SQL Server and the Sybase family. Likewise, the end dates are forced to 23:59:59.999 Hrs, so you can use a BETWEEN predicate to get the appropriate price.

```
SELECT ..
  FROM PriceHistory AS H, Orders AS O
  WHERE O.sales_date BETWEEN H.start_date
          AND COALESCE (end_date, CURRENT_TIMESTAMP);
```

It is also a good idea to have a VIEW with the current data:

```
CREATE VIEW CurrentPrices (..)
AS
SELECT ..
  FROM PriceHistory
WHERE end_date IS NULL;
```

Robert Klemme adds the caveat that if prices are entered with future start dates (e.g., "we will start selling X for $9.95 next month") the VIEW might pull a wrong current value. In that case, a different view might be better:

```
CREATE VIEW CurrentPrices (..)
AS
SELECT ..
  FROM PriceHistory
WHERE start_date <= CURRENT_TIMESTAMP
  AND (end_date IS NULL
        OR end_date > CURRENT_TIMESTAMP);
```

This will let you keep the future changes in the table, but not show them as the current values.

9.6.1   Audit Trails

Audit trails are kept outside of the schema and certainly never in the same table as the data. That means a column like "last_modified_date DATE DEFAULT CURRENT_DATE NOT NULL" should not exist.

It should be obvious that if a row in such a table is deleted, it will also destroy the audit data. This is much the reason that you do not keep the backups for the database on the same hard disk as the database. Think about what a physical disk crash would do to the data and the backup.

But it actually goes beyond that. Anyone with full access to the table can play with `last_modified_date` as well as the other attributes. Auditors do not like that. Auditors want to see at least two independent "signatures" on each and every action in the system. This means that a shipment must match to an order, so that the mailroom clerks cannot send themselves free company products.

Such a design also means that the table contains both data and metadata about whatever it is modeling. RDBMS guys do not like that.

Your best bet used to be to buy a third-party tool that can construct audit trails from the backups and log files. These log files are already in place and it is difficult, but not impossible, to disable logging. Such an action is captured and reported, however.

Backups and log files are no longer the gold standard in auditing solutions because of recent regulatory compliance requirements. Consider HIPAA, which states that medical professionals need to be able to provide, on request, information about who *even looked at the data* while backups and log files only show changes to that data. This now requires sniffing the network or database server for all SQL and logging the actions taken. Again, this detailed log has to be stored externally from the database that is being audited. Products from third-party vendors such as Guardium and Lumigent meet these requirements.

CHAPTER 10

Scrubbing Data with Non-1NF Tables

WE DO NOT always get perfect, clean data, so "data scrubbing" is an important function for a database. If you did not care about data quality, then the answer was always 42, to paraphrase Douglas Noël Adams (1952 to 2001) in the classic *Hitchhiker's Guide to the Galaxy* series. Software to extract, transform, and load (ETL) data has become a niche in the software industry all to itself, but you can do a lot in SQL itself without special tools.

There will likely be some common problems that go with data from non-SQL sources. Old file system layouts will have to be reformatted and often split into many tables. Old encodings may have to be updated to current systems; for example, the United States Census Bureau switched to the North American Industry Classification (SIC) and has replaced the U.S. Standard Industrial Classification (SIC) system so the United States, Canada, and Mexico will have comparable statistics about business activity in North America.

Not all data types match to native SQL data types if the data source is *really* old. Most programmers today have heard of Expanded Binary Coded Decimal Interchange Code (EBCDIC) for IBM mainframes and American Standard Code for Information Interchange (ASCII) for mini- and microcomputers. But these were not the only encoding schemes in use through the 1960s and early 1970s. For a lesson in geek history, read *Coded Character Sets, History and Development* by C. E. Mackenzie (ISBN 0-201-14460-3), which covers this topic.

10.1 Repeated Groups

SQL does not require that a table have unique constraints, a primary key, or anything else that would ensure data integrity. In short, you can use a table pretty much like a file if you wish. Is this a bad thing?

Well, mostly yes and a little no. You should never have such a beast in your final schema, but one common programming trick is to use a table without any constraints as a staging area. You load data from an external source into one of these pseudo-tables, scrub it, and pass it along to a real table in the actual schema. The trouble is that a lot of the time, the pseudo-table is denormalized as well as full of bad data. You can do some normalization from the staging table into another set of scrubbing tables, but you can also do some work with the table as it stands.

This example is based on material posted by a newbie on an SQL newsgroup, but his situation is not uncommon. He gets raw data from a source that can have duplicate rows and repeating groups in violation of first normal form (1NF). His scrub tables look like this:

```
CREATE TABLE PersonnelSkills
(emp_name VARCHAR(10) NOT NULL,
  skill_code1 INTEGER NOT NULL,
  skill_code2 INTEGER NOT NULL,
  skill_code3 INTEGER NOT NULL,
  skill_code4 INTEGER NOT NULL,
  skill_code5 INTEGER NOT NULL);

INSERT INTO PersonnelSkills
VALUES ('Mary', 1, 7, 8, 9, 13),
       ('Mary', 1, 7, 8, 9, 13),
       ('Mary', 1, 7, 7, 7, 13),
       ('Mary', 1, 7, 8, 9, 13),
       ('Joe', 1, 7, 8, 9, 3),
       ('Bob', 1, 7, 8, 9, 3),
       ('Larry', 22, 17, 18, 19, 113), -- non-target codes
       ('Mary', 1, 3, 2, 9, 13),
       ('Melvin', 1, 3, 2, 9, 13), -- 2 target codes
       ('Irving', 1, 8, 2, 9, 13); -- 1 target codes
```

Part of the scrubbing is to find which people have some or all of a particular code. The list can change, so we put it in a table of its own, like this:

```
CREATE TABLE TargetCodes
(skill_code INTEGER NOT NULL PRIMARY KEY,
 skill_description VARCHAR(50) NOT NULL);

INSERT INTO TargetCodes
VALUES (1, 'skill_code1'),
       (3, 'skill_code3'),
       (7, '-_code7');
```

The first goal is to return a report with the name of the employee and the number of target codes they have in their skills inventory.

The first thought of an experienced SQL programmer is to normalize the repeated group. The obvious way to do this is with a derived table, thus:

```
SELECT P1.name, COUNT(*)
FROM (SELECT emp_name, skill_code1 FROM PersonnelSkills
      UNION
      SELECT emp_name, skill_code2 FROM PersonnelSkills
      UNION
      SELECT emp_name, skill_code3 FROM PersonnelSkills
      UNION
      SELECT emp_name, skill_code4 FROM PersonnelSkills
      UNION
      SELECT emp_name, skill_code5 FROM PersonnelSkills)
      AS P1 (emp_name, skill_code) -- normalized table!
      LEFT OUTER JOIN
      TargetCodes AS T1
      ON T1.code = P1.code
GROUP BY P1.name;
```

The reason that this fools experienced SQL programmers is that they know that a schema should be in 1NF and they immediately fix that problem without looking a bit further. They want to correct the design problem first.

That chain of UNIONs can be replaced by a chain of ORs, hidden in an IN() predicate. This one is not so bad to write.

```
SELECT P1.emp_name, COUNT (DISTINCT T1.code) AS tally
  FROM PersonnelSkills AS P1
```

```
      LEFT OUTER JOIN
       TargetCodes AS T1
       ON T1.code IN (skill_code1, skill_code2,
       skill_code3, skill_code4, skill_code5)
GROUP BY name;
```

Results

```
  emp_name     tally
==================
  'Bob'          3
  'Irving'       1
  'Joe'          3
  'Larry'        0
  'Mary'         3
  'Melvin'       2
```

The trick is the use of an IN() predicate when you have a repeating group. This will give you just the names of those who have one or more target codes.

```
SELECT DISTINCT emp_name
  FROM PersonnelSkills AS P1
WHERE skill_code1 IN (SELECT code FROM TargetCodes)
   OR skill_code2 IN (SELECT code FROM TargetCodes)
   OR skill_code3 IN (SELECT code FROM TargetCodes)
   OR skill_code4 IN (SELECT code FROM TargetCodes)
   OR skill_code5 IN (SELECT code FROM TargetCodes);
```

This next modification will shown you which skills each employee has, with 1/0 flags. This has a neat trick with little-used SUM(DISTINCT <exp>) construction, but you have to know what the target codes are in advance.

```
SELECT emp_name,
       SUM(DISTINCT CASE
                  WHEN 1 IN (skill_code1, skill_code2,
                  skill_code3, skill_code4, skill_code5)
                  THEN 1 ELSE 0 END) AS skill_code1,
       SUM(DISTINCT CASE
                  WHEN 3 IN (skill_code1, skill_code2,
                  skill_code3, skill_code4, skill_code5)
```

```
                      THEN 1 ELSE 0 END) AS skill_code3,
            SUM(DISTINCT CASE
               WHEN 7 IN (skill_code1, skill_code2, skill_code3,
               skill_code4, skill_code5)
                        THEN 1 ELSE 0 END) AS skill_code7
   FROM PersonnelSkills AS P1
GROUP BY name;
```

Results

emp_name	skill_code1	skill_code3	skill_code7
===========	=============	=============	=============
'Bob'	1	1	1
'Irving'	1	0	0
'Joe'	1	1	1
'Larry'	0	0	0
'Mary'	1	1	1
'Melvin'	1	1	0

10.1.1 Sorting within a Repeated Group

Repeated groups of fields in a file system should be split out into multiple tables in a normalized schema. But on the way to that goal, you might want to check and see that values in each repeated group are sorted from left to right, because that ordering carries some meaning.

With our example, the employee's skills might be in chronological order in the five slots we have allowed. The business rule might be that you cannot become a "Class III Frammis Mechanic" as your third skill without having been a "Class II Frammis Mechanic" as your first or second skill. Putting the vector in order makes such patterns easier to find while you are scrubbing such data.

A quick way to do this sorting is the Bose-Nelson sort ("A Sorting Problem" by R. C. Bose and R. J. Nelson, *Journal of the ACM*, Vol. 9, pp. 282–296, and my article in *Dr. Dobb's Journal* back in 1985). This is a recursive procedure that takes an integer and then generates swap pairs for a vector of that size. A swap pair is a pair of position numbers from 1 to (n) in the vector that need to be exchanged if they are out of order. Swap pairs are also related to sorting networks in the literature (see *The Art of Computer Programming*, by Donald Knuth, Vol. 3).

You are probably thinking that this method is a bit weak because the results are only good for sorting a fixed number of items. But a table only has a fixed number of columns, so that is not a problem in denormalized SQL.

You can set up a sorting network that will sort five items with the minimal number of exchanges, nine swaps, like this:

```
swap (c1, c2);
swap (c4, c5);
swap (c3, c5);
swap (c3, c4);
swap (c1, c4);
swap (c1, c3);
swap (c2, c5);
swap (c2, c4);
swap (c2, c3);
```

You might want to deal yourself a hand of five playing cards in one suit to see how it works. Put the cards face down on the table and pick up the pairs, swapping them if required, then turn over the row to see that it is in sorted order when you are done.

In theory, the minimum number of swaps needed to sort (n) items is `CEILING(LOG2(n!))`, and as (n) increases, this approaches `O(n*LOG2(n))`. Computer science majors will remember that "Big O" expression as the expected performance of the best sorting algorithms, such as Quicksort. The Bose-Nelson method is very good for small values of (n). If (n < 9), then it is perfect, actually. But as things get bigger, Bose-Nelson approaches O(n ^ 1.585). In English, this method is good for a fixed-size list of 16 or fewer items and goes to Hell after that.

You can write a version of the Bose-Nelson procedure that will output the SQL code for a given value of (n). The obvious direct way to do a `swap(x, y)` is to write a chain of UPDATE statements. Remember that in SQL, the SET clause assignments happen in parallel, so you can easily write a SET clause that exchanges the two items when are out of order. Using the above swap chain, we get this block of code:

```
BEGIN ATOMIC
-- swap (skill_code1, skill_code2);
UPDATE PersonnelSkills
```

```
   SET skill_code1 = skill_code2, skill_code2 = skill_code1
WHERE skill_code1 > skill_code2;
-- swap (skill_code4, skill_code5);
UPDATE PersonnelSkills
   SET skill_code4 = skill_code5, skill_code5 = skill_code4
WHERE skill_code4 > skill_code5;

-- swap (skill_code3, skill_code5);
UPDATE PersonnelSkills
  SET skill_code3 = skill_code5, skill_code5 = skill_code3
WHERE skill_code3 > skill_code5;

-- swap (skill_code3, skill_code4);
UPDATE PersonnelSkills
  SET skill_code3 = skill_code4, skill_code4 = skill_code3
WHERE skill_code3 > skill_code4;

-- swap (skill_code1, skill_code4);
UPDATE PersonnelSkills
  SET skill_code1 = skill_code4, skill_code4 = skill_code1
WHERE skill_code1 > skill_code4;

-- swap (skill_code1, skill_code3);
UPDATE PersonnelSkills
  SET skill_code1 = skill_code3, skill_code3 = skill_code1
WHERE skill_code1 > skill_code3;

-- swap (skill_code2, skill_code5);
UPDATE PersonnelSkills
  SET skill_code2 = skill_code5, skill_code5 = skill_code2
WHERE skill_code2 > skill_code5;

-- swap (skill_code2, skill_code4);
UPDATE PersonnelSkills
  SET skill_code2 = skill_code4, skill_code4 = skill_code2
WHERE skill_code2 > skill_code4;

-- swap (skill_code2, skill_code3);
UPDATE PersonnelSkills
  SET skill_code2 = skill_code3, skill_code3 = skill_code2
WHERE skill_code2 > skill_code3;
SELECT * FROM PersonnelSkills;
END;
```

This is fully portable, Standard SQL code and it can be machine generated. But that parallelism is useful. It is worthwhile to combine some of the UPDATE statements, but you have to be careful not to change the effective sequence of the swap operations.

If you look at the first two UPDATE statements, you can see that they do not overlap. This means you could roll them into one statement like this:

```
swap (skill_code1, skill_code2)
AND swap (skill_code4, skill_code5);
```

which becomes:

```
UPDATE Foobar
    SET skill_code1 = CASE WHEN skill_code1 <= skill_code2
THEN skill_code1 ELSE skill_code2 END,
        skill_code2 = CASE WHEN skill_code1 <= skill_code2
THEN skill_code2 ELSE skill_code1 END,
        skill_code4 = CASE WHEN skill_code4 <= skill_code5
THEN skill_code4 ELSE skill_code5 END,
        skill_code5 = CASE WHEN skill_code4 <= skill_code5
THEN skill_code5 ELSE skill_code4 END
WHERE skill_code4 > skill_code5 OR skill_code1 >
skill_code2
```

The advantage of doing this is that you have to execute only one UPDATE statement and not two. Updating a table, even on nonkey columns, usually locks the table and prevents other users from getting to the data. If you could roll the statements into a single UPDATE, you would have the best of all possible worlds, but I doubt that the code would be easy to read. I'll leave that as an exercise to the reader.

10.2 Designing Scrubbing Tables

Let's assume that you are moving data from a file into a working table for scrubbing. What should the target table look like? The usual answer is to make all the columns NVARCHAR(n), where (n) is the maximum size allowed by your particular SQL product. This is the most general data type, and it can hold all kinds of garbage. It is as close to mimicking a general sequential file as you can get in SQL.

The real shame about this schema design is that people do use it in their actual database and not just as a staging area for scrubbing bad data.

The first question to ask is whether you should be using NVARCHAR(n) or simply VARCHAR(n). If you allow a Unicode character set, you can catch some errors that might not be seen in a simple Latin-1 alphabet. But most of the time, you can be sure that the file was in ASCII or EBCDIC by the time you moved it to the staging table with a utility program.

The simple way to do this is with a comma separated values (CSV) file. You can modify such a file with a text editor, and it is the closest thing we have to a universal file format. If worse comes to worst, you can even add individual "INSERT INTO <column list> VALUES (<csv record>);" code around each line and run the file as an SQL transaction with save points.

The second question is what value of (n) to use. If you have no idea what the data looks like, then setting all the columns to the maximum length in your SQL is all you can do for the first scrubbing. The next step is to run a query that looks for the minimum, maximum, and average length of each of the columns.

If a column is supposed to be a fixed length, then all three of these should be the same. That sounds simplistic, but extra and missing characters are two of the most common data entry errors. This is also the time to trim leading and trailing blanks from the fields.

If a column is supposed to be of varying length, then all three of these should be in a reasonable range. How do you define reasonable? Bigger than zero length is often a good criterion for a column being too short. This can happen when a field was skipped on an input form or if there were errors in converting it into a CSV file. In the CSV format, this would probably be two commas in a row. As an example, I moved an ACT file into SQL Server using the ACT utility program to get a CSV file and found several rows where the data had gotten shifted over one position, leaving blank or empty columns.

You generally have some idea if a varying column is too long. For example, the United State Postal Service suggestions for mailing labels use CHAR(35) lines. This is based on a 3.5-inch label prepared with a 10-pitch typewriter, so any address line longer than that is suspect (and cannot easily be used on bulk mailings).

If you have columns that are longer than expected, the first action should be to UPDATE the scrub table using TRIM() and REPLACE() functions to remove extra blanks. Extra white space is the usual culprit. You might find it is faster to do this quick cleanup in the original CSV file with a text editor. Section 5.1.3 has already shown you a SELECT statement and procedural code for parsing a simple CSV list, but those examples assumed clean data.

However, other simple edits are probably best done in SQL since a text editor does not see the individual fields. You might want to change "Street" to "St" to keep mailing addresses short, but a text editor will cheerfully make "John Longstreet" into "John Longst" as well.

In the same UPDATE, you can use UPPER() or LOWER() to be sure that your data is in the right case. Proper capitalization for text is a bit harder, and if you have to do this often, it is a good idea to write a stored procedure or user-defined function in the 4GL language that came with your SQL product.

Finally, look at the data itself. Many SQL products offer functions that test to see if a string is a valid numeric expression or to cast it into a numeric. But you have to be careful, since some of these functions stop parsing as soon as they have a numeric string; that is, given the string '123XX' your product's function might return the integer 123 and ignore the invalid characters at the end, or it might fail on 'XX123' because of the leading alpha characters.

Today, most SQL products have some kind of regular expression predicate that works like the SQL-92 SIMILAR TO predicate or the grep() utilities in UNIX. This is a great tool for validating the scrubbed data, but it has some limits. It only tells you that the data is in a validate format, but not if it is valid data.

For example, given a date of "12/11/03," you have no idea if it was supposed to be "2003-11-12" (British convention) or "2003-12-11" (American convention) without outside information. This is why we have the ISO-8601 Standards for displaying temporal data. Likewise, "2003-02-30" will pass a simple regular expression test, but there is no such date.

One of the most common errors in file systems was to load the same raw data into the file more than once. Sometimes it was literally the same data—an operator hung a magnetic tape, loaded a file, and then forgot to mark the job as having been done. The next shift would come to work and repeat the operation. Other times, a data-entry clerk simply input the same data twice or sent a correction without removing the erroneous data. Given an impatient user with a fast mouse button, you can get the same problem in the current technology, too. Look at the number of e-commerce sites that have a warning about not submitting the order form page twice.

At this point, you are ready to move the raw data to a new table with columns that have appropriate data types, but still no constraints just yet. The move can be done with an "INSERT INTO <scrub table #2> SELECT DISTINCT .. FROM <scrub table #1>;" statement to get rid of the redundant duplicates.

10.3 Scrubbing Constraints

At the point at which you have the raw data scrubbed this far, there is a temptation to simply load it into the "real tables" in the database. Resist the temptation. The syntax of the data might be acceptable, but that does not mean it is right.

We can classify errors as single-column or multicolumn errors. A single-column error might be a gender code of 'B' when only 'M' or 'F' is allowed. A multiple-column error involves individual columns that are valid, but the combination of which is invalid. For example, pregnancy is a valid medical condition; male is a valid gender; but a pregnant male is an invalid combination.

The first test is to see if your key is actually a key by running a test for NULLs and counting the occurrences of unique values:

```
SELECT key_1, key_2, ... key_n
   FROM ScrubTank
  GROUP BY key_1, key_2, ... key_n
 HAVING COUNT(*) > 1 -- dups
     OR (SIGN(key_1) + .. + SIGN(key_n) IS NULL
```

You can also use SUBSTRING(), CASE, or other functions with concatenation so that any NULL will propagate.

Assume we have a column with a code that is five characters long and we have trimmed and edited the original raw data until all the rows of that column are indeed CHAR(5). But there is a syntax rule that the code is of this format (using SQL-99 predicates):

```
CHECK (Foo_code SIMILAR TO
'[:UPPER:][:UPPER:][:DIGIT:][:DIGIT:][:DIGIT:]')
```

If you add this to your scrub table with an ALTER TABLE statement, you need to know if your SQL product will immediately test existing data for compatibility, or if the constraint will go into effect only for inserted or updated data.

Instead of adding the check constraints all at once, write case expressions that will do the testing for you. The format is simple and can be done with a text editor. Pull off the predicates from the CHECK() constraints in the target table and put them into a query like this:

```
SELECT
  CASE WHEN NOT <predicate 1> THEN 'err_###'
```

```
        WHEN NOT <predicate 2> THEN 'err_###'
        . . .
        ELSE '' END AS <test name>,
    . . .
  FROM ScrubTank;
```

A CASE expression will test each WHEN clause in the order written, so when you see one error message, you will need to correct it and then pass the data through the query again. The goal is to get a query with all blanks in the columns to show that all the rows have passed.

Rules that apply to more than one column can be tested with another query that looks for the table constraints in the same way. It is a good idea to do this as a separate step after the single-column validations. A correction in one column will often fix the multicolumn errors, too.

Hopefully, we are now ready to finally put the scrubbed data into one or more of the target tables in the actual database schema. That ought to be a simple "INSERT INTO.. SELECT.. FROM ScrubTank" statement.

Frankly, there are better tools for data scrubbing than pure SQL; this series of articles was more of a "proof of concept" than a recommendation. If you have the logical constraints in the text of your database schema, then pulling them out is a matter of a text edit, not completely new programming. While this approach is a bit of work, it gives you a script that you can reuse and does not cost you any extra money for new software.

10.4 Calendar Scrubs

When a range of possible values is limited, you can use a table for those Values that you wish to allow into the database schema.

The idea is simple enough and should have been part of the CHECK() constraints on the base tables in the schema. But when you are importing external data, you might need help.

Troels Arvin posted a problem in the DB2 newsgroup in early 2007 in which he had a non-SQL data source with CHAR(10) dates that were supposed to be in ISO-8601 format (i.e., 2006-12-24). Some of the values were known to be invalid (such as 0000-00-00 or 2006-02-45). His goal was to convert the strings to DATE values as he loaded them into his schema.

One proposed solution was to use an internal user-defined function (UDF) in SQL/PSM or an external function in a 3GL language or scripting language such as PERL to validate the strings. The body of the procedure would CAST a string to a temporal data type; if the CAST() failed, the function would return NULL.

Lennart proposed that Arvin use a calendar table instead of computational code, expressing the dates as CHAR(10) strings for the last few decades (this range was good enough for the problem). This would give us a table with less than 4,000 rows per decade, which is a very small table on modern equipment.

Such a table is simple and easy to build either in SQL or in an external spreadsheet. If this is going to be an ongoing project, then a CHAR(10) column could be added to the usual Calendar table and displayed with a VIEW.

10.4.1 Special Dates

The table lookup approach has another advantage over direct conversion to temporal data types. In many old COBOL applications, a date field would also hold special strings to indicate special temporal situations. For example, in a state prison inmate file system, we used an expected release date filed, which could be:

1.   An actual calendar in ISO-8601 format.

2.   The string 8888-88-88 was used to indicate the inmate was serving a life sentence.

3.   The string 9999-99-99 was used to indicate the inmate was serving a death sentence.

The use of all nines in COBOL application files for an unknown date was also a common COBOL and FORTRAN programming technique before SQL. This would get the special codes to sort to the end of a report.

What we had done in the COBOL file was violate 1NF by using a single column for two scalar values, namely the inmate's expected release date and the type of sentence he or she was serving.

Such special values can be added to the date format validation table, then used by the insertion statement for other actions on columns. In my example, we need to split out the release date and the type of sentence being served.

```
INSERT INTO Inmates (release_date, sentence_type, ..)
SELECT CASE WHEN R.release_date
                NOT IN ('8888-88-88', '9999-99-99')
            THEN C.date_str ELSE NULL END,
```

```
        CASE WHEN R.release_date = '8888-88-88'
             THEN 'life'
             WHEN R.release_date = '9999-99-99'
             THEN 'death'
             WHEN << other conditions>>
             THEN 'without parole'
             ELSE 'parole/probation' END,
      Etc.
  FROM RawData AS R, CalendarFormat AS C
WHERE C.date_str = R.release_date
  AND ..;
```

This same programming template can be applied to other fields that have to be split into two or more columns for normalization.

10.5 String Scrubbing

The first pass at scrubbing string data is usually to get it into the proper case. In particular, older mainframe data is in EBCDIC and it is upper-case only.

People's names are one of the hardest pieces of data to scrub because the rules are so irregular. This is one case where the best solution is to get a specialized third-party tool and use it. I strongly recommend getting a copy of *The Math, Myth & Magic of Name Search and Matching* from SSA (*www.searchsoftware.com*) for a detailed discussion of the problems.

However, there are some data elements that we can validate with a little more work. We already mentioned the SIMILAR TO predicate for regular expressions. You can find regular expressions at *http://regexlib.com/* and copy them into your code, making changes for your dialect.

For example, this regular expression checks an e-mail format against RFC 3696 and was written by David Thompson:

```
^[a-z0-9!$'*+\-_]+ (\.[a-z0-9!$'*+\-_]+)*
@
([a-z0-9]+(-+[a-z0-9]+)*\.)+
([a-z]{2}
|aero|arpa|biz|cat|com|coop|edu|gov|info|int|jobs|mil|mobi|
museum|name|net|org|pro|travel)$
```

If you do not read regular expressions, this says that a valid e-mail address is one or more groups of strings of alphanumeric characters and some limited punctuation marks, optionally separated by a period. Then there is one "little snail" or "at-sign" in the middle. This followed by more groups of strings of alphanumeric characters and a more limited set of punctuation marks separated by periods. The string finally ends with either a two-letter country code or one of several explicit domain codes.

The problem is that the "[a-z]{2}" pattern matches any two letters even when they are not a valid country code. Nor does this have a length check. Those are easy to add.

If you do not have SIMILAR TO predicates, there is another approach. Set up a CREATE TRANSLATION declaration that maps the legal postfixes into a single unique token not used in an e-mail address. This result is then passed on to another TRANSLATE (<source string USING <translation name>) expression that reduces the alphanumeric and punctuation characters to a second unique token. Eventually, you wind up with a reduced pattern made up of the two tokens and the at-sign, say '#@#?' since neither '#' nor '?' appear in an e-mail address.

A third approach is to use the TRIM(<character value expression> FROM <trim source>) function to reduce the suspect e-mail address to a single at-sign or empty string.

The same effect can be had with nested REPLACE statements, but the nesting can be pretty deep. If you are a LISP programmer, you will not mind a bit.

Are these good methods to use in place of using an external call to an external procedure in a 3GL language or SQL/PSM? Baroque as these suggestions are, they often run much faster than the external call, and they are portable. But they are ugly to maintain.

The other consideration is that you probably can accept rejecting some valid data and then scrub it by hand. Accepting bad data and letting it get into the schema is more often a problem. Thus you can aim for "good enough" for the first pass and work with the exceptions.

10.6 Sharing SQL Data

There are two simple truths that we all know about the environment that our data lives in. The first truth is that no enterprise runs on one and only one database or data source today. Any enterprise of medium to large size will have desktop databases, department-level servers, enterprise-level servers, and data warehouse servers.

If you do not have different platforms, then you are doing something wrong. While virtually all databases today run some version of SQL, they do not implement it in the same way. The same hardware and software that runs a data warehouse would be overkill for a departmental server doing OLTP.

The first part of this chapter was concerned with legacy file systems, assumed to be on magnetic tapes or disks in character formats (or formats that could be converted to character). Another assumption I made was that your goal is to get legacy data into an SQL database at some point in time.

The second truth is that no enterprise database is isolated. The connections between your enterprise and the rest of the world are now database-to-database, not on paper forms. Orders to suppliers, shipments to customers, and any other business activity require that your database talks to someone else's database. Payments are made and accepted through your bank, PayPal, or other commercial services. Shipping is done via UPS, FedEx, DHL, and other delivery companies; you track your merchandise by accessing their databases, not by building your own.

Passive data sources are now a commodity. It would be insane to try to maintain your own postal code database when you can buy the current data from the Postal Service for a few dollars. Likewise, you would use the UPC barcodes that come on packaging instead of inventing your own encoding scheme and putting your own labels on the goods you sell.

The small enterprise often has an arrogant feeling that they can ignore external data sources. The truth is they are actually more vulnerable than the larger company. The small-to-medium enterprise cannot afford the personnel, time, and resources to verify and validate data like a large enterprise. They often leave the data in the format they got it. The result is "islands of data" that communicate with spreadsheets and homemade data transfer solutions.

That is the environment. Now, let's look at the animals that live and evolve in that environment, moving data from place to place.

10.6.1 A Look at Data Evolution

We have been transferring data with tools for a long time now. We have always written small routines in C or Assembly language to convert EBCDIC to ASCII, to shift from lower to uppercase, perhaps do simple math, table lookup, and so forth.

These early creatures did one transformation in one direction and required a reasonably skilled programmer to write them. Any change in the target or the source files meant rewriting the code. As the number of file formats increased, this was simply not a workable approach; a mere 5 file formats meant 50 routines.

By the 1980s, these programs evolved into the early file transfer products, usually designed to move data between mainframes and smaller systems. There was a user interface and you did not have to be much of a programmer to use these products. The usual approach was to convert the source data into an intermediate format and then into the target format. This is a major use of XML today.

The raw speed of custom, low-level programming was traded for more flexible interfaces. Some of the products also began adding a simple programming language, usually some kind of BASIC interpreter, so some of the transforms could be customized. These are still very simple creatures.

10.6.2 Databases

A new creature appeared in the environment in the 1970s—the database. The idea was that the enterprise could have one central repository for their data. It would be a trusted source, it would remove redundancy, and the DBMS could enforce some of the data integrity rules. After a fairly brief period, proprietary navigational databases lost out to SQL databases. While there are many SQL dialects, the language is standardized enough that a programmer can quickly learn a new dialect. But this also meant that the programmers had to learn to think in a more abstract model of data instead of the more physical file model.

File systems are not anything like SQL databases. Rows are not records. A record is defined in the application program which reads it; a row is defined in the database schema and not by a program at all. The name of the field comes from the application program in the READ or INPUT statements.

Compare this to a database. A row is named, defined, and constrained in the database schema, apart from any applications that might use it. A database actively seeks to maintain the correctness of all its data. Columns have strong data types. Constraints in the Data Declaration Language (DDL) prevent incorrect data. Declarative referential integrity (DRI) says, in effect, that data in one table has a particular relationship with data in a second (possibly the same) table. It is also possible to have the database change itself via referential actions associated with the DRI.

All this means that when you move data into an RDBMS, you do not have to write code to do all this data verification and validation in a low-level language to protect yourself as you did when you wrote home-made transfer routines or used simple file transfer products.

Another simple truth is that everyone knows but will not admit that we never did much verification and validation in a low-level language when we custom-built transfer routines. Some of the most spectacular data quality failures have been the result of blindly loading data into files. Suddenly, you can find that you have absurd, illegal, and nonexistent codes in the data.

My personal favorite was a major credit card company that bought public record data that had been misaligned by one punch card column so that the letter d at the end of a town name fell into a status field where it stood for "deceased." All the holders of the credit card from that town had their cards cancelled in one day.

10.7 Extract, Transform, and Load Products

The file transfer products continued to evolve and became extract, transform, and load (ETL) products aimed at the new databases. They added fancier "mousey-click" user interfaces, libraries of functions that could be combined via that interface, and fancier custom programming languages.

But they never got over their heritage. The intermediate file format became XML or another markup language. The proprietary programming languages started to look more like Java and C++ than BASIC to reflect the "programming language du jour" syndrome. But the underlying model for the conversion remained record-at-a-time pipeline from source to target.

The connection to a database is typically ODBC, JDBC, or other session connection. Some ETL products can take advantage of bulk loading utility programs, if the data is staged to a file. At this point, the ETL products have become complex enough to require special training and certification in their proprietary language and various options.

The relational model has some implications. There is a separation of the abstraction and the physical models. A set model of data is naturally parallel, while a file is naturally sequential. There is no requirement for rows to be implemented as physically contiguous fields in files of physically contiguous records.

A declarative programming language like SQL lets a programmer tell the database engine *what* he or she wants, and leaves it to the optimizer to figure out *how* to do it. There is no one, single way to implement the logical model in hardware or software.

As a result, no two SQL engines are structurally alike internally, because they found niches in the ecology. Some are built for online transaction processing (OLTP), some for online analytical processing (OLAP), and some are for Very Large Data Base (VLDB). They all will accept SQL, but each will execute it totally differently.

The general standardized interfaces like ODBC or JDBC still exist and have their places. But the RDBMS products also evolved their own proprietary routines for moving and inserting data directly in their different architectures. These utility programs have an advantage over the external ETL packages, since they are targeted at the particular underlying architecture and can take advantage of the SQL engine.

However, the utility programs are limited and could not be used for complex transformations. The reason that you wanted to get the full power of SQL is that yet another creature suddenly appeared—the data warehouse.

10.7.1 Loading Data Warehouses

The database servers also evolved, becoming bigger, faster, and more parallel. When the cost of data storage and access was cheap enough, it became possible to build data warehouses. A data warehouse is a large database that holds huge amounts of historical data for analysis. Data warehouses are not like OLTP databases. In fact, they are almost point-for-point the opposite.

1.   Size
     a. The OLTP system wants to be small so it can be fast.
     b. The data warehouse wants to be big so it has complete information.
     c. Explanation: Wal-Mart has petabytes (yes, it's 1,024 terabytes) of data, and you do not.

2.   Users
     a. The OLTP system wants to be available to lots of users, even on the Internet.
     b. The data warehouse wants a small set of skilled users.
     c. Explanation: A data warehouse user is a statistician who knows when to use a CART algorithm, and you do not.

3.   Queries

    a. The OLTP system wants fast response to relatively simple queries on particular entities.

    b. The data warehouse can wait to get detailed answers to complex queries. These queries are for groupings and categories of entities.

    c. Explanation: An on-line user submitting an order will not wait 30 seconds to see if his or her item is in stock, while an analyst will gladly wait 30 minutes to get complete sales trends for all items for the last year.

4.   Normalization

    a. The OLTP system must be normalized so that as it changes, it preserves data integrity.

    b. The data warehouse is static, so its data must have integrity before it goes into the schema.

    c. Explanation: The OLTP database protects itself with constraints, DRI actions, triggers, assertions, and so forth. The data warehouse benefits from this, does a little data scrubbing, and assumes the data is now clean enough to use.

5.   Schema Design

    a. The OLTP should be at least third normal form (3NF), and we'd really like fifth normal form (5NF) and domain-key normal forms.

    b. The data warehouse wants a star schema or snowflake schema, which are highly denormalized, but which have data integrity because they are static.

    c. Explanation: Normalization prevents redundancy, and redundancy destroys data integrity in OLTP. Redundancy can speed up queries in the data warehouse.

6.   Temporal Frame

    a. The OLTP system is immediate and lives in the "now" of data entry and queries.

    b. The data warehouse is historic and concerned with time frames, trends, and patterns.

    c. Explanation: In OLTP, I ask if John Smith has paid his bill, while in data warehouse I ask about the breakdown of unpaid bills by 30-day, 60-day, 90-day, and greater-than-90-day intervals, without regard to particular customers. If I ask about

John Smith at all, I ask if he has paid his bill on time for the last year or two.

7.   VLDB versus RDBMS

a. The OLTP system runs on an RDBMS whose architecture is built to do traditional data processing with traditional access methods—which usually means a tree-structured index.

b. The data warehouse does much better with a Very Large Data Base (VLDB) product whose architecture is built to handle massive amounts of data with totally different access methods.

c. Explanation: DB2, Sybase, SQL Server, et al. still have contiguous physical storage and B-tree indexing that VLDB products have replaced with other techniques. VLDB uses hashing, Sand technology uses compressed bit vectors, and Model 204 uses inverted files.

The poor SQL programmer who has grown up in OLTP world is suddenly as helpless in the data warehouse world as the traditional programmer who was dropped into a nonprocedural SQL world.

10.7.2 Doing It All in SQL

The next step in the evolution is to do the data transformations inside the databases themselves. Talk to any SQL programmer and you will find that this is not a radical new idea, but a common practice that needs to be automated. SQL programmers have been creating staging or working tables to bring data into their schemas for years.

The reasons for such ad hoc techniques are that SQL programmers already have and already know SQL. There is no need to pull up a special tool and learn it for simple jobs. However, the SQL-86 and SQL-89 Standards defined a language too weak to replace the ETL tools, so code generation for data transformation was not possible.

Thank goodness everything keeps evolving, including SQL. Most of the SQL-92 Standard and parts of the SQL-99 Standard are common in all major products today. The addition of the CASE expression, OUTER JOIN, temporal functions, row constructors, common table expressions (CTE), and OLAP functions make the language complete enough to do any extractions and transformations required.

Every SQL product has a stored procedure mechanism, so we started saving these scrubbing and data transforms. When we did these ad hoc SQL routines, we noticed that they ran faster than external ETL routines. There was also a certain sense of safety, knowing that the SQL is using one and only one set of rules for rounding, truncation, math, and string handling.

Database vendors also entered the ETL market with products like Oracle's Warehouse Builder, IBM's Warehouse Manager, and Microsoft's DTS. These tools are built with one vendor's SQL engine internals. These tools are cheap or free with the database and will probably cut into the traditional ETL tool market.

However, we are back to the original problem. You have to learn the proprietary languages and conventions of the vendor's ETL tool.

10.7.3 Extract, Load, and then Transform

Stored procedures and vendor ETL tool code will not move from one product to another. There has been no way to centralize control, relocate code, or establish connections among the databases involved. We are working at too low a level for the problem.

What we want is a tool that will generate native SQL code or generic SQL on different databases with support for Standard SQL. Sunopsis (bought out by Oracle in October 2006 and made part of the Oracle Fusion Middleware offerings) is such a product and will probably have competition by the time you read this. It written in Java, so it will run on any platform from mainframe to desktop. A user without in-depth SQL experience can sit at the graphic interface and connect "boxes and pipes" to set up a flow of data from one part of the enterprise to another. It looks like a data flow diagram (DFD), so even analysts can use it.

The code is generated and compiled automatically. For example, if I decide that I want a transformation routine moved from its own stand-along server system to a large VLDB system to improve performance, I simply drag the icon to the VLDB system from hub server system.

Sunopsis will do the work to set up the connections and will create the local SQL. In many cases, you will get two to three orders of magnitude improvement in performance over a traditional ETL tool sitting on a hub server. This is especially true in the case of VLDB products that have huge amounts of parallelism.

But the real strength of Sunopsis is the ability to add your own SQL code generation to the repository. You can target the features of each RDBMS if you have an experienced programmer in that product. The system will maintain the code and can track the scripts, so that if you improve a routine, all the scripts that used the original version will get the new version.

The real question is how well this generated code works. Obviously, this is not a simple question, and results will vary. But we can get a sense of the power of the generated code with two examples from a real-life customer on a 12-node Teradata v2R5 database in 2006.

The first example is a simple Join and Aggregation process. One table of approximately 37.2 million rows is inner-joined to a second table of approximately 19.2 million rows on two columns and a MAX() is computed on a third column. This is a common insertion problem in a data warehouse and shows what bulk insertion can be like.

```
Number of rows inserted: 18,533,841
Elapsed: 2 min 7 sec
Rows/sec: 145,936
```

The second example is a complex data warehouse snapshot query. A central fact table is outer-joined to a dozen dimensional tables. The approximate table sizes and the kinds of joins are given below.

```
Fact table = 18.2 Million rows
Table 1 < 1,000 rows inner join on one column
Table 2 < 1,000 rows inner join on one column
Table 3 = 18.5 Million rows, left outer join on two columns
Table 4 = 15.9 Million rows, left outer join on two columns
Table 5 = 6.7 Million rows, left outer join on two columns
Table 6 = 1 Million rows, left outer join on two columns
Table 7 = 1 Million rows, left outer join on two columns
Table 8 = 18.2 Million rows, left outer join on two columns
Table 9 = 3,000 rows, left outer join on two columns
Table 10 = 28,000 rows, left outer join on three columns
Table 11 = 15.7 Million rows, left outer join on two columns
Table 12 = 1.5 Million rows, left outer join on two columns
```

```
Number of rows inserted: 18,207,198
Elapsed: 6 min 47 sec
Rows/sec: 44,735
```

I think that anyone who has done a job like this will agree that this query is a good "stress test" for any kind of data transfer operation.

Proprietary improvements in SQL engines will benefit data management and transfer operations. Exactly what that will mean in the future, we do not know exactly. But we do know it can only get better for us and that since each product is different, we cannot expect a generic solution, just good interfaces.

CHAPTER 11

Thinking in SQL

I HAVE BEEN telling students that you need about one year of full-time SQL programming before you have an epiphany and start thinking in SQL. Most beginners mimic their original programming language until they have their epiphany.

When DB2 was first released, you would find COBOL programmers who converted their existing file layouts into CREATE TABLE statements, the READ statements were converted into FETCH statements and so forth—a simple one-to-one mapping from one language to another. There were no JOIN operations done in the SQL. Cursors looped through data as if they were reading a magnetic tape file. Even today, people are making similar mistakes with DB2 when they try to convert old VSAM applications to DB2 without revisiting the data definitions.

This kind of programming gives horrible performance, of course, and gave SQL a bad reputation with the COBOL community back then.

Today, GUI programmers try to mimic their input screens directly in tables rather than normalize the data. Dijkstra once remarked that each generation of new IT technology repeats the mistakes of the previous ones.

This is not a new phenomenon. In fact, when I started programming we used to say "I can write FORTRAN in any language!" and it was not a joke. Jerry Weinberg in his classic book, *The Psychology of Computer Programming* (ISBN-13: 978-0932633422), reported that he could look at student PL/I programs and tell if FORTRAN, COBOL, or Algol was the first language of the programmer.

The rest of this chapter is taken from newsgroups, where people have asked for help with SQL. The answers they were given vary, but I was trying to find examples where there was a series of progressively better answers. The definition of better is a bit vague, but I was looking for things like this:

1.   Procedural code is replaced with declarative code.

2.   Proprietary code is replaced with Standard SQL.

3.   DDL and DML are used together for a solution.

4.   The solution shows a pattern that can be useful for similar problems.

11.1 Warm-up Exercises

The following mind games are to warm you up and see if you can think a little differently than the way you are used to thinking. I am assuming that the reader started his or her career as a procedural programmer and used sequential file systems for data. The classic structured programming constructs are IF-THEN-ELSE, WHILE-DO, and BEGIN-END, and they are what we have built programs from for decades. It is very hard to escape.

11.1.1 The Whole and Not the Parts

But perhaps the hardest thing to learn is thinking in sets. Consider this classic puzzle (Fig. 11.1).

Figure 11.1
Missing Bricks
Puzzle

The usual mistake people make is trying to count the $1 \times 1 \times 2$ bricks one at a time. This requires the ability to make a three-dimensional mental model of the boxes, which is really hard for most of us.

The right approach is to look at the *whole* block, as if were completely filled in. It is $4 \times 5 \times 5$ units, or 50 bricks. The corner that is knocked off is three bricks, which we can count individually, so we must have 47 bricks in the block. The arrangement inside the block does not matter at all. Starting to get the idea?

11.1.2 Characteristic Functions

Sets can be defined two ways. You can list the elements; in math this is done with a pair of curvy brackets and a comma-separated list. This method is fine for small sets, and technically that is what a table is.

The other method is to give a characteristic function that takes a value and returns a 1 or TRUE if the value is in the set and a zero or FALSE if it is not an element. That is what constraints do in SQL. For example, $\{i: \text{MOD}(i, 2) = 0\}$ will give us a test for even integers, over all possible integers.

We need both these methods to define a table properly. A properly defined table is made up of one and only one kind of entity. You do not mix Britney Spears, squids, and automobiles together.

It is possible to have sets that do not have characteristic functions in mathematics. For example, the Koch snowflake (Fig. 11.2) is a fractal that starts with an equilateral triangle, and then adds another smaller equilateral triangle to each side. This process is repeated forever.

Figure 11.2
Koch Snowflake Curve

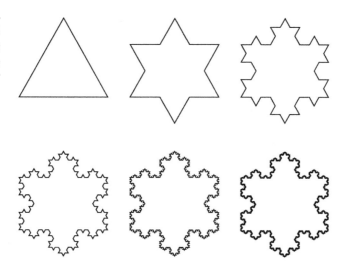

Any two points on the fractal are an infinite distance apart. Now draw a circle inside the starting triangle that touches all the sides. Draw a second circle out the starting triangle that touches all the corners. The points in the smaller circle are clearly inside the snowflake; the points outside the larger circle are clearly outside the snowflake. But you cannot determine whether certain points between the circles are inside or outside the curve, because there is no clear boundary. That makes a characteristic function impossible.

That sounds like an abstract mathematical situation that the average database designer is not likely to encounter. But there are other kinds of fuzzy boundaries and vague specifications. The W. A. Ellott Company of Toronto published a classic puzzle in 1968 called *The Vanishing Leprechaun,* which was based on an older puzzle by Sam Lloyd.

The puzzle is made of three parts that start as shown (Fig. 11.3) with 14 leprechauns. When the top two pieces are swapped (Fig. 11.4) we have 15 leprechauns, so which one vanishes or appears?

Figure 11.3
Vanishing Leprechaun Puzzle (1)

From the cartoon collection of S. Harris at *www.sciencecartoonsplus.com.*
Copyright © 2007 by Sidney Harris. Used with permission.

Figure 11.4
Vanishing Leprechaun Puzzle (2)

From the cartoon collection of S. Harris at *www.sciencecartoonsplus.com.*
Copyright © 2007 by Sidney Harris. Used with permission.

You can get a detailed discussion of the mechanics of this dissection at *http://www.roadshow.org/activities/explanation.html.*

The puzzle asks a false question. The real answer is that we never had a good definition of what makes a leprechaun in the first place. While having a clear specification has always been a major problem of software design, it is even more important in a relational database, because the data is shared, aggregated, and rearranged by many different users. You can wind up with both a 14 and 15 "Leprechaun" query in your RDBMS.

11.1.3 Locking into a Solution Early

> *No matter how far you have gone on a wrong road, turn back.*
> —*Turkish proverb*

> *Tradition is what you resort to when you don't have the time or the money to do it right.*
> —*Kirt Herbert Adler*

These are some quick lateral thinking problems that illustrate how easy it is to lock into a familiar model of the world. These were taken from an National Public Radio (NPR) segment, with a little added commentary.

Q: *What do you put in a toaster?*

A: The answer is bread. If you said "toast" then you are being fooled by words that sound alike. What is a *set* of employees? The set is Personnel, and it is made of zero or more employees (they are the elements of the Personnel set). Likewise, a bunch of trees in an ecosystem is a forest, and much different from just trees.

Q: *Say "silk" five times. Now, spell "silk." What do cows drink?*

A: Cows drink water. Most people will answer "milk" because that is the only part of the process they see or care about and the rhyme locks them into it.

Q: *If a red house is made with red bricks, a blue house is made with blue bricks, a pink house is made with pink bricks, and a black house is made with black bricks, what is a greenhouse made with?*

A: Greenhouses are made from glass. If you said "green bricks," you are looking for a similarity that does not exist. The one true lookup table (OTLT) is a prime example of cramming unrelated things that had some *very* general characteristics in common into the same table.

I often refer to this as a "Britney Spears, Squids, and Automobiles" table. Apparently, the phrase caught on and was the topic of a poll on the Internet in mid-2007 (*http://scienceblogs.com/deepseanews/2007/02/weekend_foolishness.php*).

11.2 Heuristics

The following tricks and heuristics are not exactly mathematically precise scientific methods. In fact, some of them sound pretty weird. But as Larry Constantine once remarked, a method is a list of things that tells you what to do next, when you did not know what to do next. And you hope the method at least gets you to a workable solution, if not a good solution.

11.2.1 Put the Specification into a Clear Statement

This might sound obvious, but the operative word is "clear" statement. You need to ask questions at the start. Let me give some examples from actual problem statement having to do with a schema that models a typical orders and order details database.

1. "I want to see the most expensive item in each order." How do I handle ties for the most expensive item? Did you mean the highest unit price or the highest extension (quantity * unit price) on each order?

2. "I want to see how many lawn gnomes everyone ordered." How do I represent someone who never ordered a lawn gnome in the result set? Is that a NULL or a zero? If they returned all their lawn gnomes, do I show the original order or the net results?

3. "How many orders were over $100?" Did you mean strictly greater than $100.00, or greater than or equal to $100.00?

Writing specs is actually harder than writing code. Given a complete, clear specification, the code can almost write itself.

11.2.2 Add the Words "Set of All..." in Front of the Nouns

The big leap in SQL programming is thinking in sets and not in process steps that handle one unit of data at a time. Phrases like "for the next x do .." poison your mental model of the problem. Look for set characteristics and not for individual characteristics. For example, given the task of finding all the orders that ordered exactly the same number of each item, how would you solve it?

One approach is that for each order, see if there are two values of quantity that are not equal to each other, and then reject that order.

This leads to either cursors or to a self-join. Here is a self-join version; I will not do the cursor version.

```
SELECT D1.order_nbr
  FROM OrderDetails AS D1
WHERE NOT EXISTS
      (SELECT *
         FROM OrderDetails AS D2
        WHERE D1.order_nbr = D2.order_nbr
          AND D1.qty <> D2.qty);
```

Or you can look at each order as a set with these set properties:

```
SELECT order_nbr
  FROM OrderDetails
 GROUP BY order_nbr
HAVING MIN(qty) = MAX(qty);
```

This is the block puzzle all over!

11.2.3 Remove Active Verbs from the Problem Statement

Words like "traverse," "compute," or other verbs that imply a process will poison your mental model. Try to phrase it as a "state of being" description instead. This is the other side of looking for group characteristics, but with a slight twist.

Programmers coming from procedural languages think in terms of actions. They add numbers, while declarative programmers look at a total. They think of process, while we think of completed results.

11.2.4 You Can Still Use Stubs

A famous Sydney Harris cartoon shows the phrase "Then a miracle occurs" in the middle of a blackboard full of equations, and a scientist says to the writer "I think you should be more explicit here in step 2."

We used that same trick in procedural programming languages by putting in a stub module when we did not know what do at the point in a program. For example, if you were writing a payroll program and the company had a complex bonus policy that you did not understand or have specifications for, you would write a "stub" procedure that always returned a constant value and perhaps sent out a message that it had just executed. This allowed you continue with the parts of the procedure that you did understand.

This is harder in a declarative language. Procedural language modules can be loosely coupled, whereas the clauses and subqueries of a SELECT statement are a single unit of code. You could set up a "test harness" for procedural language modules; this is harder in SQL.

Today, you can test a CTE by itself before you attach it to a query. But you can also often test a subquery in by adding the outer references to the FROM clause in a stand-alone version.

11.2.5 Do Not Worry about Displaying the Data

In a tiered architecture, display is the job of the front end, not the database. Obviously, you do not do rounding, add leading zeroes, change case, or pick a date format in the database. The important thing is to pass the front end all the data it needs to do its job.

You can add an ORDER BY clause to the cursor that passes the result set to the front-end program in a simple client/server system. But in architectures with multiple tiers, sorting and other display functions might be performed differently in several places. For example, the same data is displayed in English units sorted by department in the United States, but displayed in SI units sorted by country in Europe.

The basic principle of a tiered architecture is that display is done in the front end (i.e., client or middle tiers) and never in the back end. This is a more basic programming principle than just SQL and RDBMS. In the old days, the 3GL languages were tightly coupled to their files. Very little data was actually shared, even among programs written in the same 3GL. Each program worked with a file and used its internal declarations to give the raw data meaning.

This lack of shared data meant that old programmers who grew up with monolithic 3GL languages and tightly coupled file systems still think this way. These cowboy coders still focus on the *single* program they are working on and will argue that it is just fine to do display formatting inside the database because it is most efficient here. They never bother with the qualifiers "in my current situation in this one application, in my current programming language. Let everyone else be damned!"

Since 80% or more of the total cost of a system over its lifetime is maintenance, we want to write SQL that is clear and predictable. For example, when I call a stored procedure, I do not want to have to see who wrote it and when they did their coding. Imagine a situation where you have to read the internals of each procedure to use it safely. If Tony wrote the procedure, it returns British format dates, metric units, and uses cash accounting. If George wrote the procedure, it returns U.S. dates, English traditional units, and uses accrual accounting.

That was bad enough, but now try to make Tony's procedures work with George's procedures. This is called "engineering hell"; the parts look fine by themselves, but they cannot be put together to make a system.

It is far more maintainable and cost effective in the long run to set up a data dictionary that includes the physical formats, industry and internal standards, and scales used for the data so that *all* programs know that, say, we *always* use UTC dates and times, metric units to three decimal places, and accrual accounting following GAAP standards.

11.2.6 Your First Attempts Need Special Handling

Henry Ledgard put it very nicely:

> Pruning and restoring a blighted tree is almost an impossible task. The same is true of blighted computer programs. Restoring a structure that has been distorted by patches and deletions, or fixing a program with a seriously weak algorithm isn't worth the time. The best that can result is a long, inefficient, unintelligible program that defies maintenance. The worst that could result, we dare not think of.

This is especially true with SQL. But handling restarts in DDL and DML is different because of the declarative nature of the two sublanguages. DDL execution is static once it is put into place, while DML is dynamic. That is, if I issue the same CREATE <schema object> statement twice in a row, it will have the same results each time. Namely, the first statement will make changes in the schema information tables and storage system; the second statement will fail and leave the schema unchanged.

But if I issue the same SELECT, INSERT, UPDATE, or DELETE statement twice in a row, the execution plan could change each time, based on the current statistics, cached data, and other users. And I will get a result back, if the statement is valid.

11.2.7 Do Not Be Afraid to Throw Away Your First Attempts at DDL

Bad DDL will distort all the code based on it. Just consider a schema with a proprietary BIT data type used for gender. The code would not port to other SQL dialects. The host languages would have to handle low-level bit manipulation. It would not interface to other data sources that use ISO Standard sex codes.

Designing a schema is very hard work. It is unlikely that you will get it completely right in one afternoon. Yes, rebuilding a database will take time and require fixing existing data. But the other choices are worse.

When I lived in Salt Lake City, a programmer I met at a user group meeting had gotten into this situation. The existing database was falling apart as the workload increased thanks to poor design at the start. The updates and insertions for a day's work were taking almost 24 hours at that time and the approaching disaster was obvious to the programmers. Management had no real solution, except to yell at the programmers. They used the database to send medical laboratory results to hospitals and doctors. This is not the kind of data that you want to get too late to act upon it.

A few months later, I got to see how an improperly declared column resulted in the wrong quantities of medical supplies being shipped to an African disaster area. The programmer tried to save a little space by violating First Normal Form (1NF) by putting on the package sizes into one column as a comma-separated list and pulling them out with SUBSTRING() operations. It made the database look like the display screen and matched an enumerated data structure in his host language.

The suppliers later agreed to package smaller quantities to help with the fantastic expense of shipping to a war zone. Now the first "subfield" in the quantity column was one unit and not five, but the tightly coupled front did not know this. Would you like to pick which four children will die because of sloppy programming? See what we mean by the last sentence in Ledgard's quote?

11.2.8 Save Your First Attempts at DML

Bad DML can run several orders of magnitude more slowly than good DML. The bad news is that it is hard to tell what is good and what is bad in SQL. Even worse, from a performance perspective, what executes quickly in one SQL product may painfully slow in other SQL products.

The procedural programmers had a deterministic environment in which the same program ran the same way every time. SQL decides how to execute a query based on statistics about the data and the resources available. They can and do change over time. Thus, what was the best solution today could be the poorer solution tomorrow.

In 1988, Fabian Pascal published a classic article on PC database systems at the time, "SQL Redundancy and DBMS Performance" in *Database Programming & Design* (Vol. 1, No. 12, December 1988, pp. 22–28).

Pascal constructs seven logical equivalent queries for a database. Both the database and the query set were very simple, and were run on the same hardware platform to get timings.

The Ingres optimizer was smart enough to find the equivalence, used the same execution plan, and gave the best performance for all the queries. The other products at the time gave very uneven performances. The worst timing was an order of magnitude more than the best. In the case of Oracle, the worst timing was over 600 times the best. Yes, things have gotten better in all products, but you still have to be aware of possible problems.

I recommend that you save your working attempts so that you can reuse them when the world and/or your optimizer change. Put the code for one of the candidate queries in as a comment, so that the maintenance programmer can find and try it.

11.2.9 Do Not Think with Boxes and Arrows

This is going to sound absolutely insane, but some of us like to doodle when we are trying to solve a problem. Even an informal diagram can be a great conceptual help, especially when you are learning something new. We are visual creatures.

The procedural programmers had the original ANSI X3.5 Flowchart symbols as an aid to their programming. This standard was a first crude attempt at a visual tool that evolved into structure charts and data flow diagrams (DFD) in the 1970s. All of these tools are based on boxes and arrows—they show the flow of data and/or control in a procedural system.

If you use the old tools, you will tend to build the old systems. You might write the code in SQL, but the design will tend toward the procedural. Here is "Mother Celko's Heuristics" for doodling on the back of a paper napkin.

11.2.10 Draw Circles and Set Diagrams

If you use set-oriented diagrams, you will tend to produce set oriented solutions. For example, draw a GROUP BY as small disjoint circles inside a larger containing circle so you see them as subsets of a set. Use a time line with half-open intervals on it to model temporal queries. In a set-oriented model, nothing flows; it exists in a state defined by constraints.

Probably the clearest example of boxes an arrows versus set diagrams is the adjacency list model versus the nested sets model for trees. You can Google these models or buy a copy of my book *Trees and Hierarchies in SQL* for details. The diagrams for each approach look like this.

Figure 11.5
*Graph vs.
Nested Sets Tree
Diagram*

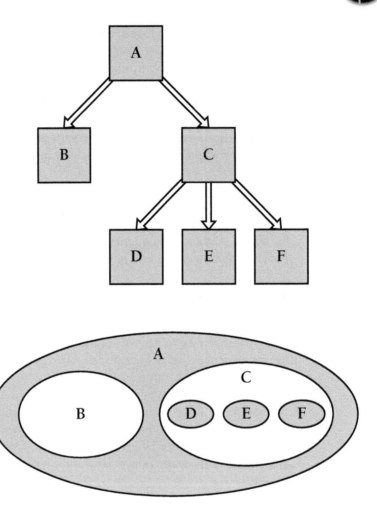

The nesting of the sets suggests storing the hierarchy with ranges on a number line, the boxes and arrows diagram suggest keeping the end points of the directed graph for a physical traversal. As an aside, younger programmers who learned XML, HTML, and other markup languages find the nested sets model to be very natural (it's tags in a thin disguise!) while procedural programmers find the adjacency list model more natural (it's pointer chains in a thin disguise!).

11.2.11 Learn Your Dialect

While you should always try to write Standard SQL, it is also important to know what constructs your particular dialect and release favor.

For example, constructing indexes and keys is very important in older products that are based on sequential file structures. At the other extreme, the Nucleus engine from Sand Technology represents the entire database as a set of compressed bit vectors and has no indexing because in effect everything is automatically indexed. Teradata uses hashing. WX_2 also has no indexing, and so forth.

11.2.12   Imagine that Your WHERE Clause Is "Super Amoeba"

That is the weirdest section title in this chapter, so bear with me. Your "Super Amoeba" computer can split off a new processor at will, and assign it a task, in a massively parallel fashion. Imagine that every row in the working table that was built in the FROM clause is allocated one of these "amoeba processors" that will test the WHERE clause search condition on just that row. This is a version of Pournelle's rule: "One task, one processor".

If each and every row in your table can be independently tested against simple, basic search conditions, then your schema is probably a good relational design. But if your row needs to reference other rows in the same table or an external source, or if it cannot answer those simple questions, then you probably have some kind of normalization problems.

You have already seen the nested sets model and the adjacency list model for trees. Given one row in isolation from the rest of the table, can you answer simple, basic questions about the tree being modeled? This of course leads to what we mean by basic simple questions. Here is a short list that applies to trees in graph theory:

1.   Is this a leaf node?

2.   Is this the root node?

3.   How big is the subtree rooted at this node?

4.   Given a second node in the same tree, is this node superior, subordinate, or at the same level as my node? (This will require two nodes, obviously.)

Question #4 is particularly important, since it is the basic comparison operation for hierarchies. As you can see, the nested sets model can answer all of these questions and more, while the adjacency list model can only detect the root node by looking for a row where (`parent_node IS NULL`).

11.2.13 Use the Newsgroups, Blogs, and Internet

The Internet is the greatest resource in the world, so learn to use it. You can find a whole range of newsgroups devoted to your particular product or to more general topics. If you ask a question on a newsgroup or blog, please post DDL, so that people do not have to guess what the keys, constraints, declarative referential integrity, data types, and so forth in your schema are.

Sample data is also a good idea, along with clear specifications that explain the results you wanted.

Most SQL products have a tool that will spit out DDL to a text file in one keystroke. Unfortunately, the output of these tools is generally less than human-readable. You should prune the real tables down to just what is needed to demonstrate your problem—no sense posting a 100-column `CREATE TABLE` statement when all you want is two columns. Then clean up the constraints and other things in the output using the rules given in this book. You are asking people to do your job for you for free. At least be polite enough to provide them with sufficient information.

If you are a student asking people to do your homework for you, please be advised that presenting the work of other people as your own is a valid reason for expulsion and/or failure at a university. When you post to a blog of newsgroup, announce that this is homework, the name of your school, your class, and your professor. This will let people verify that your actions are allowed.

11.3 Do Not Use BIT or BOOLEAN Flags in SQL

The `BIT` and `BIT VARYING` data type were deprecated in the SQL:2003 Standards, but they have survived some products, along with `BYTE` data types. While `BOOLEAN` had not yet been deprecated as of this writing, it also has problems with the rules about NULLs and the three-valued logic of SQL. The NULL cannot be treated as an UNKNOWN because one of the basic rules of NULLs is that they propagate. The resulting four-valued logic is inconsistent:

```
UNKNOWN AND TRUE  = UNKNOWN
UNKNOWN AND FALSE = FALSE
```

```
NULL AND FALSE = NULL
NULL AND TRUE = NULL
```

But there are other problems with flags.

11.3.1 Flags Are at the Wrong Level

In SQL, a row in a properly designed table should represent a single complete fact, expressed as values of attributes that make up the entity modeled by the table.

Machine-level things like a BIT or BYTE data type have no place in a high-level language like SQL. SQL is abstract and defined without regard to *physical* implementation. This basic principle of data modeling is called data abstraction.

Bits and bytes are the lowest units of hardware-specific, physical implementation you can get. Are you on a high-end or low-end machine? Does the machine have 8-, 16-, 32-, 64-, or 128-bit words? Twos-complement or ones-complement math? Hey, the standards allow decimal machines, so bits do not exist at all!! What about NULLs? To be an SQL data type, you have to have NULLs, so what is a NULL bit? By definition, a bit is on or off and has no NULL.

What does the implementation of the host languages do with bits? Did you know that $+1$, $+0$, -0, and -1 are all used for BOOLEANs, but not consistently (look at C# and VB from Microsoft; they had to use a kludge in .NET to handle the differences in the interface)? That means all the host languages—present, future, and not-yet-defined.

There are two situations in practice. Either the bits are individual attributes, or they are used as a vector to represent a single attribute. In the case of a single attribute, the encoding is limited to two values, which do not port to host languages or other SQLs, cannot be easily understood by an end user, and cannot be expanded. Even a "yes/no" question grows to need "Not Answered", "Not Applicable", "Impossible because of a Prior Answer", and so forth.

In the second case, what some newbies, who are still thinking in terms of second- and third-generation programming languages or even punch cards, do is build a vector for a series of "yes/no" status codes, failing to see the status vector as a single attribute. Did you ever play the children's game "20 Questions" when you were young? Bingo!!

Imagine you have six components for a loan approval, so you allocate bits in your second generation model of the world. You have 64 possible vectors, but only 5 of them are valid (i.e., you cannot be rejected for bankruptcy and still have good credit). For your data integrity, you can:

1.   Ignore the problem. This is actually what most newbies do.

2.   Write elaborate CHECK() constraints with user-defined functions or proprietary bit-level library functions that cannot port and that run like cold glue.

Now we add a seventh condition to the vector—which end does it go on? Why? How did you get it in the right place on all the possible hardware that it will ever use? Did all the code that references a BIT in a word by its position do it right after the change?

You need to sit down and think about how to design an encoding of the data that is high-level, general enough to expand, abstract, and portable. For example, is that loan approval a hierarchical code? Concatenation code? Vector code? Did you provide codes for unknown, missing, and N/A values? It is not easy to design such things!

The results are often mixed signals. Imagine a Personnel table that uses a zero amount to show that an employee does not get paid a salary and/or commission. But now add in a flag:

```
CREATE TABLE Personnel
(emp_id INTEGER NOT NULL PRIMARY KEY,
salary_amt DECIMAL(12,2) DEFAULT 0.00 NOT NULL,
commission_amt DECIMAL(12,2) DEFAULT 0.00 NOT NULL,
is_salaried BOOLEAN NOT NULL,
..);
```

What do I do when the salary amount is set to $0.00 and the BOOLEAN is set to TRUE? What is value of the flag when someone has both a salary and a commission? To get a count of the salaried people, I might look at the flag, but it would be easier and more accurate to use SIGN(salary_amt). The flag is a redundant summary of the state of being in the data that can be computed.

11.3.2 Flags Confuse Proper Attributes

Here is a slightly cleaned-up version of a newsgroup posting. The schema is supposed to model a shared collection of articles that users can browse with some limitations.

The UNIQUE_IDENTIFIER is a huge proprietary, system-generated string that cannot ever be a relational key, or ported, or remembered by a human being. We have users with 100-character names; audit trail dates are mixed in with the tables they are supposed to track. The data element names were worse than shown here. In short, there is not much right with this skeleton schema.

```
CREATE TABLE Users
(user_id UNIQUE_IDENTIFIER NOT NULL PRIMARY KEY,
-- not a real key
user_name VARCHAR (100), -- nullable??
date_added TIMESTAMP NOT NULL); -- audit info
mixed with data

CREATE TABLE Articles
(article_id UNIQUE_IDENTIFIER NOT NULL PRIMARY KEY,
-- not a key
user_id UNIQUE_IDENTIFIER NOT NULL, -- he is an attribute?
article_comment VARCHAR (1000),
date_added TIMESTAMP NOT NULL, -- audit info
mixed with data
private_flag BIT NOT NULL);

CREATE TABLE ArticleFavorites -- no key given
(user_id UNIQUE_IDENTIFIER NOT NULL,
article_id UNIQUE_IDENTIFIER NOT NULL,
active_flag BIT NOT NULL);

CREATE TABLE UserFriends
(user_id UNIQUE_IDENTIFIER NOT NULL, -- no ref to Users?
friend_id UNIQUE_IDENTIFIER NOT NULL -- two names,
one data element
  REFERENCES Users (user_id), -- no actions given
active_flag BIT NOT NULL); -- why have this at all?
```

The problem is when any user browses through the favorites of another user they are only allowed to see articles that are not private unless the browser is already a friend of the content owner. If an article is not private, then anyone can see it.

You might want to stop and try this query with the above schema.

The questions will be easier with better DDL. What, did you think a user is an attribute of an article? It is an entity! Why are you using BIT flags in SQL as if you were still in a magnetic tape system? What do audit dates have to do with this data—putting them in here is illegal. Why would you use UNIQUE_IDENTIFIERS—you do know that they are never relational keys, don't you? People will actually use character string ids before they earn an insanely long integer value. The friends are also users, but they get a role prefix on the basic data element name to become "friend_user_id" instead of a new data element with its own name. Let's try again:

```
CREATE TABLE Users
(user_id CHAR(8) NOT NULL PRIMARY KEY, -- UNIX recommendation
user_name VARCHAR(35) NOT NULL); -- USPS recommendation

CREATE TABLE Articles
(article_id INTEGER NOT NULL PRIMARY KEY,
-- need industry standard
article_comment VARCHAR(1000));

CREATE TABLE SharedArticles
(user_id CHAR(8) NOT NULL
    REFERENCES Users (user_id)
    ON UPDATE CASCADE
    ON DELETE CASCADE,
 friend_user_id CHAR(8) DEFAULT '**PUBLIC**' NOT NULL
    REFERENCES Users (user_id)
    ON UPDATE CASCADE
    ON DELETE CASCADE,
 article_id INTEGER NOT NULL
   REFERENCES Articles (article_id)
   ON UPDATE CASCADE
   ON DELETE CASCADE,
 PRIMARY KEY (user_id, friend_user_id, article_id));
```

Now always make sure the user is among his or her own friends when you do an insert. You can either do that with a simple housekeeping routine, like this:

```
INSERT INTO SharedArticles (user_id, friend_user_id,
article_id)
SELECT S1.user_id, S1.user_id, S1.article_id
   FROM SharedArticles AS S1
 WHERE NOT EXISTS
     (SELECT *
        FROM SharedArticles AS S2
      WHERE S1.user_id = S1.friend_user_id);
```

Or hide the extra row in a procedure that creates new rows in the shared articles table:

```
INSERT INTO SharedArticles (user_id, friend_user_id,
article_id)
VALUES (:my_user_id, :my_friend_user_id, :my_article_id),
(:my_user_id, :my_user_id, :my_article_id);
```

This is a 3-ary relationship (2 people, 1 article). The poster seemed to only think in 2-ary relationships and got into higher normal form problems because of it.

Quoting: "When any user browses through the favorites of another user, they are only allowed to see articles that are not private unless the actual user browsing the content is already a friend of the content owner."

This query will let the browser see all of his friend's articles:

```
SELECT :browser_id, A.user_id, A.artcle_id,
A.article_comment
 FROM Articles AS A,
      SharedArticles AS S
 WHERE A.article_id = S.article_id
    AND :browser_id = S.friend_user_id;
```

Quoting: " .. but it won't show anything at all if the user is not a friend (which is bad) when in this case I want to display the non-private user articles."

The word "nonprivate" is a strange word in English. We would usually say "public" instead. But once caught in a "Boolean brain trap," it is hard to shake it. Let's create a dummy user called '**PUBLIC**' (same word you have in SQL's DCL language) and let users assign that special friend to articles they wish to expose to the world. Now your query is simply:

```
SELECT DISTINCT :browser_id, A.user_id, A.artcle_id,
A.article_comment
  FROM Articles AS A,
       SharedArticles AS S
WHERE A.article_id = S.article_id
  AND S.friend_user_id IN (:browser_id, '**PUBLIC**');
```

Notice the use of the SELECT DISTINCT in case an article is both private and public.

CHAPTER 12

Group Characteristics

LEARNING TO THINK in terms of SQL is a jump for most programmers. Most of your career is spent writing procedural code, and suddenly you have to deal with nonprocedural code. The thought pattern has to change from sequences to sets of data elements. Things happen to various units of work "all at once" in a table, but in file systems and procedural code, records are input from left to right, in sequential order, to be processed by sequential program steps.

Here is how a SELECT works in SQL—at least in theory. Real products will optimize things, but the code has to produce the same results.

a.   Start in the FROM clause and build a working table from all of the joins, unions, intersections, exceptions, and whatever other table constructors are there. You can get the details in other sections of this book.

b.   Execute the WHERE clause (if any) and remove rows that do not pass criteria; that is, that do not test to TRUE (i.e., reject UNKNOWN and FALSE search criteria). A missing WHERE clause returns the entire working table. The WHERE clause is applied to the working set in the FROM clause; the other clauses have not been applied yet.

Figure 12.1
Original Set

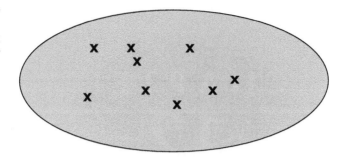

c. Execute the optional GROUP BY clause, partition the original table into groups and reduce each grouping to a single row, replacing the original working table with the new grouped table. The rows of a grouped table must be only group characteristics:

1. Grouping Columns, as given in the GROUP BY clause

2. Statistics about each grouping (i.e., aggregate functions)

3. Functions or Constants

4. Expressions made up of only those three items

The original table no longer exists and you cannot reference anything in it.

d. Execute the optional HAVING clause and apply it against the grouped working table; if there was no GROUP BY clause, treat the entire table as one group.

Figure 12.2
Make Groups

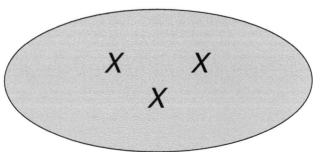

Figure 12.3
Reduce Groups
to a Single *Row*

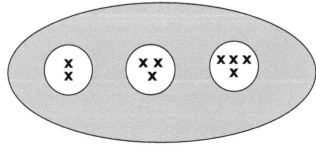

e.   Execute the SELECT clause and construct the expressions in the list. This means that the scalar subqueries, function calls, and expressions in the SELECT are done after all the other clauses are done. The expressions in the SELECT clause list can be given names with the AS operator. These new names come into existence all at once, but after the WHERE clause, GROUP BY clause, and HAVING clause have been executed, you cannot use them in the SELECT list or the WHERE clause for that reason.

f.   Nested query expressions follow the usual scoping rules you would expect from a block-structured language like C, Pascal, Algol, and so forth. Namely, the innermost queries can reference columns and tables in the queries in which they are contained.

12.1 Grouping Is Not Equality

Go back to step c in the last section. A grouping is not exactly defined by equality. Equality is a comparison between two scalar values, and it follows the rules for that data type.

First of all, consider how equality of strings is defined in SQL. The shorter string is padded out with blanks on the right side until it is the same length as the longer string. The characters are matched position for position, so that 'Smith' = 'Smith   ' and so forth. Given a subset of different length strings that all test equal under that rule, which one represents the "Smith group" in the working table?

Second, consider floating-point numbers. Two FLOATs can actually be different but test equal if they are within a certain difference of each other. The problems of floating-point rounding were discussed in Sections 5.3.1 and 9.1.2. Given a subset of different floating-point numbers that all test equal under the IEEE rules, which one represents the group in the working table?

This is why you try to group on exact numeric data type columns and fixed length character strings.

The other convention in a GROUP BY that does not hold in equality is the rules for NULLs. While (x = NULL) is UNKNOWN for all values of x in all data type and (NULL = NULL) is UNKNOWN for all data types, we group all NULLs into their own grouping, which has the appropriate data type for that column.

Grouping rules also apply to the SELECT DISTINCT, which removes redundant duplicate rows. Two rows are duplicates if their values match column for column. For purposes of defining a duplicate row, NULLs are treated as matching, just like in the GROUP BY.

This same difference in operations done at different levels of abstraction also applies to aggregate functions. Before the SUM(), AVG(), MIN(), MAX(), or COUNT() are computed, the NULLs are removed from the set they aggregate. If the set is empty, then the aggregates return a NULL.

This rule does not apply to COUNT (*), which is a very different animal in spite of similar syntax. It finds the cardinality of a set, without regard to columns or expression in individual columns. It probably should have been written as CARD(<set constructor>), much like the [NOT] EXISTS (<set constructor>) predicate.

This convention is not as strange as it seems. Think about addition (+) versus summation (Σ). Addition is a binary operation; summations are defined for a set of values. That set can be empty, finite, or countably infinite. The finite set behaves like repeated addition. The infinite set may or may not converge to a limit. The sum of an empty set is not defined, but it is often dropped or placed by zero in a summation to get the effect of dropping it.

12.2 Using Groups without Looking Inside

Much like the convergence of a summation, you can often deduce characteristics of a set of data elements as a whole without seeing each individual element.

As an example of what I mean, consider a posting made on December 22, 1999, by J. R. Wiles to a Microsoft SQL Server newsgroup: "I need help with a statement that will return distinct records [sic: rows are not records] for the first three fields [sic: columns are not fields] where all values in field [sic] four are all equal to zero."

What do you notice about this program specification? The first thing is that it is vague. But this is very typical of what people put out on the Internet when they ask for SQL help. More importantly, the poster is confusing fields with columns. That means he is still thinking in terms of a file system and not in RDBMS. The next problem is that he does not give any DDL for the table he wants us to use for the problem. This means we have to guess what the column data types are, what the constraints are, and everything else about the table.

However, he did give some sample data in the posting that lets us guess that the table looks like this and has no keys, so it is not even a proper table:

```
CREATE TABLE Foobar -- non-table
(coll INTEGER NOT NULL,
```

```
col2 INTEGER NOT NULL,
col3 INTEGER NOT NULL,
col4 INTEGER NOT NULL);

INSERT INTO Foobar
VALUES (1, 1, 1, 0),
       (1, 1, 1, 0),
       (1, 1, 1, 0),
       (1, 1, 2, 1),
       (1, 1, 2, 0),
       (1, 1, 2, 0),
       (1, 1, 3, 0),
       (1, 1, 3, 0),
       (1, 1, 3, 0);
```

Then he tells us that the query should return these two rows:

```
(1, 1, 1, 0)
(1, 1, 3, 0)
```

While it is total violation of RDBMS rules not to have a declared PRIMARY KEY on a table, just ignore that slip for the moment. Let's look for approaches to solutions.

12.2.1   Semiset-Oriented Approach

At this point, people started sending in possible answers. Tony Rogerson at Torver Computer Consultants Ltd. came up with this answer:

```
SELECT *
  FROM (SELECT col1, col2, col3, SUM(col4)
          FROM Foobar
         GROUP BY col1, col2, col3)
       AS F1(col1, col2, col3, col4)
 WHERE F1.col4 = 0;
```

Using the assumption, which is not given anywhere in the specification, Tony decided that col4 has a constraint "col4 INTEGER NOT NULL CHECK (col4 IN (0, 1)", based on the sample data. Notice how doing this INSERT INTO statement would ruin his answer:

```
INSERT INTO Foobar (col1, col2, col3, col4)
VALUES (4, 5, 6, 1), (4, 5, 6, 0), (4, 5, 6, -1);
```

But there is another problem. This is a semiprocedural approach to the query. The innermost query builds groups based on the first three columns and gives you the summation of the fourth column within each group. That result, named F1, is then passed to the containing query that then keeps only groups with all zeros, under his assumption about the data. We really want to do this in one step.

Another approach from Erik Lennart depends on the implementation having the SQL-92 row constructors and comparison predicates.

```
SELECT DISTINCT F1.col1, F1.col2, F1.col3, F1.col4
  FROM Foobar AS F1
 WHERE NOT EXISTS
       (SELECT *
          FROM Foobar AS F2
         WHERE (F1.col1, F1.col2, F1.col3)
             = (F2.col1, F2.col2, F2.col3)
           AND COALESCE (F2.col4, 1) < 0);
```

The EXISTS() could be quite fast with the proper indexing. But we still have two levels of queries.

12.2.2 Grouped Solutions

Now, students, what do we use to select groups from a grouped table? The HAVING clause! Mark Soukup noticed this was a redundant construction and offered this answer:

```
SELECT col1, col2, col3, 0 AS col4zero
  FROM Foobar
 GROUP BY col1, col2, col3
HAVING SUM(col4) = 0;
```

Why is this improvement? The HAVING clause does not have to wait for an entire subquery to be built before it can go to work. In fact, with a good optimizer, it does not have to wait for an entire group to be built before dropping it from the results. Given parallelism and hashing, you can get an answer as soon as a hash bucket has something in it.

However, there is still that assumption about the values in col4. Roy Harvey came up with answer that gets around that problem:

```
SELECT col1, col2, col3, 0 AS col4_zero
  FROM Foobar
```

```
GROUP BY col1, col2, col3
HAVING COUNT(*)
       = SUM(CASE WHEN col4 = 0
                  THEN 1 ELSE 0 END);
```

Using the CASE expression inside an aggregation function this way is a handy trick. The idea is that you count the number of rows in each group and count the number of zeros in col4 of each group; if they are the same, then the group is one we want in the answer.

However, when most SQL compilers see an expression inside an aggregate function like SUM(), they have trouble optimizing the code.

12.2.3 Aggregated Solutions

I came up with two approaches. Here is the first:

```
SELECT col1, col2, col3
  FROM Foobar
 GROUP BY col1, col2, col3
HAVING MIN(col4) = MAX(col4) -- one value in table
   AND MIN(col4) = 0; -- has a zero
```

The first predicate is to guarantee that all values in column four are the same. Think about the characteristics of a group of identical values. Since they are all the same, the extremes will also be the same. The second predicate assures us that col4 is all zeros in each group. This is the same reasoning; if they are all alike and one of them is a zero, then all of them are zeros.

However, these answers make assumptions about how to handle NULLs in col4. The specification said nothing about NULLs, so we have two choices: (1) discard all NULLs and then see if the known values are all zeros, or (2) keep the NULLs in the groups and use them to disqualify the group. To make this easier to see, let's do this statement:

```
INSERT INTO Foobar (col1, col2, col3, col4)
VALUES (7, 8, 9, 0), (7, 8, 9, 0), (7, 8, 9, NULL);
```

Tony Rogerson's answer will drop the last row in this statement from the SUM(), and the outermost query will never see it. This group passes the test and gets to the result set.

Roy Harvey's answer will convert the NULL into a zero in the SUM(), the SUM() will not match COUNT(*), and thus this group is rejected.

My first answer will give the "benefit of the doubt" to the NULLs, but I can add another predicate and reject groups with NULLs in them.

```
SELECT col1, col2, col3
  FROM Foobar
 GROUP BY col1, col2, col3
HAVING MIN(col4) = MAX(col4)
   AND MIN(col4) = 0
   AND COUNT(*) = COUNT(col4); -- No NULL in the column
```

The advantage of using simple aggregate functions is that SQL engines are tuned to produce them quickly and to optimize code containing them. For example, the MIN(), MAX(), and COUNT(*) functions for a base table can often be determined directly from an index or from a statistics table used by the optimizer, without reading the base table itself. If you are a little luckier, the individual columns have a histogram in the Statistics tables that will let you look up the COUNT(<column name>) for each value (remember that COUNT(<column name>) drops NULLs and COUNT(*) does not).

12.3 Grouping over Time

This problem shows up in some form every few years in a newsgroup. You are given a table of some event, say sales, with just the date of the sale and customer columns. The problem is to calculate the average number of days between purchases for each customer. It is a good useful statistic for predicting future behavior and budgeting in a lot of situations. Let's use a simple table that assumes nobody makes more than one purchase on the same day:

```
CREATE TABLE Sales
(customer_name CHAR(5) NOT NULL,
sale_date DATE NOT NULL,
PRIMARY KEY (customer_name, sale_date));
```

Let's take a look at the data for the first week in June 2008:

```
Sales

 customer_name      sale_date
==============================
 'Fred'            '2008-06-01'
 'Mary'            '2008-06-01'
```

```
customer_name    sale_date
============================
   'Bill'         '2008-06-01'
   'Fred'         '2008-06-02'
   'Bill'         '2008-06-02'
   'Bill'         '2008-06-03'
   'Bill'         '2008-06-04'
   'Bill'         '2008-06-05'
   'Bill'         '2008-06-06'
   'Bill'         '2008-06-07'
   'Fred'         '2008-06-07'
   'Mary'         '2008-06-08'
```

The data shows that Fred waited one day, then waited five days, for an average of three days between his visits. Mary waited seven days for an average of seven days. Bill is a regular customer every day.

12.3.1 Piece-by-Piece Solution

The first impulse is to construct an elaborate VIEW that shows the number of days between each purchase for each customer. The first task in this approach is to get the sales into a table with the current sale_date and the date of the last purchase:

```
CREATE VIEW Lastsales (customer_name, this_sale_date,
last_sale_date)
AS
SELECT S1.customer_name, S1.saledate,
       (SELECT MAX(sale_date)
          FROM Sales AS S2
         WHERE S2.saledate < S1.saledate
           AND S2.customer_name = S1.customer_name)
  FROM Sales AS S1, Sales AS S2;
```

This is a greatest lower bound query—we want the highest date in the set of dates for this customer that comes before the current date.

Now we construct a VIEW with the gap in days between this sale and their last purchase. You could combine the two views in one statement, but it would be unreadable and would not optimize any better. Just to keep the code simple, assume that we have a DAYS() function that returns an integer to do the temporal math.

```
CREATE VIEW SalesGap (customer_name, purchase_gap)
AS
SELECT customer_name, sale_date
        - MIN (sale_date) OVER (ORDER BY sale_date
ROWS 1 PRECEDING)
  FROM Sales;
```

The final answer is one query:

```
SELECT customer, AVG(purchase_gap)
  FROM SalesGap
 GROUP BY customer_name;
```

You could combine the two views into the AVG() parameter, but it would be totally unreadable, or it might blow up and would run like molasses.

With the new OLAP syntax, this can be written to run a bit faster.

```
CREATE VIEW SalesGap (customer_name, purchase_gap)
AS
SELECT X.customer_name, AVG(X.purchase_gap)
  FROM (SELECT customer_name, sale_date,
                (sale_date - MIN (sale_date)
                  OVER (PARTITION BY customer_name
                        ORDER BY sale_date DESC
                        ROWS 1 PRECEDING))
          FROM Sales)
        AS X (customer_name, sale_date, purchase_gap)
GROUP BY customer_name;
```

The OLAP functions allow you to grab pairs of sequenced dates, and you can probably find a lot of other ways to write this same query with the OLAP extensions.

12.3.2 Data as a Whole Solution

I showed you answer one because it demonstrates how you can be too smart for your own good. Because we only need the total duration and the number of events in that duration for the average number of days a customer waits between purchases, there is no need to build an elaborate VIEW. Simply count the number of lapsed days and then divide by the number of sales.

```
SELECT customer_name, (MAX(sale_date) - MIN(sale_date)) /
(COUNT(*)-1) AS avg_purchase_gap
```

```
   FROM Sales
  GROUP BY customer
 HAVING COUNT(*) > 1;
```

The (COUNT(*) -1) works because there is always one less purchase than orders, if you do not consider the time gap between the date of the last order and today's date. These one-shot customers can be included by changing MAX(sale_date) to CURRENT_DATE in the SELECT statement.

```
SELECT customer_name,
   CASE WHEN COUNT(*) > 1
        THEN DAYS(MAX(sale_date) - MIN(sale_date)) /
             (COUNT(*)-1)
        ELSE DAYS(CURRENT_TIMESTAMP - MIN(sale_date))
   END AS avg_purchase_gap
  FROM Sales
 GROUP BY customer_name;
```

Incidentally, with either approach, you can have more than one sale per day per customer.

12.4 Other Tricks with HAVING Clauses

You can use the aggregate functions and the HAVING clause to determine certain characteristics of the groups formed by the GROUP BY clause. For example, given a simple grouped table, you can determine the following properties of the groups with these HAVING clauses:

HAVING COUNT (DISTINCT col_x) = COUNT (col_x)— col_x has all distinct values.

HAVING COUNT(*) = COUNT(col_x);—There are no NULLs in the column.

HAVING MIN(col_x - <const>) = -MAX(col_x - <const>)— col_x deviates above and below const by the same amount.

HAVING MIN(col_x) * MAX(col_x) < 0—either MIN or MAX is negative, not both.

HAVING MIN(col_x) * MAX(col_x) > 0—col_x is either all positive or all negative.

HAVING MIN(SIGN(col_x)) = MAX(SIGN(col_x))—col_x is all positive, all negative, or all zero.

HAVING MIN(ABS(col_x)) = 0;—col_x has at least one zero

HAVING MIN(ABS(col_x)) = MIN(col_x)—col_x >= 0
(although the where clause can handle this, too).

HAVING MIN(col_x) = -MAX(col_x)—col_x deviates above
and below zero by the same amount.

HAVING MIN(col_x) * MAX(col_x) = 0—either one or both of
MIN or MAX is zero.

HAVING MIN(col_x) < MAX(col_x)—col_x has more than one
value (may be faster than COUNT(*) > 1).

HAVING MIN(col_x) = MAX(col_x)—col_x has one value or
NULLs.

HAVING (MAX(seq) - MIN(seq)+1) = COUNT(seq)—the
sequential numbers in seq have no gaps.

Tom Moreau contributed most of these suggestions.

Let me remind you again that if there is no GROUP BY clause, the HAVING clause will treat the entire table as a single group. This means that if you wish to apply one of the tests given above to the whole table, you will need to use a constant in the SELECT list.

This will be easier to see with an example. You are given a table with a column of unique sequential numbers that start at 1. When you attempt to insert a new row, you must use a sequence number that is not currently in the column; that is, fill the gaps. If there are no gaps, then and only then can you use the next highest integer in the sequence.

```
CREATE TABLE Foobar
(seq_nbr INTEGER NOT NULL PRIMARY KEY
        CHECK (seq > 0),
junk CHAR(5) NOT NULL);

INSERT INTO Foobar
VALUES (1, 'Tom'), (2, 'Dick'), (4, 'Harry'), (5, 'Moe');
```

How do I find if I have any gaps?

```
EXISTS (SELECT 'purchase_gap'
         FROM Foobar
        HAVING COUNT(*) = MAX(seq_nbr))
```

You could not use "SELECT seq_nbr" because the column values will not be identical within the single group made from the table, so the subquery fails with a cardinality violation. Likewise, "SELECT *" fails because the asterisk is converted into a column name picked by the SQL engine. Here is the insertion statement:

```
INSERT INTO Foobar (seq_nbr, junk)
VALUES (CASE WHEN EXISTS -- no gaps
                 (SELECT 'no gaps'
                    FROM Foobar
                   HAVING COUNT(*) = MAX(seq_nbr))
            THEN (SELECT MAX(seq_nbr) FROM Foobar) + 1
            ELSE (SELECT MIN(seq_nbr) -- gaps
                    FROM Foobar
                   WHERE (seq_nbr - 1)
                         NOT IN (SELECT seq_nbr FROM Foobar)
                     AND seq_nbr > 0) - 1,
        'Celko');
```

The ELSE clause has to handle a special situation when 1 is in the seq_nbr column, so that it does not return an illegal zero. The only tricky part is waiting for the entire scalar subquery expression to compute before subtracting one; writing "MIN(seq_nbr - 1)" or "MIN(seq_nbr) -1" in the SELECT list could disable the use of indexes in many SQL products.

12.5 Groupings, Rollups, and Cubes

OLAP functions add the GROUPING, ROLLUP, and CUBE extensions to the GROUP BY clause. They can be written in older Standard SQL using GROUP BY and UNION operators, so they are really shorthand and not brand-new functionality.

They return a single result set that has mixed levels of aggregation. In some ways, the mixed levels are a violation of "relational purity," but they are handy for basic hierarchical reporting. You will see those clauses called "super groups" in the literature.

12.5.1 GROUPING SET Clause

The first member of the family is the GROUPING SET. It is really just shorthand for a UNION of several similar grouped queries. It might be easier to see if we build up the options in this subclause.

1.   No GROUP BY clause is the same as GROUP BY GROUPING
      SET(). It returns the whole working table.

2.   GROUP BY a is the same as GROUP BY GROUPING
      SET((a)).

3.   GROUP BY a, b, c is the same as GROUP BY GROUPING
      SET((a, b, c)).

4.   A table has to have a fixed number of columns per row, and
      all the columns must have one and only one data type. These
      new grouping functions generate NULLs for each grouping set
      element at the levels to preserve the "shape" of the rows.

The elements in the grouping set list are set to NULL in all possible
combinations with the appropriate data types. For example:

```
SELECT dept_name, job_title, COUNT(*)
  FROM Personnel
 GROUP BY GROUPING SET (dept_name, job_title);
```

This gives a COUNT(*) on just dept_name and on just job_title. This is
shorthand for this query in SQL-92.

```
SELECT dept_name, CAST(NULL AS CHAR(10)) AS job_title,
COUNT(*)
  FROM Personnel
 GROUP BY dept_name
UNION ALL
SELECT CAST(NULL AS CHAR(8)) AS dept_name, job_title,
COUNT(*)
  FROM Personnel
 GROUP BY job_title;
```

If a grouping set element is a multicolumn list, then the members of
the list are all kept or all set to generated NULLs. Thus, GROUP BY
GROUPING SET((a, b), c) is not like GROUP BY GROUPING
SET(a, (b, c)) when executed.

How do you tell the difference between a real NULL that was in the
original data and a generated NULL? There is a GROUPING() function
that returns 0 for NULLs in the original data and 1 for generated NULLs
that indicate a subtotal.

Here is a little trick to get a human-readable output:

```
SELECT CASE GROUPING(dept_name)
  WHEN 1 THEN 'department total'
  ELSE dept_name END AS dept_name,
  CASE GROUPING(job_title)
  WHEN 1 THEN 'job total'

  ELSE job_title_name END AS job_title
 FROM Personnel
GROUP BY GROUPING SETS (dept_name, job_title);
```

As an aside, in his book on the second version of the relational model, Dr. Codd introduced two kinds of NULLs: one when the attribute is present but the value is presently unknown (a-mark) and one when the attribute is not present so it can never have a value (i-mark). For example, you can model the color of my feathers as an "i-mark NULL" since I am a mammal and not a bird. However, you could model my hair color as an "a-mark NULL" under the assumption that some day I might grow it back.

12.5.2 The ROLLUP Clause

A ROLLUP grouping is shorthand for a series of grouping-sets.

```
GROUP BY ROLLUP (a, b, c)
```

is equivalent to

```
GROUP BY GROUPING SETS (
(a, b, c), -- most detailed level
(a, b),
(a),
()) -- grand total
```

Order of specification of list elements is important for ROLLUPs. This is really the classic control break reporting from the earliest days of data processing. The difference is that the output is not necessarily sorted unless you do it with an ORDER BY clause.

12.5.3 The CUBE Clause

In 25 words or less, a CUBE grouping is a cross tabulation in disguise. It is also shorthand for a GROUPING SET.

```
GROUP BY CUBE (a, b, c)
```

is equivalent to

```
GROUP BY
 GROUPING SETS ((a, b, c), (a, b), (a, c), (b, c), (a),
 (b), (c), ())
```

Notice that the three elements of this CUBE example translate to $8 = (2^3)$ grouping sets. Yes, cubes get really big, really fast. The order of specification of elements does not matter for CUBE. It is going to generate all possible combinations.

12.5.4 A Footnote about Super Grouping

Statistical packages have been doing these sorts of aggregations for decades, but with their own proprietary syntax. These extensions were proposed by a group at Microsoft led by Jim Gray, with help from a smaller group at IBM ("Data Cube: A Relational Aggregation Operator Generalizing GROUP BY, Cross-Tab and Sub-Totals," *Data Mining and Knowledge Discovery*, Vol. 1, No. 1, 1997, ISSN 1384-5810). This was an attempt to bring basic statistical concepts into SQL but not to make SQL a full-blown stat package language.

Optimization for the super grou ping operators is pretty straightforward. As each row in the working table is constructed, it can be sent to a bucket for each of the aggregations done on it. This is a natural problem for parallel processing.

Cubes are already used in specialized data warehousing products and have a literature of their own. If you want an overview, you can get a copy of my book, *Analytics and OLAP in SQL*, ISBN-13:978-0123695123.

An interesting question is whether or not the GROUPING() function will work with the NULLs generated by OUTER JOINs in your particular SQL product. You will want to test it.

12.6 The WINDOW Clause

Partition functions in SQL were developed by Oracle and IBM representatives on the SQL Standards Committee, and some of their work was also picked up in SQL Server 2005. The basic idea is to make aggregate functions work in a partition built by ordering the rows of a table. The syntax is a bit complicated with a lot of options to it.

Figure 12.4
WINDOW
Clause

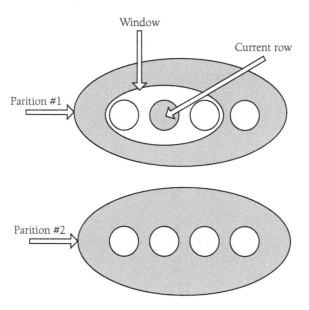

Any of the usual aggregate functions (MIN(), MAX(), AVG(), SUM(), or COUNT()) simply has an OVER clause added to it, thus:

```
<Aggregate function> ([DISTINCT]<exp>) OVER
(<window clause>) [[AS] <column name>]
```

The WINDOW clause describes how a partition of rows will be constructed around the current row. Since it is a function, it will return one value per row. The options within the window are:

```
OVER ([<partition clause>]
[<range clause>]
[<order by clause>])
```

The subclauses do not make sense without the ORDER BY subclause.

12.6.1 The PARTITION BY Clause

The syntax is:

```
PARTITION BY <exp> [, <exp>] ..
```

The PARTITION BY <column list> clause acts as a sort of local GROUP BY clause. If it is not given, the whole result set is one partition. The table is partitioned into a working table like the GROUP BY clause would do, but the groups are not consolidated into a single value. The other clauses act within each partition.

Here is a very simple example of the clause:

```
SELECT emp_id, dept_nbr, salary_amt,
       AVG(salary_amt) OVER (PARTITION BY dept_nbr)
       AS dept_avg_salary
 FROM Personnel;
```

An alternative syntax, if the same window is to be used in several places in the same query is to add a WINDOW clause at

```
SELECT emp_id, dept_nbr, salary_amt,
       AVG(salary_amt) OVER W1 AS dept_avg_salary
  FROM Personnel
WINDOW W1 AS (PARTITION BY dept_nbr);
```

12.6.2 The ORDER BY Clause

The syntax is:

```
ORDER BY <exp> [ASC | DESC] [,<exp> [ASC | DESC]] ..
```

This gives the sorting order within each partition. If it is not given, then that order is unpredictable. The RANGE clause does not make sense without this clause, so you should expect to use them both. It looks like the usual ORDER BY clause, with the ASC and DESC options after each column name in the sort list.

Let us add a bit more to the first example. We have a bonus history that shows the bonuses paid each month for each employee.

```
SELECT emp_id, bonus_amt, bonus_date,
       AVG(bonus_amt)
         OVER (PARTITION BY emp_id,
               ORDER BY bonus_date ASC
               RANGE 2 PRECEDING) AS moving_avg_bonus
 FROM BonusHistory;
```

This will look back for the current and previous two months to compute the average amount paid to each employee in that time frame.

It is worth mentioning that the ORDER BY clause now has an optional [NULLs FIRST | NULLs LAST] final clause. Before the OLAP functions, the sort order of NULLs was implementation defined.

12.6.3 The RANGE Clause

The RANGE clause says how many rows before and after the current row to apply the aggregate function. It does not make sense without an ORDER BY subclause.

This is the most complicated one of the trio. Imagine that you have a clear glass window in a frame and you are moving it over the rows in the partition. The RANGE clause decides how big that window is. You specify the rows that come before and/or after the current row for which the aggregate is being computed.

```
{ROWS | RANGE} {window frame start | window frame between}]

<window frame start> ::=
{UNBOUNDED PRECEDING | <unsigned integer> PRECEDING |
CURRENT ROW}

<window frame between> ::=
BETWEEN <window frame bound> AND <window frame bound>

<window frame bound> ::= <window frame start> | UNBOUNDED
FOLLOWING| <unsigned integer> FOLLOWING
```

The term "CURRENT ROW" explains itself. The window frame start is based on the rows within the current partition. You can start with first row in the partition using "UNBOUNDED PRECEDING", or you can count a fixed number of rows backwards from the current row. Likewise, UNBOUNDED FOLLOWING anchors the window at the highest element and "<unsigned integer> FOLLOWING" gives a fixed number of rows ahead.

12.6.4 Programming Tricks

You can adjust the window size pretty much as you wish. However, when a window has fewer rows that the size you originally asked for, the computation is still done on the smaller set. If this is a problem, you can use a CASE expression to avoid it.

```
CASE WHEN COUNT(*) OVER W1 > 3
THEN NULL -- or whatever you want
ELSE AVG(bonus_amt) OVER W1
 END
```

The WINDOW clause can take a list of window expressions in the same way that the WITH clause can take a list of CTE expressions. An empty list item is the whole table as one partition.

```
WINDOW Company AS (),
        Department AS (PARTITION BY dept_nbr),
        People AS (PARTITION BY emp_id)
```

The ANSI spec allows for one window declaration to reference a previous one, but as of this writing that feature has not been implemented. Since it is just shorthand, this is not a loss.

CHAPTER 13

Turning Specifications into Code

ONE OF MY frequent rants is that it takes about a year of full-time SQL to unlearn procedural thinking and move to a pure SQL view of the world. You will gradually build up a set of heuristics and patterns that you see over and over.

13.1 Signs of Bad SQL

The phrase "original sin" always seemed to be an oxymoron; originality is an attribute that is usually missing when people—and programmers—sin. Programmers tend to make the same kinds of errors in their designs and their code over and over. They confuse RDBMS with the file systems and 3GL- or OO-oriented programming environments they first learned. The same thing happens with a spoken natural language—you first use your old grammar and syntax rules with the new words. Eventually, you use the new grammar and syntax rules with the new words.

Here are a few diagnostics you can apply simply by looking at the code. These are not in-depth analyses, but immediately visible symptoms of deeper problems. This is like a doctor who sees a patient with red spots and has a pretty good idea what their real problem is before sending cultures to the lab. Is this always right? No, but it is how the smart money bets.

13.1.1 Is the Code Formatted Like Another Language?

Look at the physical layout of the SQL on the page. Does it look like another programming language? Programmers from the C family of languages tend to put the entire program in lowercase as if they were still using a teletype on a UNIX system. Mainframe programmers tend to put the entire program in uppercase as if they were still using punch cards or a 3270 video monitor for input. Look for "camelCase" and "PascalCase" words in the text. All of these styles have been shown to be bad for humans to read, but they are hard habits to break. You can find some details on this in my other book, *SQL Programming Style* (ISBN 10: 0-12-088797-5).

Along the same lines, look for the use of proprietary features even when ANSI/ISO Standard options are available. The worst offenders are SQL Server programmers who use ISNULL() when they have COALESCE(), SELECT for assignment when they have SET, CONVERT() when they have CAST(), and so forth. You will also find Oracle programmers who use DECODE() when they have CASE, and much the same sort of thing in DB2 where there are explicit data type conversion functions that predate the generic ANSI/ISO Standard CAST() function. This gives you an idea which SQL they know and how long they have used it.

13.1.2 Assuming Sequential Access

Does the programmer assume that they have sequential access to a table? It means that they have no idea what a table is and are still thinking in terms of a sequential file. Look for a lot of ORDER BY clauses in VIEWs and subqueries, if the SQL implementation, such as T-SQL, will allow it. Look for specifications that ask for the first, last, or n-th row in a table rather than asking for a maximum or minimum defined by some rule.

13.1.3 Cursors

Does the code have cursors? This is the one place that an ORDER BY clause makes sense in SQL. But you should only need to write a few cursors inside the database; my rule of thumb is five database-sides in your entire career. The ANSI/ISO cursor model is directly based on the old magnetic tape commands on IBM and other mainframe systems. That is what a cursor is mimicking almost every time. If you are embedding SQL in a 3GL language like COBOL, you must use cursors to get around the "impedance mismatch"—the data in SQL is returned in sets, while data in COBOL is returned in records.

Of course, sometimes COBOL programmers use too many cursors instead of doing the work in SQL before it is sent to a CURSOR to be read into the COBOL program.

Worse, programmers will nest one cursor inside another to mimic a tape file merge. If they wrote data to a temporary table, then put a cursor on it, they have written a scratch tape in SQL. The worst situation is dynamic cursors. They combine the slow performance of cursors with the unpredictable nature of dynamic code. Even without using cursors, you will see programs that use temporary tables as scratch tapes. Each temporary table holds the output of one step in a sequential process so it can pass it along to the next step.

13.1.4 Poor Cohesion

Cohesion is how well a module of code does one and only one thing, that it is logically coherent. There are several types of cohesion. The original definitions have been extended from procedural code to include OO and class hierarchies. I will not go into details—you can look them up in any software engineering book.

The symptom in DDL is a table with lots of NULLable columns. It is probably two or more entities crammed into a single table. People commonly do this when they have a relationship that is 1:1 or 0:1 and they model the 0:1 case as NULLs. For example, a Personnel table with all of the attributes we want to know about a spouse as well as the employee should be put into a Spouses table, separate from the employee's personnel data.

The symptom in DML is a query or other statement that tries to do too many things. When the same procedure or query checks inventory and builds a personnel report, you have cohesion problems.

Another symptom in a procedure is a lot of IF-THEN-ELSE-END IF logic or strange CASE expressions to detect the intended targets and computations. The most common version of this is trying to pass a table as a parameter. This means that the procedure or query will work on Squids, Automobiles, or any kind of entity in the universe modeled by a table in the schema. If you want to manipulate a table qua table, then you are into metadata tools and not an application.

13.1.5 Table-Valued Functions

The table-valued function shows that the programmer still wants to see procedural coding complete with parameters. An SQL programmer would think in terms of VIEWs and CTEs. It is also still very proprietary, so the programmer is probably using the model known from his or her old programming language.

13.1.6 Multiple Names for the Same Data Element

In an RDBMS, a data element has one and only one name that is used anywhere the data element appears. In a file system, a field name is determined by the application program reading that file. You will constantly see newbies using different names or abbreviations for the same thing—for example, "cust_id" and "customer_nbr" might be exactly the same data element. But if they are actually different data elements, then if customer attributes use "cust_" and "customer_", you use the same prefix everywhere.

Another classic example is having a magical, universal "id" in every table (even worse if it is an autonumbering feature). The programmers maintaining the code are supposed to figure out from context which identifier is meant. Thus, "student_id" and "Student.id" are two names for the same data element.

13.1.7 Formatting in the Database

You never format data in the back end. The output of the database is in a known, consistent data type and pattern. The basic principle of a tiered architecture is that display is done in the front end and never in the back end. This is a more basic programming principle than just SQL and RDBMS.

Dates are probably the worst offenders, since many vendor products have formatting options in their standard function library. The ANSI/ISO Standards are all based on UTC and ISO-8601 without any local options. That is what you want to pass to the next tier, where it can be converted to a U.S. British, or Chinese display format, with or without Daylight Saving Time as needed.

People's names are the next victim—should it be three columns, or concatenated "<last name>, <first name> <initial>", or be concatenated "<first name> <last name> <initial>" in the SELECT clause list? The argument that doing the concatenation in the database will save time is absurd in this day and age.

Another symptom of bad design is the use of CAST() in too many places. Either the DDL is a nightmare of improperly chosen data types or the programmer is formatting the data for output.

13.1.8 Keeping Dates in Strings

Related to formatting dates in the back end, you will find programmers who are not comfortable with temporal data types. They keep the dates in character strings, thus costing themselves data integrity, wasted storage, and more complex code. While rarer, you will sometimes see numeric data kept in strings, then cast for computations.

13.1.9 BIT Flags, BOOLEAN, and Other Computed Columns

BIT and BIT VARYING were deprecated from Standard SQL, but some still have them (exactly what a NULL means is weird). Likewise, you will see Booleans either in a proprietary data type or faked with {'y', 'n'} or {0, 1}. The programmer is probably still back in a low-level language or even assembly language programming. A "yes/no" question needs more than two values—"yes", "no", "not answered", "not applicable", and so forth depending on the status of the question.

But more often than not, the flag can be computed from the values of other attributes in the schema. Why waste time storing it? Why risk data corruption from not updating all of the components of the computation? In particular, keeping a timestamp for a status change instead of a flag preserves information at very little cost.

13.1.10 Attribute Splitting Across Columns

Attribute splitting is a class of design flaws where an attribute is split into more than one location in the schema. You can split it into columns in the same row, across multiple rows, or across tables.

The simplest form is to have one column that holds more than one data element. If it were something as simple putting shoe size or hat size, you would see it at once—a person can have both those attributes. But if the two attributes exclude each other, say various currencies, it might not get noticed. The currency symbol in a string or a second column tells us what this column means.

13.1.11 Attribute Splitting Across Rows

This is when a single data element is spread across two (or more) rows in the same column. The most common form of this is to have a single column with the arrival and the departure time of an event to mimic the lines on sign-in sign-out sheets on a clipboard. The result is that you are constantly doing self-joins to get the duration of the event that was the split data element.

13.1.12 Attribute Splitting Across Tables

If you saw tables for "MalePersonnel" and "FemalePersonnel", you would recognize immediately that the gender attribute had been used to split a "Personnel" table apart. However, you will constantly see table split on temporal attributes—a table for each month or year of some entity. The result is that you will UNION or UNION ALL things together constantly to get the table you should have had in the first place.

Do not confuse a split table with a partitioned table. A partitioned table is physically split on disk storage to improve access. The RDBMS system maintains a logical view of the data that makes it looks like we have a single logical table. A split table is logically split on an attribute, and the programmer has to maintain the data integrity.

13.2 Methods of Attack

This is a simple problem, but the replies to it illustrate approaches to solutions in any SQL. The problem is a single-column table that holds the time in seconds from some starting time (time zero or t_0) of some event. For simplicity, the event times are captured in even seconds from a time zero.

```
CREATE TABLE Events
(event_time DECIMAL(4,1) NOT NULL PRIMARY KEY
 CHECK(event_time = ((10 * event_time)/ 10))
 -- whole seconds);
INSERT INTO Events
VALUES (500), (505), (510), (535),
       (910), (939), (944), (977);
```

I need to assign a group number to the above values, based on a time interval of 30 seconds. The numbering does not matter, just as long as the numbering increases with the event times. For example, this is a correct result for the given data:

GroupedEvents

event_time	grp_id
500	1
505	1
510	1
535	2
910	3
939	3
944	4
977	5

So, how do we attack the problem? I can think of three basic approaches. (1) We use a cursor and mimic a magnetic tape file system, with nested loops. (2) We use SQL statements to construct the ranges on the fly from the Events table. (3) We can construct the ranges independently of the Events table and do a join. Let's look at each answer.

13.2.1 Cursor-Based Solution

The most basic procedural solution, with a hint of SQL syntax! This approach to the problem views the table as a sequential file. The structure is a simple loop within a loop. Sort the event times, read them in one at a time. Grab one as the start of a group. Get the next (n) event times and give them the same group id if they are within 30 seconds of the starting event time. When a value goes over the limit, then start another group. Here is a simple version of the algorithm in Standard SQL. Assume that the my_grp_cursor is allocated and deallocated outside the module.

```
BEGIN
DECLARE my_grp_cursor CURSOR FOR
 SELECT event_time
   FROM Events
  ORDER BY event_time;

DECLARE my_group_id INTEGER;
DECLARE my_grp_start INTEGER;
```

```
DECLARE my_grp_end INTEGER;
SET my_group_id = 1; -- or other value
DELETE FROM Results; -- clean out results table
OPEN my_grp_cursor;

FETCH event_time INTO my_grp_start;
WHILE SQLSTATUS = '00000'
DO
SET my_grp_end = my_grp_start;
  WHILE my_grp_end - my_grp_start < 30
  DO
   INSERT INTO Results (event_time, group_id)
   VALUES (my_grp_end, my_group_id);
   FETCH event_time INTO my_grp_end;
 END WHILE;
SET my_group_id = my_group_id + 1; -- next group
SET my_grp_start = my_grp_end; -- restart group
END WHILE;

CLOSE my_grp_cursor;
END;
```

There are a few problems with this. First of all, cursors are slow and the syntax in each vendor's product is highly proprietary. If you add new data, the Results table has to be recalculated with this code.

13.2.2 Semiset-Oriented Approach

The term "semiset-oriented" is a bit weird and needs some explaining. You can write SQL that depends on heavy use of functions, proprietary extensions, and computations.

Instead of trying to find a portable, simple SQL statement, we get nested "nightmare SQL" that is trying to mimic the same algorithms we has in a procedural solution. This example is in Microsoft's T-SQL dialect. I have put in some comments about the dialect, which depends on a simple one-pass compiler based on C and Algol.

```
BEGIN
-- @ marks local variable in T-SQL dialect
DECLARE @interval INTEGER;
SET @interval = 30; -- could have been hardwired
```

```
DECLARE @result_table TABLE; -- proprietary temp table
syntax
(start_time INTEGER NOT NULL,
 end_time INTEGER NOT NULL,
 grp_id INTEGER IDENTITY(1,1) -- proprietary auto numbering
   NOT NULL PRIMARY KEY CLUSTERED);

-- Build the grouping table with insanely complex code
INSERT INTO @result_table (start_time, end_time)
-- identity is automatically filled in
SELECT MIN(start_time) AS start_time, end_time
 FROM
  (SELECT CASE
     WHEN D.start_time IN
       (SELECT DISTINCT
        (SELECT TOP 1 event_time -- proprietary max()
           FROM Events
          WHERE event_time >= B.event_time
            AND event_time < B.event_time + @interval
          ORDER BY event_time DESC) AS end_time
        FROM Events AS B)
     THEN D.end_time
     ELSE D.start_time
     END AS start_time,
   end_time
   FROM SELECT A.event_time AS start_time,
             (SELECT TOP 1 event_time -- proprietary max()
                FROM Events
               WHERE event_time >= A.event_time
                 AND event_time < A.event_time +
                     @interval
               ORDER BY event_time DESC) AS end_time
         FROM Events AS A) AS D) AS E
       GROUP BY end_time;

SELECT event_time, grp_id
 FROM Events
     INNER JOIN
     @result_table
     ON event_time BETWEEN start_time AND end_time;
END;
```

This sets up ranges on the fly, uses insanely proprietary T-SQL syntax, and has five copies of the base table and three levels of nesting. I could translate it into Standard SQL with a common table expression (CTE), but that would defeat the purpose of this example. I will leave that as an exercise to the reader.

13.2.3 Pure Set-Oriented Approach

This is an example of using an auxiliary table to get the ranges. Consider the problem of loading the time groups table. The typical approach is to write a loop as in the cursor solution, but if you have an auxiliary Sequence table, you can write this. The Sequence table is a list of integers from 1 to (n) and perhaps other columns with sequence-related data such as ordinal or cardinal number names, functions, and so forth.

```
INSERT INTO TimeGroups (group_id, start_time, end_time)
SELECT seq, (seq + :my_start_value),
             (seq + :my_start_value) + 029.9
  FROM Sequence AS S
 WHERE S.seq < :my_size;
```

The parameter `my_size` can be adjusted. But a whole year of 30-second intervals will require about one million rows.

You can also use this select as a derived table in the other query. But if you only want to use the groupings once, then write it as one query:

```
SELECT G.group_id, E.event_time
  FROM (SELECT S.seq, (S.seq + :my_start_value),
                      (S.seq + :my_start_value) + 029.9
          FROM Sequence AS S
         WHERE S.seq < :my_size)
        AS G (group_id, start_time, end_time),
       Events AS E
 WHERE E.event_time BETWEEN G.start_time AND G.end_time;
```

13.2.4 Advantages of Set-Oriented Code

This set-oriented approach has many advantages over the other two. Adding new event data is not a problem. Unlike the previous solutions, the group identifiers will stay the same for existing events.

The groupings can also be used with other tables, so that other reports will be consistent with each other.

It is impossible to predict which approach will run faster with actual data on a particular product. The set-oriented code is completely portable; at least it will run on any SQL. The join between Events and Groupings can be done in parallel if your product supports that feature.

13.3 Translating Vague Specifications

This problem was posted in mid-2007 on a newsgroup. The poster wanted to set up a system for controlling access to articles in some context. Here are his specifications. (Note: this example was used in Chapter 11, but we will be discussing different aspects of it here and in more depth.)

- The Users table stores information about users.

- The Articles table stores information about articles.

- Each Article belongs to a User.

- Each Article can be marked private. When an article is marked private, only the article owner and his or her friends can see them.

- The ArticleFavorites table stores information about user's bookmarked articles.

- The UserFriends tables keeps track of which users are friends.

The schema for the tables he first posted, cleaned up a bit, were:

```
CREATE TABLE Users
(user_id PRIMARY KEY INTEGER NOT NULL,
 user_name VARCHAR(100) NOT NULL,
 date_added TIMESTAMP DEFAULT CURRENT_TIMESTAMP NOT NULL);

CREATE TABLE Articles
(article_id PRIMARY KEY INTEGER NOT NULL,
 user_id INTEGER NOT NULL,
 comment_txt VARCHAR(1000),
 date_added TIMESTAMP DEFAULT CURRENT_TIMESTAMP NOT NULL,
 private_flag BIT NOT NULL);

CREATE TABLE ArticleFavorites
(user_id INTEGER NOT NULL,
```

```
article_id INTEGER NOT NULL,
active_flag BIT NOT NULL);

CREATE TABLE UserFriends
(user_id INTEGER NOT NULL
  REFERENCES Users(user_id),
 friend_id INTEGER NOT NULL
  REFERENCES Users(user_id),
 active_flag BIT NOT NULL);
```

Obviously, this skeleton would want to have a standard citation method and a much better user identifier than integers. The assembly language proprietary `BIT` flags and the `date_added` columns are also poor design.

Notice that we have no idea whether the same article can belong to many different users. We have no idea what to do if it is not marked `private`—does that make it `public` to everyone? Being `private` is not an attribute of an article per se. It is a relationship of a user to the article. The poster never used the word `public` in his narrative. He also never explained what a bookmark was supposed to do.

The `user_id` is all over the place in many different roles. It gets renamed `friend_id` in the UserFriends table; it is the article owner in the ArticleFavorites and the UserFriends tables.

The problem he was facing is when any user browses through the favorites of another user, they are only allowed to see articles that are "not `private`" unless the actual user browsing the content is already a friend of the content owner. We need better specifications.

1.   If I am looking at my own favorites, I want to be able to see them all (`private` and not `private`), if assuming I have any favorites.

2.   If I am looking at someone else's favorites and I am their friend, I should see them all.

3.   If I am looking at someone else's favorites and I am not their friend, I should only see the "not `private`" articles.

The proposed answers became more and more nested queries and dependent on the proprietary `BIT` flags.

13.3.1 Go Back to the DDL

Your questions will be easier with better DDL. Why did you think a user is an attribute of an article? It is an entity in its own right. Why are you using BIT flags in SQL as if you were still in a magnetic tape system? What do dates have to do with this data?

Let's try again:

```
CREATE TABLE Users
(user_id CHAR(8) NOT NULL PRIMARY KEY,
 user_name VARCHAR(35) NOT NULL);
```

The choice for a user_id is based on the size of a password in UNIX, but probably ought to be an e-mail address or something easy to learn. There ought to be a password, too. The choice of the length of the user's name is from the old U.S. Service address label recommendations.

None of these choices are written in concrete, but each has a rationale that can be explained to the client. The client is then in the mindset of thinking about what is appropriate in his situation.

```
CREATE TABLE Articles
(article_id INTEGER NOT NULL PRIMARY KEY,
 article_comment VARCHAR(1000));
```

The article identifier should be some industry-standard citation code, but for now, we will just use an integer. The client needs to tell you what to actually use. Medical, legal, and computer science are all slightly different, so I cannot make a subject area decision without more specs.

Now we have another design question. Is an article owned by one and only one user who should be shown as a foreign key in the Articles table? Or is ownership a relationship between an article and a user? The latter would imply that an article can appear in the portfolio of more than one user.

We need to show that relationship with a table of shared articles, something like this:

```
CREATE TABLE OwnedArticles
(owner_user_id CHAR(8) NOT NULL
  REFERENCES Users (user_id)
  ON UPDATE CASCADE
  ON DELETE CASCADE,
 friend_user_id CHAR(8) DEFAULT '*PUBLIC*' NOT NULL
  REFERENCES Users (user_id)
   ON UPDATE CASCADE
   ON DELETE CASCADE,
 article_id INTEGER NOT NULL -- industry standard citation?
```

```
REFERENCES Articles(article_id)
  ON UPDATE CASCADE
  ON DELETE CASCADE,
PRIMARY KEY (owner_user_id, friend_user_id, article_id));
```

This is a 3-ary relationship (2 users, 1 article) and a lot of things are
happening here. The `user_id` has one of two roles, so they need to get a
role prefix on their data element name. I am going to assume that nobody
suffers from self-loathing, so that an owner is also his or her own friend.

That is easy with an assertion if you actually want to materialize this
relationship.

```
CREATE ASSERTION
CHECK
((SELECT COUNT(*)
    FROM OwnedArticles
  WHERE friend_user_id = owner_user_id)
 = (SELECT COUNT(*) FROM Users)
);
```

This is important because it gets rid of the proprietary, low-level bit
flag logic. Instead, we use logic based on those two roles. But why
materialize this at all? Put it into a VIEW instead.

```
CREATE VIEW SharedArticles (owner_user_id, friend_user_id,
article_id)
AS
SELECT owner_user_id, friend_user_id, article_id
FROM SharedArticles
UNION
SELECT owner_user_id, owner_user_id, article_id
FROM SharedArticles;
```

We have also created a dummy user, *PUBLIC*, whose name is taken
from SQL's DCL language. This is the friend's user id that owners assign
to articles they wish to expose to the world. Here is where another
assumption was smuggled into the design; the default is *PUBLIC*, and
not an insertion error.

Now your query is simply:

```
SELECT DISTINCT :my_browser_user_id, A.user_id,
A.article_id, A.article_comment
```

```
FROM Articles AS A, SharedArticles AS S
WHERE A.article_id = S.article_id
  AND (:my_browser_user_id = S.friend_user_id
        OR S.friend_user_id = '*PUBLIC*');
```

Notice the use of the SELECT DISTINCT in case an article is both private and public.

13.3.2 Changing Specifications

The poster then changed the specs again. If all friendships work in both directions, this is not a good design. If an owner has 100 friends and this owner adds an article and makes it private, I would have to add 200 new rows into this table (one for each direction of the friendship).

This is not a good way to control access; you want to control each friend and article separately in most secure environments. Mother should not get access to my porno collection, but my brother can. What will happen is that you will get a "foaf" (friend of a friend) collapse of security.

However, Hugo Kornelis pointed out that this is what government agencies in the Netherlands want. A document can be *strictly* private to the agency using it, or it is *totally* public once released. At that point, the article does not belong to anyone in particular but the public in general.

If friendship works both directions, then have user_id_1 and user_id_2 since they are equals and add CHECK (user_id_1 < user_id_2) to the table. Your query can use a VIEW that flips these columns or encode it in the SELECT. But that is another elaborate set of constraints.

He proposed a schema something like this instead:

```
CREATE TABLE Users
(user_id INTEGER NOT NULL PRIMARY KEY,
 user_email VARCHAR(100) NOT NULL UNIQUE,
 -- Other columns);
```

The user's e-mail address was used as the "real" key for the users.

```
CREATE TABLE Articles
(article_id INTEGER NOT NULL PRIMARY KEY,
 owner_user_id INTEGER NOT NULL
    REFERENCES Users (user_id),
 article_visibility CHAR(10) DEFAULT '*PUBLIC*' NOT NULL,
```

```
      CHECK (article_visibility IN ('*PUBLIC*', '*PRIVATE*')),
   article_comment VARCHAR(1000) NOT NULL,
   ..   );
```

Ownership becomes a `unique` attribute that makes sense only with an article visibility status of `private` assigned to it.

```
CREATE TABLE Friends
(friend1_user_id INTEGER NOT NULL
   REFERENCES Users (user_id),
 friend2_user_id INTEGER NOT NULL
    REFERENCES Users (user_id),
 CHECK (friend1_user_id <= friend2_user_id),
 PRIMARY KEY (friend1_user_id, friend2_user_id),
   ..   );
```

Now create a `VIEW` with both columns switched to give you all the possible pairs.

```
CREATE TABLE UserFavorites
(user_id INTEGER NOT NULL
    REFERENCES Users (user_id),
 article_id INTEGER NOT NULL
    REFERENCES Articles (article_id)
PRIMARY KEY (user_id, article_id),
  ..   );
```

This table is a list of articles that a user likes, `public` or `private`.

Based on this schema, we can now proceed to write the queries. It is very easy to find your own favorites now.

```
SELECT A.article_id, article_owner_id, ..
  FROM Articles AS A, UserFavorites AS UF
 WHERE UF.user_id = :my_user_id
   AND UF.article_id = A.article_id;
```

Oops! What if the articles you own are not in your favorites list? Do you want to show them anyway?

```
SELECT DISTINCT A.article_id, article_owner_id, ..
  FROM Articles AS A, UserFavorites AS UF
 WHERE (UF.user_id = :my_user_id
```

```
            AND UF.article_id = A.article_id)
    OR A.owner_user_id = :my_user_id;
```

The other two bullet points depend on which of the two interpretations of the requirement is correct. Does the answer depend on whether the visibility of private articles is determined by the friendship status of owner of the favorites list or the article owner? I will leave that as an exercise for the reader.

CHAPTER 14

Using Procedure and Function Calls

EVERY SQL PROGRAMMER should makes friends with an APL, LISP, or FP programmer and pump them for programming tricks. These programming languages make heavy use of nesting function calls and recursion.

While computational languages (such as FORTRAN) and specialized statistical and mathematical languages have very rich function libraries, most SQL implementations are much poorer. This is not a bad thing; SQL is a data management and retrieval language, and it was never meant for string handling, numerical computations, or application development.

All that having been said, you can still use its function library to good advantage to scrub and manipulate data.

14.1 Clearing out Spaces in a String

This problem comes up on newsgroups about once a year. Given a VARCHAR(n) column with words in it, how do you squeeze out the extra spaces so that each word is separated by only one space? You can assume that you have a REPLACE (<target string>, <old string>, <new string>) function and a SPACES(n) function.

14.1.1 Procedural Solution #1

The obvious procedural code is a loop.

```
BEGIN
DECLARE i INTEGER;
SET i = (SELECT DATALENGTH(col_x) FROM Foobar);
WHILE i > 1
  DO UPDATE Foobar
        SET col_x = REPLACE (col_x, SPACES(i), SPACES(1));
  SET i = i - 1;
END WHILE;
END;
```

I have seen code like this in production. It is quick and easy to write, but it keeps doing UPDATE statements that require table locking, logging, and a lot of overhead. When this was pointed out, the proposed solution was to do the work in different procedural code. The core of the procedure was like this:

```
BEGIN
DECLARE i INTEGER; -- loop counter
DECLARE working_string VARCHAR(8000); -- huge safe size
SET i = DATALENGTH(working_string);
SET working_string
    = (SELECT col_x
         FROM Foobar
        WHERE Foobar.foo_id = :foo_id); -- one row!
WHILE i > 1
  DO SET working_string
     = REPLACE (col_x, SPACES(i), SPACES(1));
  SET i = i - 1;
END WHILE;
UPDATE Foobar
        SET col_x = working_string;
END;
```

This is the way that most procedural language programmers would do it. This algorithm still needs to be passed a key to locate which row it is working on. The next step was to loop through the table, calling this body of code in a stored procedure. But that only hides the "single record at a time" programming model.

14.1.2 Functional Solution #1

You can nest function calls many levels deep in SQL products, so the answer is something like this skeleton statement:

```
BEGIN
DECLARE i INTEGER;
SET i = (SELECT DATALENGTH(col_x) FROM Foobar);
WHILE i > 1
   DO UPDATE Foobar
        SET col_x = REPLACE (col_x, SPACES(i), SPACES(1));
   SET i = i - 1;
END WHILE;
END;
BEGIN
DECLARE i INTEGER; -- loop counter
DECLARE working_string VARCHAR(8000); -- huge safe size
SET i = DATALENGTH(working_string);
SET working_string
    = (SELECT col_x
         FROM Foobar
        WHERE Foobar.foo_id = :foo_id); -- one row!
WHILE i > 1
   DO SET working_string
       = REPLACE (col_x, SPACES(i), SPACES(1));
SET i = i - 1;
END WHILE;

UPDATE Foobar
   SET col_x
       = REPLACE (
          REPLACE (
           REPLACE (
            ..
            REPLACE(col_x, SPACES(2), SPACES(1)),
            ..
            SPACES(x), SPACES(1)),
         SPACES(y), SPACES(1)),
SPACES(z), SPACES(1));

UPDATE Foobar
   SET col_x = working_string;
END;
```

This is faster than hanging in a loop, and it is pure SQL, which will log only one UPDATE statement and not use excessive row locking. But now, a math problem for you: let col_x be VARCHAR(n). What is the optimal mix of nested replace function calls, and what should they look like for the general case of (n)?

Analysis of the Problem

There can be more than one word in the string, so you can have varying sized substrings, which are all spaces that need to be reduced to a single space.

Let (j –> k) mean "replace SPACES(j) with SPACES(k)", and consider these strategies:

a.   Use (SPACES(2) -> SPACES(1)) repeated LOG2(n) times?

b.   Use SPACE FLOOR(SQRT(n)) -> SPACES(1) as the starter?

c.   Use a decreasing Fibonacci series?

The first approach of simply doing a 2-to-1 space replacement has an upper bound for a VARCHAR(n); we would need CEILING(LOG2(n)) nested REPLACE() calls. For example, SQL Server's VARCHAR(n) can have a maximum length of 8,000 characters, so 13 ($2^13 = 8,192$) successive 2-to-1 space replacements will always be sufficient. But most products cannot nest anywhere near that depth.

John Gilson wrote a stored procedure to return all sequences of divisors that will reduce a VARCHAR of a given length. The procedure can be called to find all such sequences, regardless of length, for a VARCHAR of a given length or simply the shortest sequences. Without going into the details, the choice of replacement sizes for removing spaces in a VARCHAR(10) string were either three or four levels deep. But there is not a unique answer—for example, (4, 3, 2) works.

```
UPDATE Foobar
SET col_x
    = REPLACE (
        REPLACE (
        REPLACE(col_x, SPACES(4), SPACES(1)),
      SPACES(3), SPACES(1)),
    SPACES(2), SPACES(1));
```

For a VARCHAR (8000), the shortest sequences are of length 6. And there are over 200,000 to choose from!

Ernst-Udo Wallenborn also did a good job of experimental math. He looked at VARCHAR(64) strings and came up with the following series of operations, which will all result in single spaced strings:

```
1) (2 -> 1), (2 -> 1), (2 -> 1), (2 -> 1), (2 -> 1), (2 -> 1)
2) (3 -> 1), (3 -> 1), (3 -> 1), (3 -> 1), (2 -> 1)
3) (55 -> 1), (34 -> 1), (21 -> 1), (13 -> 1), (8 -> 1),
   (5 -> 1), (3 -> 1), (2 -> 1)
4) (64 -> 1), (32 -> 1), (16 -> 1), (8 -> 1), (4 -> 1),
   (2 -> 1)
5) (65 -> 1), (33 -> 1), (17 -> 1), (9 -> 1), (5 -> 1),
   (3 -> 1), (2 -> 1)
```

As is easily seen, $(2 -> 1)$ will prune the string in at most LOG2(n) rounds. This is not always the lowest number of rounds. $(3 -> 1)$ will arrive at a string with at most two consecutive spaces in FLOOR(LOG3(2^n))+1 rounds (that's 4 rounds in this case, which reduce a string of 63 spaces to 21, then 7, then 3, then 1 space, and a string of 64 spaces to 22, then 8, then 4, then 2). An additional $(2 -> 1)$ step then removes the remaining consecutive spaces.

Which poses the question: what is the number of string replacements needed by the algorithms above to reduce a string of (k) spaces $(1 <= k <= 2^n)$ to a single space? This can easily be evaluated, and it is clear that (1) is O(n) and (2) O(n/2), but (3) through (5) are nearly constant. In fact, the average number of string replacement operations for reducing a string of length (k) with $(1 <= k <= 64)$ to a single space are:

```
1) 31.50
2) 16.00
3) 2.39
4) 3.09
5) 3.00
```

This seems to support the Fibonacci series theory. However, real-life strings do not consist of spaces only. The spaces in real-life strings are not randomly distributed either. But let us assume they were, so we can construct strings that consist of characters that are SPACES(1) with probability (p) and not SPACES(1) with probability (1-p). Then, running through 10,000 randomly created VARCHAR(64) strings, the 5 algorithms above need the following number of string replacement operations.

(mean and standard deviations in parentheses)

	p=0.1	p=0.25	p=0.5	p=0.75	p=0.9
1)	0.63 (0.84)	3.95 (2.29)	15.74 (4.42)	35.40 (5.36)	51.04 (4.30)
2)	0.57 (0.74)	3.17 (1.67)	10.54 (2.55)	20.38 (2.53)	27.07 (1.85)
3)	0.57 (0.74)	3.13 (1.63)	9.40 (2.17)	13.13 (2.01)	10.22 (2.47)
4)	0.57 (0.73)	3.03 (1.56)	9.01 (2.04)	13.60 (1.98)	11.60 (2.71)
5)	0.57 (0.74)	3.13 (1.64)	9.48 (2.19)	13.78 (2.04)	11.30 (2.63)

The more spaces there are in a string, the worse are 1) and 2), for an obvious reason. It is very inefficient to prune an (n) space string two or three spaces at a time. The other three seem to be similar, with the Fibonacci series getting a slight edge for large strings. Why? Well, the minimum number of string replacement operations in a string with (n) substrings consisting of more than one space is, of course, n, with the series:

```
6) (64 -> 1), (63 -> 1), (62 -> 1), (61 -> 1), ...,
   (2 -> 1)
```

at the cost of having $(n-1)$ nested rounds, instead of $O(LOG2(n))$. Fibonacci has more rounds, and the Fibonacci numbers are denser than (2^k), so the probability of a particular substring being pruned to SPACES(1) in only very few steps is higher.

So it all comes down to the relative costs of nesting depth versus string operations.

14.1.3 Functional Solution #2

A completely different functional solution depends on having a maximum VARCHAR(n) that is twice the size of the string you are trying to reduce. Assume that '<' and '>' do not appear in col_x.

```
UPDATE Foobar
SET col_x
    = REPLACE (
        REPLACE (
          REPLACE(col_x, SPACES(1), '<>'),
        '><', SPACES(0)),
        '<>', SPACES(1));
```

This is due to someone named Carnegie in a newsgroup posting. The only problem is that it fails if the first function call overflows the maximum string length. You might get errors or truncation depending on your SQL.

```
UPDATE Foobar
SET col_x
  = REPLACE(
      REPLACE (
        REPLACE (
          REPLACE(col_x, SPACES(2), '<>'),
          '><', SPACES(0)),
        '<>', SPACES(1)),
      SPACES(2), SPACES(1));
```

This is still a problem if you have the '<' or '>' in the string. Here is a solution to that problem, at the expense of more nesting levels.

```
UPDATE Foobar
SET col_x
  = REPLACE (
      REPLACE (
        REPLACE (
          REPLACE (
            REPLACE (
              REPLACE (
                REPLACE (
                  REPLACE (col_x, '>', '\>\'),
                  '<', '\<\'),
                SPACES(2), '<>'),
              '><', SPACES(0)),
            '<>', SPACES(1)),
          SPACES(2), SPACES(1)),
        '\>\', '>'),
      '\<\', '<');
```

Basically, you are "escaping" the '>' and '<' on the right and left by protecting them with the '\' character. Doing this does expand the string slightly, so you do get back to the possibility of overflowing the maximum string size.

14.2 The PRD() Aggregate Function

If you were a math major, you would write capital sigma (Σ) for summation and capital Pi (Π) for product for the aggregate summation and aggregate product, respectively. The SUM() and SUM() PO OVER() functions are the SQL versions of the sigma. We do not have an aggregate function in SQL, but if we did the syntax for it would look something like:

```
PRD ([DISTINCT] <expression>) [<window clause>]
```

You can create such an aggregate from the LN() natural log function and LOG10() base ten logarithm function. But you will need CASE expressions to handle some special situations.

1. If there is a zero anywhere in the column, the answer is zero. Oh, the logarithm is not defined for zero.

2. If the values are all positive, you are fine.

3. If there are negative numbers in the list, then you have two subcases. An even number of negatives make the product positive, and an odd number of negatives make the results negative.

4. SQL has two rules about aggregates—NULLs are dropped before computations are started, and the DISTINCT option in the parameter list removes redundant duplicate values.

Here is a version with a little algebra and logic:

```
SELECT CASE MIN (SIGN (nbr))
WHEN 1 THEN EXP (SUM (LN (nbr)))  -- all positive numbers
WHEN 0 THEN 0.00                  -- some zeros
WHEN -1                           -- some negative numbers
THEN (EXP (SUM (LN (ABS(nbr))))
          * (CASE WHEN
                  MOD (SUM (ABS (SIGN(nbr)-1/ 2)), 2) = 1
                  THEN -1.00 ELSE 1.00 END))
       ELSE CAST (NULL AS FLOAT) END AS big_pi
FROM NumberTable;
```

The logarithm, exponential, mod, and sign functions are not standards, but they are very common. You might also have problems with data types. The SIGN() function should return an INTEGER. The LN()

function should cast nbr to FLOAT or DOUBLE PRECISION but beware.

The idea is that there are three special cases—all positive numbers, one or more zeros, and some negative numbers in the set. You can find out what your situation is with a quick test on the SIGN() of the minimum value in the set.

Within the case where you have negative numbers, there are two subcases: (1) an even number of negatives or (2) an odd number of negatives. You then need to apply some high school algebra to determine the sign of the final result.

Itzak Ben-Gan had problems implementing this in SQL Server that are worth passing along in case your SQL product also has them. The query as written returns a domain error in SQL Server even though it should not, had the result expressions in the CASE expression been evaluated after the conditional flow had performed a short circuit evaluation. Examining the execution plan of the above query, it looks like the optimizer evaluates all of the possible result expressions in a step prior to handling the flow of the CASE expression.

This means that in the expression after WHEN 1 ... the LN() function is also invoked in an intermediate phase for zeros and negative numbers, and in the expression after WHEN −1 ... the LN(ABS()) is also invoked in an intermediate phase for zeroes. This explains the domain error.

To handle this, I had to use the ABS() and NULLIF() functions in the positive numbers when CLAUSE, and the NULLIF() function in the negative numbers when CLAUSE:

```
   . . .
   WHEN 1 THEN EXP(SUM(LN(ABS(NULLIF(result, 0.00)))))
and
   . . .
   WHEN -1
   THEN EXP(SUM(LN(ABS(NULLIF(result, 0.00)))))
         * CASE ...
```

If you are sure that you will have only positive values in the column being computed, then you can use

```
PRD(<exp>) = EXP(SUM(LN (<exp>)))
```

or

```
PRD(<exp>) = POWER(CAST (10.00 AS FLOAT),
SUM(LOG10(<exp>)))
```

depending on your vendor functions. This last version assumes that 10.00 would need to be cast as a FLOAT to work with LOG10 (), but you should read the manual to see what the assumed data types are.

14.3 Long Parameter Lists in Procedures and Functions

A parameter is the formal name for a value passed to a procedure; an argument is the actual value that a parameter takes. If you check with the vendor of your SQL database product, you will find that functions written in the vendor's proprietary 4GL can handle a huge number of parameters. The maximum number of arguments for stored procedures in Sybase is 2,048, MS SQL Server can have 2,100 arguments, and in DB2 the maximum number of arguments is 32,767 (for DARI-style procedures only; for GENERAL style, the limit is 90).

If you are an old C programmer, you might remember when the ANSI Standard C changed the way that an array was passed on the stack from a pointer to the actual array elements. This is the classic "pass by values" or "pass by reference" question in early programming languages. The syntax stayed the same, but the execution changed.

There is a good rule about keeping a parameter list at or below seven parameters (*http://www.musanim.com/miller1956/*) to avoid human conceptual processing limits. However, there is another human factor called "chunking"—we aggregate things into "chunks" or sets of related things and deal with the chunk as a unit. For example, you do not think about the 35 individual kids in Ms. Kowalski's third-grade class, but you make "Ms. Kowalski's third-grade class" a chunk and think of it as a whole. This is why passing an array name does not cause the same concern that passing all the elements does.

A large number of parameters is often an attempt to fake an array in a scalar parameter list, since SQL/PSM (and the proprietary 4GLs) do not have arrays, lists, or other data structures that are not part of SQL. In fact, passing a table is problematic.

If you look at the Sudoku example in this book, you will see the use of a "row# || column#" template to construct an array. FORTRAN programmers will recognize this as a version of the EQUIVALENCE statement, which gave a name to each cell in an n-dimensional FORTRAN array ("Plus ça change, plus c'est la même chose." The more things change, the more they are the same.—Alphonse Karr).

The repeated code structure is easy to maintain with a text editor that has pattern recognition test (that usually means a regular expression parser). You can generate a huge repetitive parameter list with a single macro. And because of mathematical induction, you know the code is correct.

A good rule of thumb is to have not more than 10 to 25 parameters. People will not consistently fill out a GUI form with more than that many values. When you have to send a large number of human provided values, load a table and scrub the data first. A weird fact of life is that you may not show more than 12 input lines on a screen form. Superstitious input clerks will not enter the unlucky 13th line. You should show 10 lines and renumber them on a second display page. I wish I were making that up.

If you are worried about scalability and other issues, then compare those virtues to having correct data. The longer the input streams from a human, the higher the error rate. Scrubbing data might be a scalability issue if the validation and verification are complicated. But usually, you look for uniqueness, a check digit, and perhaps a table lookup—a simple validation of some kind.

14.3.1 The IN() Predicate Parameter Lists

This problem gets it own section because it is so common. Programmers coming from procedural languages want to pass an array as a parameter, but cannot do it in SQL/PSM or most of the proprietary 4GLs. The usual solutions are:

1.   Use dynamic SQL (with the possibility of SQL injection problems).

2.   Write a simple parser in SQL/PSM, a proprietary 4GL or an external 3GL language.

3.   Write a query that does the parsing, but without any real error handling.

The skeleton of a procedure with an IN() predicate from parameter is usually like this:

1.   Accept a list of parameters—again, 10 to 25 is usually more than enough. Let the T-SQL, SQL/PSM, Informix 4GL, or whatever procedural language do its parsing per the rules of the vendor's provided functions. If there are bad parameters,

the compiler should throw an exception. I assume we want that behavior, rather than having to do that work in our own code.

2.   Clean out a data scrubbing table and load it with the parameter as a column. This will probably be a local temporary table, so that more than one user can invoke the procedure.

3.   Insert any values that have to be there by default—this is usually CURRENT_TIMESTAMP or CURRENT_USER, but it could be anything. It might be a dummy value with special meaning in the schema; it could come from other tables or whatever. This is an optional step.

4.   Apply any data validations, like (i > 0) or (i BETWEEN 0 AND 100). I could throw an exception, but I have tended to simply remove bad data from the list and proceed. That decision is open to criticism.

Do the query with the IN() predicate, which is the meat of the procedure. Here is the skeleton with INTEGER data types:

```
CREATE PROCEDURE Foobar (IN p1 INTEGER, IN p2 INTEGER, ..
IN pn INTEGER)
LANGUAGE SQL
BEGIN ..
DELETE FROM ScrubTable; -- local temp table
INSERT INTO ScrubTable (i) VALUES (p1), (p2),.. (pn);
  ..
INSERT INTO ScrubTable (i)
VALUES (<< required value if any>>);
 -- Or
INSERT INTO ScrubTable (i)
SELECT << required value if any>>
  FROM ..;
  ..
 DELETE FROM ScrubTable -- do some data scrubbing
  WHERE << bad data test >>
      OR i IS NULL; -- assuming nulls are dropped

  ..
 SELECT a, b, c -- finally, the meat of the procedure!
```

```
 FROM Bar
 WHERE x IN (SELECT i FROM ScrubTable);
END;
```

The template does not show exception handling or a lot of details, but there are no loops or IF-THEN-ELSE-END IF logic or highly proprietary code.

Numbering Rows

PROCEDURAL PROGRAMMERS CANNOT seem to shake the idea of a physical row number being exposed to them. The idea that there is no sequential access or ordering in an RDBMS, so "first," "next," and "last" are totally meaningless, is lost on them.

The bad news is that many vendors provide such numberings by exposing their underlying physical storage model. The most common method is to auto-increment a counter as new rows are added to a table. This assumes that the SQL product inserts whole rows in a sequence, just as we added records to the end of a magnetic tape. This is not true for SQL engines with parallelism or that work with columns rather than rows.

If you want an ordering, then you need to have a column that defines that ordering. Dr. Codd called this the Information Principle, which says that all information in the database has to be represented in one and only one way, namely by values in column positions within rows of tables.

The other classic choice was to get out of SQL and use a file system for sorting and numbering the data in the application. The real problems come when the user tries to rearrange and renumber the rows by inserting new data or deleting old.

15.1 Procedural Solutions

The usual replacement for renumbering is to move the data from the current table to a temporary working table with an auto-increment on it. This will close up gaps, and if you do it with a cursor, you can pick the sort order. In SQL Server dialect, it usually looked like this:

```
CREATE TABLE #temptable
(row_num INTEGER IDENTITY (1, 1) PRIMARY KEY NOT NULL,
   cola INTEGER NOT NULL,
   colb INTEGER NOT NULL,
..);

-- insert the transactions
INSERT INTO #temptable (cola, colb, ..)
SELECT cola, colb, ..
  FROM Mytable -- same structure as #temptable
 ORDER BY cola;
```

The # prefix creates a local temporary table that disappears at the end of the session. IDENTITY is the dialect syntax for their auto-increment. And, yes, this eats up a lot of storage. Each table can have one and only one IDENTITY, and it is nearly impossible to change once set.

Each vendor will have a slightly different version of this "feature," but it is fairly common to see tables with an explicit ordering column in them. This can be a natural attribute like sequential check numbers, or it can be a very artificial thing created purely for display. The second approach is bad programming. The basic principle of a tiered architecture is that display is done in the front end and never in the back end. This is a more basic programming principle than just SQL and RDBMS.

You might be thinking that since IDENTITY is declared, it is not procedural. Not so. The first practical consideration is that IDENTITY is proprietary and nonportable, so you know that you will have maintenance problems when you change releases or port your system to other products. Newbies actually think they will never port code! Perhaps they only work for companies that are failing and will be gone before they have to consider growth problems. Perhaps their code is so bad nobody else wants their application.

But let's look at the logical problems. First, try to create a table with two columns and try to make them both IDENTITY. If you cannot declare more than one column to be of a certain data type, then that thing is not a data type at all, by definition. It is a property that belongs to the PHYSICAL table, not the LOGICAL data in the table.

Next, create a table with one column and make it an IDENTITY. Now try to insert, update, and delete different numbers from it. If you cannot insert, update, and delete rows from a table, then it is not a table by definition.

Finally, the ordering used is unpredictable when you insert with a SELECT statement.

```
INSERT INTO Foobar (a, b, c)
SELECT x, y, z
  FROM Floob;
```

Since a query result is a table, and a table is a set that has no ordering, what should the IDENTITY numbers be? The entire, whole, completed set is presented to Foobar all at once, not a row at a time. There are (n!) ways to number (n) rows, so which permutation did you pick? The answer has been to use whatever the physical order of the result set happened to be. That nonrelational phrase "physical order" again!

But it is actually worse than that. If the same query is executed again, but with new statistics or after an index has been dropped or added, the new execution plan could bring the result set back in a different physical order. Indexes and statistics are not part of the logical model.

The second family is to expose the physical location on the disk in an encoded format that can be used to directly move the read/ writer head to the record. This is the Oracle ROWID. If the disk is defragmented, the location can be changed, and the code will not port. This approach is dependent on hardware.

The third family is a function. This was originally done in Sybase SQL Anywhere (née WATCOM SQL) and was the model for the Standard SQL ROW_NUMBER() function.

This function computes the sequential row number of the row within the window defined by an ordering clause (if one is specified), starting with 1 for the first row and continuing sequentially to the last row in the window. If an ordering clause, ORDER BY, isn't specified in the window, the row numbers are assigned to the rows in arbitrary order as returned by the subselect. In actual code, the numbering functions are used for display purposes rather than adding line numbers in the back end.

15.1.1   Reordering on a Numbering Column

Imagine a motor pool with sequentially numbered parking spaces; you want to move the automobiles around using their old parking space number and the new target space. All the cars between those spaces have to slide up or down a space to make room.

The simplest table to illustrate this problem is:

```
CREATE TABLE Motorpool
(parking_space INTEGER NOT NULL
   CHECK (parking_space > 0),
 vin CHAR(17) NOT NULL,
PRIMARY KEY (parking_space, vin));
```

Rearrange the display order based on the parking_space column:

```
CREATE PROCEDURE SwapVehicles
(IN old_parking_space INTEGER, IN new_parking_space
INTEGER)
DETERMINISTIC
LANGUAGE SQL
UPDATE Motorpool
   SET parking_space
      = CASE parking_space
         WHEN old_parking_space
         THEN new_parking_space
         ELSE parking_space + SIGN(old_parking_space -
         new_parking_space)
         END
 WHERE parking_space BETWEEN old_parking_space AND
 new_parking_space
    OR parking_space BETWEEN new_parking_space AND
    old_parking_space;
```

When you want to drop a few rows, remember to close the gaps with this:

```
CREATE PROCEDURE CloseMotorpoolGaps()
DETERMINISTIC
LANGUAGE SQL
UPDATE Motorpool
   SET parking_space
      = (SELECT COUNT (M1.parking_space)
           FROM Motorpool AS M1
          WHERE M1.parking_space <= Motorpool.parking_
          space);
```

If you really wanted to use the SwapVehicles() procedure to do a sort, say by VIN, you could do it. In effect, you would be treating the table like an array in a procedural programming language. A much quicker way is to use the new OLAP functions in SQL-99.

```
CREATE PROCEDURE SortMotorpool()
DETERMINISTIC
LANGUAGE SQL
UPDATE Motorpool
   SET parking_space
       = ROW_NUMBER() OVER(ORDER BY vin);
```

The problem with this answer is that it is not currently available in all SQL implementations.

15.2 OLAP Functions

The introduction of OLAP functions in Standard SQL made it possible to do all kinds of row numberings easily. I would like to stress that these are functions, and they behave like other SQL functions in spite of their strange syntax.

15.2.1 Simple Row Numbering

The ROW_NUMBER() OVER() is pretty simple to understand. The window clause works the same way. PARTITION BY creates partitions, just as it did with the aggregate functions. The ORDER BY clause sorts the rows within the partition and assigns a number from 1 to (n); if no ORDER BY clause is given, then the results are unpredictable. Since the ORDER BY applies to the whole partition, a RANGE clause makes no sense.

It does not make much sense to use a ROW_NUMBER() without an ORDER BY, for obvious reasons. In the event of ties in the sort, the results are unpredictable.

Median Computation

A cute trick for the median is to use two ROW_NUMBER()s with an OVER() clause.

```
SELECT AVG(x),
       ROW_NUMBER() OVER(ORDER BY x ASC) AS hi,
       ROW_NUMBER() OVER(ORDER BY x DESC) AS lo
  FROM Foobar
 WHERE hi IN (lo, lo+1, lo-1);
```

This handles both the even and old number of cases. If there is an odd number of rows, then (hi = lo). If there is an even number of rows, then we want the two values in the two rows to either side of the middle. I leave it to the reader to play with duplicate values in column x and getting a weighted median, which is a better measure of central tendency.

```
x      hi      lo
==================
1       1       7
1       2       6
2       3       5
3       4       4 <= median - 4.0
3       5       3
3       6       2
3       7       1
```

The median for an even number of cases:

```
x      hi      lo
==================
1       1       6
1       2       5
2       3       4 <= median
3       4       3 <= median = 3.5
3       5       2
3       6       1
```

15.2.2 RANK() and DENSE_RANK()

So far, we have talked about extending the usual SQL aggregate functions. There are special functions that can be used with the window construct.

The RANK() OVER() assigns a sequential rank of a row within a window. The RANK() OVER() of a row is defined as one plus the number of rows that strictly precede the row. Rows that are not distinct within the ordering of the window are assigned equal ranks. If two or more rows are not distinct with respect to the ordering, then there will be one or more gaps in the sequential rank numbering. That is, the results of RANK may have gaps in the numbers resulting from duplicate values.

x	RANK
1	1
2	3
2	3
3	5
3	5
3	5
3	5
3	5
3	5

DENSE_RANK() OVER() also assigns a sequential rank to a row in a window. However, a row's DENSE_RANK() OVER() is one plus the number of rows preceding it that are distinct with respect to the ordering. Therefore, there will be no gaps in the sequential rank numbering, with ties being assigned the same rank. The RANK() OVER() and DENSE_RANK() OVER() require an ORDER BY clause.

x	DENSE_RANK
1	1
2	2
2	2
3	3
3	3
3	3
3	3
3	3

15.3 Sections

This problem is an old classic, but with a new OLAP solution from Itzak Ben-Gan. You are given a generic table with a key column that also provides an ordering and a nonkey column with some value in it. The key column can be dates, sequential numbers, or whatever, and likewise the value column can be anything. The problem is to identify sections or runs of consecutive rows that share the same value. A common example might be the days for which a bank account stayed at the same amount.

For each section, we want the minimum or starting key, the maximum or ending key, the value that defines the section, a count of rows in the section, and possibly other aggregates.

For purpose of discussion, let's use this short table and load some sample data.

```
CREATE TABLE Runs
(seq_nbr INTEGER NOT NULL PRIMARY KEY,
 val VARCHAR(10) NOT NULL);

INSERT INTO Runs(seq_nbr, val)
 VALUES (1, 'a'), (2, 'a'), (3, 'a'), (5, 'a'),
        (7, 'b'), (9, 'b'), (11, 'a'), (13, 'a'),
        (17, 'b'), (19, 'b'), (23, 'b'), (29, 'a'),
        (31, 'b'), (37, 'b');
```

The classic subquery method takes the current row, looks ahead in the sequence, and finds the first row where the value changes. This gives the end of the section to which the current row belongs.

```
SELECT seq_nbr, val,
       (SELECT MIN(seq_nbr)
          FROM Runs AS R1
         WHERE R1.seq_nbr > R2.seq_nbr
           AND R1.val <> R2.val) AS section
  FROM Runs AS R2;
```

Working from that, we can then find the starting values and pair them up. YOU can find similar solutions for similar problems in *SQL for Smarties, Third Edition* (ISBN-13: 978-0-12-369379-2), Chapter 24.

```
SELECT MIN(seq_nbr) AS start_section,
       MAX(seq_nbr) AS end_section,
       COUNT(*) AS row_cnt
  FROM (SELECT seq_nbr, val,
               (SELECT MIN(seq_nbr)
                  FROM Runs AS R1
                 WHERE R1.seq_nbr > R2.seq_nbr
                   AND R1.val <> R2.val)
          FROM Runs AS R2) AS R3(seq_nbr, val, section)
 GROUP BY section;
```

But can we use the new OLAP functions to get the same answer? Yes, of course; otherwise this would not be much of a chapter. Use the ROW_NUMBER() function to order all the rows by the key and call that the "row number for sequence key," or "rn_seq_nbr" for short. Now order all the values by their sequential position in the table, using the horrible name "rn_val_seq_nbr" for the results. That might be a little hard to see at first, but (11, 'a') is the seventh row in the table and the fifth occurrence of 'a' as a value.

```
SELECT seq_nbr, val,
       ROW_NUMBER() OVER(ORDER BY seq_nbr) AS rn_seq_nbr,
       ROW_NUMBER() OVER(ORDER BY val, seq_nbr)
       AS rn_val_seq_nbr,
       (ROW_NUMBER() OVER(ORDER BY seq_nbr)
         - ROW_NUMBER() OVER(ORDER BY val, seq_nbr))
           AS diff
   FROM Runs;
```

When I subtract (rn_seq_nbr - rn_val_seq_nbr), the difference is a constant within each section. A slightly different version of the same idea involves a table with ranges instead of simple sequence numbers. The goal is to combine overlapping runs to get a minimal representation of the data.

```
CREATE TABLE Foobar
(seq_nbr CHAR(10) NOT NULL,
 start_seq INTEGER NOT NULL,
 end_seq INTEGER NOT NULL,
 CHECK (start_seq <= end_seq),
 PRIMARY KEY (seq_nbr, start_seq));

INSERT INTO Foobar
VALUES ('A', 0, 5), ('B', 2, 5), ('A', 5, 8), ('C', 8, 10),
       ('B', 11, 12), ('A', 13, 14), ('B', 12, 15), ('A', 16, 18),
       ('A', 18, 24), ('A', 26, 30);
```

The query becomes:

```
SELECT seq_nbr, MIN(start_seq) AS "start", MAX(end_seq)
AS "end"
  FROM (SELECT F1.seq_nbr, F1.start_seq, F1.end_seq,
               F1.start_seq + F1.end_seq - MIN(F2.
               start_seq)
           FROM Foobar AS F1
```

```
            LEFT OUTER JOIN
            Foobar AS F2
            ON F2.seq_nbr = F1.seq_nbr
               AND F2.start_seq > F1.start_seq
         GROUP BY F1.seq_nbr, F1.start_seq, F1.end_seq)
        AS D(seq_nbr, start_seq, end_seq, diff)
GROUP BY seq_nbr, diff;
```

CHAPTER 16

Keeping Computed Data

THIS IS BASED on a posting in a DB2 newsgroup. Whenever a row is inserted into an Accounts table, the poster wants to either update an existing row in a separate tally table or insert a row into that tally table with the new account and batch number for every 100th batch within an account. Here is a skeleton schema:

```
CREATE TABLE Accounts
(account_id INTEGER NOT NULL,
 batch_nbr INTEGER NOT NULL,
 PRIMARY KEY (account_id, batch_nbr));
```

and put the last qualifying batch number into another table:

```
CREATE TABLE Accounts_100
(account_id INTEGER NOT NULL,
 batch_nbr INTEGER NOT NULL PRIMARY KEY,
 PRIMARY KEY (account_id, batch_nbr));
```

16.1 Procedural Solution

The obvious way to do this is to write a procedure that scans the batch numbers and throws them into the Account when they are a multiple of 100.

New SQL programmers do not think of TRIGGERs as procedural code, but they are. Unlike declarative code, they also do nothing for the optimizer.

```
CREATE TRIGGER AccountBatchTally
AFTER UPDATE ON Accounts
REFERENCING NEW AS N
MERGE INTO Accounts_100
USING LATERAL(VALUES(N.account_id, N.batch_nbr
                - (N.batch_nbr/100)))
     AS X (account_id, batch_nbr)
ON X.account_id = Accounts_100.account_id
WHEN MATCHED
THEN UPDATE SET Accounts_100.batch_nbr = X.batch_nbr
WHEN NOT MATCHED
THEN INSERT VALUES (X.account_id, X.batch_nbr);
```

The use of the LATERAL table construct is to get to the NEW table, which is used with a VALUES() clause to do math on the batch_nbr. This looks very nice and modern, but under the covers it is hiding a simple procedural program.

```
BEGIN
INSERT INTO Accounts (account_id, batch_nbr)
VALUES (:my_account_id, :my_batch_nbr);
IF NOT EXISTS
   (SELECT *
      FROM Accounts AS A
    A.account_id = :my_account_id)
THEN INSERT INTO Accounts_100 (account_id, 0)
ELSE UPDATE Accounts_100
       SET batch_nbr
           = :my_batch_nbr - (:my_batch_nbr/100)
     WHERE account_id = :my_account_id;
IF END;
END;
```

But both of these solutions have another problem; the definition of "every 100th batch" is vague. If we assume that batch numbers are sequential, then the math we have shown will work.

But what if the batch numbering is not really sequential? There might be gaps in the numbering, or they might be generated in a pseudo-random order, or whatever. Pulling out the 100th row also begs the question as to how to determine which row is the 100th insertion, since rows are inserted as sets, so a timestamp is not a solution. Then there is the question about dropped rows changing the count that was never explained.

16.2 Relational Solution

The use of redundant tables is a way to mimic a physical file. We immediately know, using our "set-oriented thinking," that the table Accounts_100 needs to become a VIEW.

```
CREATE VIEW Accounts_100s (account_id, batch_nbr, rn)
AS
(SELECT account_id, batch_nbr, rn
   FROM (SELECT account_id, batch_nbr,
                ROW_NUMBER()
                OVER (PARTITION BY acct_nbr
                      ORDER BY posting_date, batch_nbr)
          FROM Accounts) AS A1 (account_id, batch_nbr, rn)
  WHERE MOD(A.rn, 100) = 0;
```

Computed data is built on the fly, rather than persisted in a base table that requires storage and has to be constantly updated to be correct. The exception to this is the data warehouse where the data will not change and needs to be accessed in the aggregate as fast as possible. In that situation, materializing and indexing the summary data will probably work much better.

16.3 Other Kinds of Computed Data

Programmers coming from procedural languages are surprised to learn the SQL does not have a BOOLEAN data type. Their reaction is to use a proprietary BIT or BINARY data type to store flags, if their product has them, or to use a CHAR(1) with a constraint to allow only two values.

Flags like this should be replaced with the data that set them to their current state. For example, do not have an "is_delivered" flag when you could have the delivery date.

In the old punch card days, we would compute line totals in commercial application by multiplying the item quantity and unit price and punching the results in the right side of the card with special equipment. There was no place to keep the data except the cards. But you will still see this pattern mimicked in modern system.

Triggers for Constraints

THERE IS A myth that triggers have to be used for complex constraints. While there is a place for triggers in a few situations, they are usually avoidable. But more than that, they are procedural code and should be avoided in favor of declarative code that the optimizer can use.

Furthermore, while there is an ANSI/ISO Standard for triggers, most vendors have highly proprietary implementations, so the code will not easily port. In Standard SQL, a trigger name is unique in the whole schema even though it is attached to a particular base table. It is executed before or after an INSERT, UPDATE, and/or DELETE action. The INSTEAD OF trigger is used on VIEWs that would not otherwise be updatable to change the underlying base tables.

The model used in Standard SQL is that the action will create a working table named OLD (reserved word) of the rows that qualified for the UPDATE or DELETE action and a table named NEW (reserved word) of the created rows for the INSERT or UPDATE action. The ANSI/ISO Standard is a bit more complex than just this, but this will serve for our discussion.

17.1 Triggers for Computations

If you look at posting in newsgroups, you can easily find examples of table declarations with computed columns. The values in these columns are provided by a computation done in a trigger.

```
CREATE TABLE Boxes
(box_name CHAR(5) NOT NULL PRIMARY KEY,
box_length INTEGER NOT NULL,
box_height INTEGER NOT NULL,
box_width INTEGER NOT NULL,
box_volume INTEGER NOT NULL);
```

This is accompanied by a trigger that has the statement:

```
SET box_volume = box_length * box_height * box_width;
```

Depending on your SQL product, you might have to update the table as a whole, or just update the modified rows. The reasoning given for this trigger is to be sure that an UPDATE is always run to keep the box's volume correct. It is a way to ensure that an expensive, slow-running waste of storage is at least correct.

In this case, the error of that reasoning is easy to see because the computation is so simple that it can easily be done in the query. But for more complex math, you are better off with a VIEW. SQL Server 2005 introduced computed columns in their product, which are a shorthand for a VIEW without the need to use a CREATE VIEW statement.

17.2 Complex Constraints via CHECK() and CASE Constraints

This problem was posted on a newsgroup by Patrick L. Nolan at Stanford University. He has a small database with the following business rules:

1. Every person in the database is uniquely defined by a single key, their user_id.

2. Everyone is assigned a job category—call them A, B, and X.

3. Everyone in job category X has a supervisor, who must be in either job category A or job category B.

4. Let's assume that nobody can be their own supervisor.

This is a minimal set of rules that we expect to become more and more complex over time.

One proposal was to divide job category X into two categories; call them XA and XB, respectively. All the XA people would have A supervisors, and all the XB people would have B supervisors.

Mr. Nolan immediately noticed that there is redundancy and the possibility of inconsistency. Suppose somebody in job category XA somehow gets assigned to a supervisor in job category B, contrary to the definition of XA—Murphy's Law would require this to happen after a while.

```
CREATE TABLE Users
(user_id INTEGER NOT NULL PRIMARY KEY,
job_cat CHAR(2) NOT NULL
  REFERENCES JobCategories(job_cat),
super_job_cat CHAR(2) NOT NULL
  REFERENCES JobCategories(job_cat),
Etc);

CREATE TABLE JobCategories
(job_cat CHAR(2) NOT NULL PRIMARY KEY,
-- {'A', 'B', 'X', 'XA', 'XB'}
job_cat_description VARCHAR(50) NOT NULL);
```

The rules could be validated with a trigger, and then trigger code would be modified as the rules become more complex.

But this is not a good answer. The better answer is that Users and Job Assignments are fundamentally different. Users are entities and Job Assignments are relations, thus we need two tables. The current job categories are so short you could put them in a CHECK() constraint, but let's allow for expansion and flexibility.

The first trick is to have a super key in the Users table that can be referenced by the job assignments. This adds the business rule that a user has one and only one job category.

```
CREATE TABLE Users
(user_id INTEGER NOT NULL PRIMARY KEY, -- key
job_cat CHAR(1) NOT NULL
   REFERENCES JobCategories(job_cat),
UNIQUE (user_id, job_cat), -- super key!
etc.);

-- this could be a CHECK() in Users table right now

CREATE TABLE JobCategories
(job_cat CHAR(1) NOT NULL PRIMARY KEY, -- {'A', 'B', 'X'}
job_cat_description VARCHAR(50) NOT NULL);
```

The job assignments use the super key as their foreign key. Notice the use of a role prefix on the data element names.

```
CREATE TABLE JobAssignments
(sub_user_id INTEGER NOT NULL,
 sub_job_cat CHAR(1) NOT NULL,
 FOREIGN KEY (sub_user_id, sub_job_cat)
  REFERENCES Users(user_id, job_cat),

super_user_id INTEGER NOT NULL,
super_job_cat CHAR(1) NOT NULL,
FOREIGN KEY (super_user_id, super_job_cat)
 REFERENCES Users(user_id, job_cat),

-- the tricky part!!

CHECK (sub_user_id <> super_user_id), -- assumed

CHECK (CASE WHEN sub_job_cat = 'X' AND super_job_cat
IN ('A', 'B')
            THEN 'T'
            WHEN sub_job_cat = 'A' AND <<other rules??>
            THEN 'T'
            WHEN sub_job_cat = 'B' AND <<other rules??>
            THEN 'T'
            ELSE 'F' END = 'T'),

PRIMARY KEY (sub_user_id, super_user_id),
etc.);
```

This ensures that nobody is their own supervisor and that everyone in job category X has a supervisor, who must be in either job category A or job category B. But again we do not know what to do about A and B users. You can easily expand the CASE expression to as complicated a set of rules as you wish. CASE expressions can be nested inside each other, too.

The question is whether to use positive or negative logic. That is, should the WHEN clauses test for TRUE conditions and accept a row, or test for FALSE conditions and reject a row? For example, in this problem, what if we only reject an X category user without a proper supervisor and accept any other situation?

```
CHECK (CASE WHEN sub_job_cat = 'X' AND super_job_cat
NOT IN ('A', 'B')
            THEN'F' ELSE 'T' END = 'T')
```

In this example, we have a more compact CASE expression, but that is not always true. When you have really complicated rules, I strongly recommend

getting a copy of Logic Gem (*http://www.catalyst.com/products/logicgem/*).
This is a Windows-based decision table tool. You fill in a spreadsheet-like
form with conditions and actions that create your business rules. Once
you've defined the rules, the editor will automatically analyze them. It will
add missing rules, and remove those rules that are redundant or contradic-
tory. You know for certain that you have logically complete business rules
from which you can automatically generate source code.

17.3 Complex Constraints via VIEWs

This was posted by a newbie on an SQL Server newsgroup in a very
different format because of the dialect not being close to ANSI Standards.
While the dialect is a problem, there was another and bigger problem.
The poster was still thinking in terms of procedural code and was forced
by the dialect to write a CURSOR inside the body of the original trigger
code to get the equivalent of a FOR EACH ROW clause. Here is my simplified literal translation, including the original flag code and error message.

```
CREATE TRIGGER InsertStocks
BEFORE INSERT ON Portfolio
REFERENCING NEW ROW AS N
FOR EACH ROW
IF (SELECT P.disabled_flag
      FROM Portfolio AS P
    WHERE P.stock_sym = N.stock_sym) = 1 -- uses a flag!
OR (SELECT P.share_qty - P.max_qty
      FROM Portfolio AS P
      WHERE P.stock_sym = N.stock_sym) <= N.purchase_qty
THEN RETURN ('stock is disabled or maximum level exceeded');
    ROLLBACK;
END IF;
```

This will loop through each row in whatever order the data happens to
be in. A CURSOR could have an ORDER BY clause and force an order
of execution, but in this case, it is not so important because we have a
stock symbol and a purchase number to use as a key.

You can debate the quality of the procedural code inside the cursor.
This modification will probably run faster:

```
CREATE TRIGGER InsertStocks
BEFORE INSERT ON Portfolio
```

```
REFERENCING NEW AS N
IF EXISTS
    (SELECT *
       FROM N, Portfolio AS P
      WHERE P.share_qty + N.purchase_qty <= P.max_qty
        OR P.disabled_flag = 1)
THEN RETURN ('stock is disabled or maximum level exceeded');
    ROLLBACK;
END IF;
```

But they both have the flaw of not returning an exact error message.

17.3.1 Set-Oriented Solutions

Let's look for declarative solutions. The rule about purchasing too much of one stock can be put into an ASSERTION or a table-level CHECK() constraint.

```
CREATE ASSERTION No_Overstock -- pun!
CHECK (NOT EXISTS
        (SELECT *
           FROM Portfolio AS P
          WHERE P.tot_share_qty > P.max_qty));
```

or

```
CREATE TABLE Portfolio
(stock_sym CHAR(5) NOT NULL,
 purchase_nbr INTEGER NOT NULL,
 tot_share_qty DECIMAL(7,4) NOT NULL,
 max_qty DECIMAL(7,4) NOT NULL,
   CHECK (tot_share_qty <= max_qty),
..);
```

The table constraint is probably a better choice. It will be checked only when the Portfolio table is changed, while an assertion works at a global level and tests for empty tables as well as those with rows. Also, the CREATE ASSERTION statement is not widely implemented yet.

The poster never explained the definition of the disabled flag, so it is hard to guess what was meant by it in his or her data model. A Boolean flag simply does not give enough information. But the point is that it served to block a purchase, even if we have no idea what the business rule is. I would tend to favor having a date or date range during which we are only going to buy up to a certain number of shares. This is a more realistic description of how a portfolio is filled over time. You balance supply and demand in such a way as to avoid creating a rush on a stock.

```
Target_qty = shares we want to buy in this period
Tot_share_qty = What we currently hold
Tot_target_qty = What we want to hold

CREATE TABLE StockRestrictions
(stock_sym CHAR(5) NOT NULL,
target_qty DECIMAL(7,4) NOT NULL
    CHECK(target_qty> 0),
purchase_start_date DATE DEFAULT CURRENT_DATE NOT NULL,
purchase_end_date DATE, -- null means ongoing
PRIMARY KEY (stock_sym, start_date);

CREATE TABLE Portfolio
(stock_sym CHAR(5) NOT NULL,
tot_share_qty DECIMAL(7,4) NOT NULL
    CHECK(tot_share_qty > 0),
tot_target_qty DECIMAL(7,4) NOT NULL
    CHECK(tot_target_qty > 0),
..);
```

Let's create a VIEW to show us what stocks we can buy and how many shares of them are allowed today. We count how many shares we already have and compare it to how many shares we want to buy within this time period.

```
CREATE VIEW AllowedStockPurchases (stock_sym, target_qty)
AS
SELECT R.stock_sym, R.target_qty
  FROM StockRestrictions AS R, Portfolio AS P
WHERE R.stock_sym = P.stock_sym
  AND CURRENT_TIMESTAMP BETWEEN R.purchase_start_date
          AND COALESCE (R.purchase_end_date, CURRENT_DATE)
  AND (P.tot_share_qty - R.target_qty) > 0
WITH CHECK OPTION;
```

The bad news is that this VIEW is not updatable and would require an INSTEAD OF trigger to update the portfolio with a new purchase.

17.4　Operations on VIEWs as Constraints

VIEWs are virtual, logical tables that are from base tables in the physical schema. Ideally, the user should not be aware of the differences between a VIEW and a base table. Unfortunately, UPDATE, DELETE, or INSERT operations cannot be done directly on a VIEW. The operations have to resolve down to persistent base tables.

17.4.1　The Basic Three Operations

A base table is always updatable, but VIEWs are not always updatable. All an SQL engine knows about a VIEW is its definition, namely the query that specifies the table derived by the VIEW. An optimizer might be able to detect indexing and constraints on the base tables to construct an execution plan, but this can be pretty complicated.

There are three operations we need to worry about:

■ DELETE Operations: A row in a VIEW must map to one and only one row in a base table.

■ UPDATE Operations: A row in a VIEW must map to one and only one row in a base table, just like a deletion. This only makes sense because an update is modeled as a deletion followed by an insertion. But the VIEW must also map each column to be updated to a column in a base table.

■ INSERT Operations: The new row to be inserted into a VIEW must have all the columns specified in the target base table. This means that a VIEW that can handle an INSERT can be updated, which also implies that you can also delete from it.

17.4.2　WITH CHECK OPTION Clause

If WITH CHECK OPTION is specified in a VIEW declaration, the viewed table has to be updatable. This is actually a fast way to check how your particular SQL implementation handles updatable VIEWs. Try to create a version of the VIEW in question using the WITH CHECK OPTION and see if your product will allow you to create it. The WITH CHECK OPTION is part of the SQL-89 standard, which was extended in Standard SQL by adding an optional <levels clause>. CASCADED is implicit if an explicit LEVEL clause is not given. Consider a VIEW defined as

```
CREATE VIEW V1
AS SELECT *
   FROM Foobar
   WHERE col1 = 'A';
```

and now UPDATE it with

```
UPDATE V1 SET col1 = 'B';
```

The UPDATE will take place without any trouble, but the rows that were previously seen now disappear when we use V1 again. They no longer meet the WHERE clause condition! Likewise, an INSERT INTO statement with VALUES (col1 = 'B') would insert just fine, but its rows would never be seen again in this VIEW. VIEWs created this way will always have all the rows that meet the criteria, and that can be handy. For example, you can set up a VIEW of rows with a status code of "to be done", work on them, and change a status code to "finished", and they will disappear from your view. The important point is that the WHERE clause condition was checked only at the time when the VIEW was invoked.

The WITH CHECK OPTION makes the system check the WHERE clause condition upon insertion or UPDATE. If the new or changed row fails the test, the change is rejected and the VIEW remains the same. Thus, the previous UPDATE statement would get an error message and you could not change certain columns in certain ways. For example, consider a VIEW of salaries under $30,000 defined with a WITH CHECK OPTION to prevent anyone from giving a raise above that ceiling.

The WITH CHECK OPTION clause does not work like a CHECK constraint.

```
CREATE TABLE Foobar (col_a INTEGER);

CREATE VIEW TestView (col_a)
AS
SELECT col_a FROM Foobar WHERE col_a > 0
WITH CHECK OPTION;

INSERT INTO TestView VALUES (NULL); -- This fails!

CREATE TABLE Foobar_2 (col_a INTEGER CHECK (col_a > 0));
INSERT INTO Foobar_2(col_a)
VALUES (NULL); -- This succeeds!
```

The WITH CHECK OPTION must be TRUE while the CHECK constraint can be either TRUE or UNKNOWN. Once more, you need to watch out for NULLs.

Standard SQL has introduced an optional <levels clause>, which can be either CASCADED or LOCAL. If no <levels clause> is given, a <levels clause> of CASCADED is implicit. The idea of a CASCADED check is that the system checks all the underlying levels that built the VIEW, as well as the WHERE clause condition in the VIEW itself. If anything causes a row to disappear from the VIEW, the UPDATE is rejected. The idea of a WITH LOCAL check option is that only the local WHERE clause is checked. The underlying VIEWs or tables from which this VIEW is built might also be affected, but we do not test for those effects.

Consider two VIEWs built on each other from the salary table:

```
CREATE VIEW Lowpay
AS SELECT *
    FROM Personnel
  WHERE salary <= 250;

CREATE VIEW Mediumpay
AS SELECT *
    FROM Lowpay
  WHERE salary >= 100;
```

If neither VIEW has a WITH CHECK OPTION, the effect of updating Mediumpay by increasing every salary by $1,000 will be passed without any check to Lowpay. Lowpay will pass the changes to the underlying Personnel table. The next time Mediumpay is used, Lowpay will be rebuilt in its own right and Mediumpay rebuilt from it, and all the employees will disappear from Mediumpay.

If only Mediumpay has a WITH CASCADED CHECK OPTION on it, the UPDATE will fail. Mediumpay has no problem with such a large salary, but it would cause a row in Lowpay to disappear, so Mediumpay will reject it. However, if only Mediumpay has a WITH LOCAL CHECK OPTION on it, the UPDATE will succeed. Mediumpay has no problem with such a large salary, so it passes the change along to Lowpay. Lowpay, in turn, passes the change to the Personnel table and the UPDATE occurs. If both VIEWs have a WITH CASCADED CHECK OPTION, the effect is a set of conditions, all of which have to be met. The Personnel table can accept UPDATEs or INSERTs only where the salary is between $100 and $250.

This can become very complex. Consider an example from an ANSI X3H2 paper by Nelson Mattos of IBM (Celko 1993). Let us build a five-layer set of VIEWs, using xx and yy as place holders for CASCADED or LOCAL, on a base table T1 with columns c1, c2, c3, c4, and c5, all set to a value of 10, thus:

```
CREATE VIEW V1 AS SELECT * FROM T1 WHERE (c1 > 5);

CREATE VIEW V2 AS SELECT * FROM V1 WHERE (c2 > 5)
       WITH xx CHECK OPTION;

CREATE VIEW V3 AS SELECT * FROM V2 WHERE (c3 > 5);

CREATE VIEW V4 AS SELECT * FROM V3 WHERE (c4 > 5)
       WITH yy CHECK OPTION;

CREATE VIEW V5 AS SELECT * FROM V4 WHERE (c5 > 5);
```

When we set each one of the columns to zero, we get different results, which can be shown in this chart, where S means success and F means failure:

```
      xx/yy           c1   c2   c3   c4   c5
====================================
  cascade/cascade     F    F    F    F    S
  local/cascade       F    F    F    F    S
  local/local         S    F    S    F    S
  cascade/local       F    F    S    F    S
```

To understand the chart, look at the last line. If xx = CASCADED and yy = LOCAL, updating column c1 to zero via V5 will fail, whereas updating c5 will succeed. Remember that a successful UPDATE means the row(s) disappear from V5.

Follow the action for UPDATE V5 SET c1 = 0; VIEW V5 has no WITH CHECK OPTIONs, so the changed rows are immediately sent to V4 without any testing. VIEW V4 does have a WITH LOCAL CHECK OPTION, but column c1 is not involved, so V4 passes the rows to V3. VIEW V3 has no WITH CHECK OPTIONs, so the changed rows are immediately sent to V2. VIEW V2 does have a WITH CASCADED CHECK OPTION, so V2 passes the rows to V1 and awaits results. VIEW V1 is built on the original base table and has the condition c1 > 5, which is violated by this UPDATE. VIEW V1 then rejects the UPDATE to the base table, so the rows remain in V5 when it is rebuilt. Now the action for

```
UPDATE V5 SET c3 = 0;
```

VIEW V5 has no WITH CHECK OPTIONs, so the changed rows are immediately sent to V4, as before. VIEW V4 does have a WITH LOCAL CHECK OPTION, but column c3 is not involved, so V4 passes the rows to V3 without awaiting the results. VIEW V3 is involved with column c3 and has no WITH CHECK OPTIONs, so the rows can be changed and passed down to V2 and V1, where they UPDATE the base table. The rows are not seen again when V5 is invoked, because they will fail to get past VIEW V3. The real problem comes with UPDATE statements that change more than one column at a time. For example,

```
UPDATE V5 SET c1 = 0, c2 = 0, c3 = 0, c4 = 0, c5 = 0;
```

will fail for all possible combinations of <levels clause>s in the example schema.

Standard SQL defines the idea of a set of conditions that are inherited by the levels of nesting. In our sample schema, these implied tests would be added to each VIEW definition:

```
local/local
V1 = none
V2 = (c2 > 5)
V3 = (c2 > 5)
V4 = (c2 > 5) AND (c4 > 5)
V5 = (c2 > 5) AND (c4 > 5)

cascade/cascade
V1 = none
V2 = (c1 > 5) AND (c2 > 5)
V3 = (c1 > 5) AND (c2 > 5)
V4 = (c1 > 5) AND (c2 > 5) AND (c3 > 5) AND (c4 > 5)
V5 = (c1 > 5) AND (c2 > 5) AND (c3 > 5) AND (c4 > 5)

local/cascade
V1 = none
V2 = (c2 > 5)
V3 = (c2 > 5)
V4 = (c1 > 5) AND (c2 > 5) AND (c4 > 5)
V5 = (c1 > 5) AND (c2 > 5) AND (c4 > 5)

cascade/local
V1 = none
V2 = (c1 > 5) AND (c2 > 5)
V3 = (c1 > 5) AND (c2 > 5)
```

```
V4 = (c1 > 5) AND (c2 > 5) AND (c4 > 5)
V5 = (c1 > 5) AND (c2 > 5) AND (c4 > 5)
```

17.4.3 WITH CHECK OPTION as CHECK() clause

Lothar Flatz, an instructor for Oracle Software Switzerland, made the observation that while Oracle cannot put subqueries into CHECK() constraints, and triggers would not be possible because of the mutating table problem, you can use a VIEW that has a WITH CHECK OPTION to enforce subquery constraints.

For example, consider a hotel registry that needs to have a rule that you cannot add a guest to a room that another is or will be occupying. You could write the constraint directly, like this:

```
CREATE TABLE Hotel
(room_nbr INTEGER NOT NULL,
arrival_date DATE NOT NULL,
departure_date DATE NOT NULL,
guest_name CHAR(30) NOT NULL,
CONSTRAINT schedule_right
CHECK (H1.arrival_date <= H1.departure_date),
CONSTRAINT no_overlaps
CHECK (NOT EXISTS
      (SELECT *
         FROM Hotel AS H1, Hotel AS H2
        WHERE H1.room_nbr = H2.room_nbr
          AND H2.arrival_date < H1.arrival_date
          AND H1.arrival_date < H2.departure_date)));
```

The schedule_right constraint is fine, since it has no subquery, but many products will choke on the no_overlaps constraint. Leaving the no_overlaps constraint off the table, we can construct a VIEW on all the rows and columns of the Hotel base table and add a WHERE clause which will be enforced by the WITH CHECK OPTION.

```
CREATE VIEW Hotel_V (room_nbr, arrival_date,
departure_date, guest_name)
AS SELECT H1.room_nbr, H1.arrival_date, H1.departure_date,
H1.guest_name
     FROM Hotel AS H1
    WHERE NOT EXISTS
          (SELECT *
             FROM Hotel AS H2
```

```
            WHERE H1.room_nbr = H2.room_nbr
              AND H2.arrival_date < H1.arrival_date
              AND H1.arrival_date < H2.departure_date)
        AND H1.arrival_date <= H1.departure_date
   WITH CHECK OPTION;
```

For example,

```
INSERT INTO Hotel_V
VALUES (1, '2006-01-01', '2006-01-03', 'Ron Coe');
COMMIT;
INSERT INTO Hotel_V
VALUES (1, '2006-01-03', '2006-01-05', 'John Doe');
```

will give a WITH CHECK OPTION clause violation on the second
INSERT INTO statement, as we wanted.

17.4.4 How VIEWs Behave

Let's now define a few simple tables and then investigate the updatability of various VIEWs of those tables. Using an example from Serge
Rielau, consider these two very simple tables and VIEW.

```
CREATE TABLE Foo -- not a proper table!
(c1 INTEGER NOT NULL,
 c2 DECIMAL(3,1));
INSERT INTO Foo VALUES (5, 6.0), (6, 7.0), (5, 6.0);

CREATE TABLE Bar -- not a proper table!
(c1 INTEGER NOT NULL,
 c2 DECIMAL(3,1));
INSERT INTO Bar VALUES (5, 9.0), (5, 4.0), (7, 5.0);

CREATE VIEW V1(c1)
AS SELECT c1 FROM Foo WHERE c2 > 0;
```

This is a very simple VIEW. The derived table contains a subset of the
rows and a subset of the columns of Foo. Neither of these tables has a
key declared, but the statement:

```
DELETE FROM V1 WHERE c1 = 6;
```

Can find one row and remove it from Foo. However, the statement:

```
DELETE FROM V1 WHERE c1 = 5;
```

References the two rows where `Foo.c1` equals 5, so you have no idea which one or both should be deleted.

This VIEW is also updatable:

```
UPDATE V1 SET c1 = c1 + 5 WHERE c1 = 5;
```

because `V1.c1` can be directly mapped to `Foo.c1`.

What about INSERT? Without key or other constraints, I can insert any row inserted into V1 that could be inserted into Foo. But I have no idea what to use for `Foo.c2`. If I had a DEFAULT clause, I could use that value explicitly. When a VIEW is defined its column defaults are inherited from the underlying base tables for updatable columns. If a column is not updatable (without the help of an INSTEAD OF trigger) then the DEFAULT is effectively NULL.

Assigning Expressions

What happens when there is an expression? Let's create a second VIEW.

```
CREATE VIEW V2(c1, c2)
AS SELECT c1, (c2 * c2) FROM Foo;
```

SQL still knows which row in the VIEW was produced by which row in the base table. The `V2.c1` column is updatable, and therefore the VIEW is updatable. However, `V2.c2` is not updatable. The reason is that there is no way to decide the value of `Foo.c2` from any given `V2.c2`.

Maybe you could use a square root algorithm to find the inverse of the multiplication for a value. But this is not practical and makes no sense in theory. Can you think of a universal algorithm for getting an inverse function based on only the data?

Watch out for vendor differences. Prior to DB2 version 8, a VIEW was required to have all columns updatable for an insertion, but in DB2 version 8 it is sufficient to have just one updatable column.

```
INSERT INTO V2(c1) VALUES (7);
```

The system will insert (7, NULL) into Foo. Note that you could delete from the VIEW, even if no column is updatable. By the same reason, the only argument against inserting into a VIEW with no updatable columns is that neither VALUES nor SELECT is defined without a single column.

Try another VIEW:

```
CREATE VIEW V3(c1, c2, c3)
AS SELECT Foo.c1, Foo.c2, Bar.c2
```

```
FROM Foo, Bar
WHERE Foo.c1 = Bar.c1;
```

This VIEW is derived from a JOIN. In this case, its result is:

```
 c1   c2    c3
===============
  5   6.0   4.0
  5   6.0   4.0
  5   6.0   9.0
  5   6.0   9.0
```

You cannot delete from this VIEW. While each row in the VIEW can be traced back to one row in each of the tables Foo and Bar, deleting the first row (5, 6.0, 4.0) by deleting the respective rows in Foo and Bar would also indirectly delete the second (5, 6.0, 4.0) and one of the two (5, 6.0, 9.0) rows. This behavior is hard to understand if you do not know the VIEW definition.

There are cases in which a deleted row in the VIEW results in one row deleted in the base table without having an undesired impact on the VIEW. This would be the case if, for example, both Foo.c1 and Bar.c1 were unique. SQL today does not consider this a special case.

A quick inspection will convince you that V3 is not updatable.

17.4.5 UNIONed VIEWs

```
CREATE VIEW V4(c1, c2)
AS SELECT c1, c2 FROM Foo
   UNION ALL
   SELECT c1, c2 FROM Bar;
```

Every row in V4 clearly originated from one row in a specific table. Therefore, you can delete from a VIEW based on UNION ALL. If a column is not based on an expression, then the column is also updatable.

However, you cannot insert into V4 for the obvious reason that you have no idea to which base table any given row should be inserted. It makes no sense to put it in both base tables, because a subsequent SELECT from the VIEW would show the row twice. To allow INSERT through UNION ALL, constraints are required on the base tables that dispatch any given row to exactly one table. But then your SQL engine has to be able to detect that. It gets worse; a column of a UNION ALL VIEW might not be updatable because of hidden CAST() functions.

```
CREATE VIEW V5(c1, c2)
AS SELECT c2, c1 FROM Foo
   UNION ALL
   SELECT c1, c2 FROM Bar;
```

SQL had to cast both `Bar.c1` and `Foo.c1` to `DECIMAL(3, 1)`.
Both `V5.c1` and `V5.c2` are now based on expressions and thus not
updatable. Nonetheless, you can still delete rows in V5.

Let's try a self-UNIONed VIEW like this:

```
CREATE VIEW V6(c1, c2)
AS SELECT c1, c2 FROM Foo
   UNION ALL
   SELECT c1, c2 FROM Foo;
```

A VIEW like V6 is also called a "diamond" because the processing fans
out from a single source into two operations (SELECT) and then
comes back together again (UNION ALL). Diamonds are read-only.
The rows cannot even be deleted. The reason is that each row from Foo
is represented twice in V6. So it is not possible to delete just one row
in V6. Also, it is not possible to update one row only.

The reverse problem arises when a UNION (or DISTINCT) is used.
Now each row in the VIEW can be mapped to potentially many rows in
the base table. Should only one row or all matching rows in the base
table be deleted?

17.4.6 Simple INSTEAD OF Triggers

The solution for all of the complications mentioned above is the
INSTEAD OF trigger. An INSTEAD OF trigger catches the INSERT,
UPDATE, or DELETE action and does a body of procedural code instead
of the expected actions.

```
CREATE VIEW V7(c1, c2)
AS SELECT DISTINCT c1, c2 FROM Foo;
```

An INSTEAD OF trigger can be defined to delete all rows in Foo
matching a given row in V7 or to delete only one according to some
predetermined rule. Let's define a trigger that deletes all matching rows
in the base table:

```
CREATE TRIGGER V7_delete INSTEAD OF DELETE ON V7
REFERENCING OLD AS O FOR EACH ROW
```

```
DELETE FROM Foo
 WHERE O.c1 = c1 AND O.c2 = c2;
```

Superficially, only two clauses have changed compared to a normal trigger. First, we defined the keywords INSTEAD OF. Second, we specified the name of a VIEW rather than a base table.

INSTEAD OF is a very clear clause. It does not mean execute the trigger before attempting the delete. It does not mean do it after. It literally means forget about the delete and execute this piece of code instead.

In some products, the INSTEAD OF triggers are always created for VIEWs, never for base tables. Other products treat them as BEFORE triggers on base tables. Vendors may also disagree on uses of the FOR EACH ROW options. This means the trigger is executed once for each row that qualifies for the DELETE, UPDATE, or INSERT operation against the VIEW. It is not so important for a DELETE, but could make problems if INSERT and UPDATE actions are performed multiple times.

A typical scenario requiring joins and updates to all tables (at the same time) is the vertical partitioning of the data. To keep things simple, we use a schema of Persons. Some Persons are employed, others are enrolled as students. Some Persons are both employed and students.

```
CREATE TABLE Persons
(ssn CHAR(9) NOT NULL PRIMARY KEY,
person_name VARCHAR(20) NOT NULL);

CREATE TABLE Workers
(ssn CHAR(9) NOT NULL PRIMARY KEY
    REFERENCES Persons(ssn),
company_name VARCHAR(20) NOT NULL,
salary_amt DECIMAL(9,2)NOT NULL);

CREATE TABLE Students
(ssn CHAR(9) NOT NULL PRIMARY KEY
    REFERENCES Persons(ssn),
university_name VARCHAR(20) NOT NULL,
major CHAR(5) NOT NULL);
```

To join all these tables together in the application can be annoying. So we create a VIEW:

```
CREATE VIEW Everybody(ssn, person_name, company_name,
                salary_amt, university_name, major)
```

```
AS SELECT P.ssn, P.person_name, W.company_name,
          W.salary_amt, S.university_name, S.major
FROM Persons AS P
     LEFT OUTER JOIN
     Workers AS W
     ON P.ssn = W.ssn
      LEFT OUTER JOIN
      Students AS S
       ON P.ssn = S.ssn;
```

This VIEW cannot be INSERTed into, UPDATEd, or DELETEd from, so we will need all three kinds of INSTEAD OF triggers.

Insertion with INSTEAD OF

The usual template uses conditional logic to determine which tables will get new rows.

```
CREATE TRIGGER Insert_Everybody
INSTEAD OF INSERT ON Everybody
REFERENCING NEW AS N FOR EACH ROW
BEGIN ATOMIC
-- the new guys will always be in Persons
 INSERT INTO Persons VALUES (N.ssn, N.person_name);
-- he is a student, if he has a school
 IF N.university_name IS NOT NULL
 THEN INSERT INTO Students
     VALUES (N.ssn, N.university_name, N.major);
 END IF;
-- he is a worker if he has a company
 IF N.company_name IS NOT NULL
 THEN INSERT INTO Workers
     VALUES (N.ssn, N.company_name, N.salary);
 END IF;
 END;
```

That handles insertions; now let's do deletions.

Deletion with INSTEAD OF

This is a little easier, since the WHERE clause does all the work.

```
CREATE TRIGGER Delete_Everybody
INSTEAD OF DELETE ON Everybody
```

```
REFERENCING OLD AS O FOR EACH ROW
BEGIN ATOMIC
DELETE FROM Students WHERE ssn = O.ssn;
DELETE FROM Workers WHERE ssn = O.ssn;
DELETE FROM Persons WHERE ssn = O.ssn;
END;
```

Updating with INSTEAD OF

Updates are trickier. If a person graduates or enters school, gets a job or loses a job, then we have to update one or both of those tables.

```
CREATE TRIGGER Update_Everybody
INSTEAD OF UPDATE ON Everybody
REFERENCING OLD AS O NEW AS N
FOR EACH ROW
BEGIN ATOMIC
UPDATE Persons
   SET ssn = N.ssn, person_name = N.person_name
 WHERE ssn = O.ssn;
IF N.university_name IS NOT NULL
   AND O.university_name IS NOT NULL
THEN
 UPDATE Students
    SET ssn = N.ssn,
        university_name = N.university_name,
        major = N.major
    WHERE ssn = O.ssn;
ELSE IF N.university_name IS NULL
     THEN DELETE FROM Students WHERE ssn = O.ssn;
     ELSE INSERT INTO Students
          VALUES (N.ssn, N.university_name, N.major);
     END IF;
END IF;
IF N.company_name IS NOT NULL
   AND O.company_name IS NOT NULL
THEN UPDATE Workers
        SET ssn = N.ssn,
            company_name = N.company_name,
            salary_amt = N.salary_amt
     WHERE ssn = O.ssn;
ELSE IF N.company_name IS NULL
```

```
            THEN DELETE FROM Workers WHERE ssn = O.ssn;
            ELSE INSERT INTO Workers
                  VALUES (N.ssn, N.company_name, N.salary_amt);
            END IF;
     END IF;
     END;
```

17.4.7 Warnings about INSTEAD OF Triggers

This is a relatively new feature in SQL and each vendor will have some differences in semantics and syntax because they have to support their proprietary TRIGGER syntax. Most of the current implementations are row-level triggers that are executed once for each row. However, it is possible to have table-level triggers. Recursive triggers are also a problem.

The best approach is to keep them as simple and direct as possible. Declare INSERT, DELETE, and UPDATE triggers on important nonupdatable VIEWs, even if you do not think you will do all of the three operations. You are probably wrong.

CHAPTER 18

Procedural and Data-Driven Solutions

WE USED TO joke that SQL stands for "Scarcely Qualifies as a Language" because it lacks input and output formatting as well as special functions that other languages have to do particular jobs. What is forgotten is that SQL is a data management language, and it was never meant to do certain jobs.

Statistical and mathematical packages can handle floating-point rounding errors and provide libraries of complex functions. String and document base languages can search and manipulate character data far faster and easier than SQL. The only data structure in SQL is a multiset, so you cannot easily do operations that involve arrays.

This does not mean that you cannot do some of these things in SQL; but you need to know when you will hit a limit or have complicated code to maintain. There are problems that are better solved in other programming languages.

18.1 Removing Letters in a String

We had previously seen an example of how to remove extra blanks from a string of characters in pure SQL. Consider another version of that kind of problem. Given a string of characters, remove all the redundant duplicate letters from it, in left-to-right order. An example will make this clear: "abcbdabcbcc" would reduce to "abcd" because those four letters appear one or more times to the left of their n-th occurrence (n > 1) in the string of characters.

Let's create some sample data and expected results.

```
CREATE TABLE Wordlist
(word_key INTEGER NOT NULL PRIMARY KEY,
 word_txt VARCHAR(25) NOT NULL);

INSERT INTO Wordlist VALUES (1, 'aaaaaa'); -- 'a'
INSERT INTO Wordlist VALUES (2, 'abababa'); -- 'ab'
INSERT INTO Wordlist VALUES (3, 'abcdeaccc'); -- 'abcde'
INSERT INTO Wordlist VALUES (4, 'abbcdeab'); -- 'abcde'
INSERT INTO Wordlist VALUES (5, 'abcdefg'); -- 'abcdefg'
```

18.1.1   The Procedural Solution

Assuming that we have a replacement function in the SQL we are using, the obvious way to do this for one word at a time is:

```
CREATE PROCEDURE TrimDups (my_word VARCHAR(50))
LANGUAGE SQL
DETERMINISTIC
BEGIN
DECLARE i INTEGER;
SET i = 1;
WHILE i <= CHARLENGTH (my_word)
DO SET my_word
     = SUBSTRING (my_word FROM 1 FOR i)
        || REPLACE (SUBSTRING (my_word FROM i+1
                                FOR CHARLENGTH (my_word)),
                    SUBSTRING (my_word FROM i FOR 1), '');
SET i = i + 1;
END WHILE;
END;
```

The idea is to move a pointer for the current letter from left to right, look at the current letter, and replace it with an empty string in the remaining right side of the word. Since we are moving from left to right, we know the current letter is its first occurrence in the word.

But if I were writing in ICON or SNOBOL, this problem would be one statement. Those languages are designed for string manipulations.

18.1.2 Pure SQL Solution

Let us start by considering how we can classify a letter in the word as a "keeper" or a "kill" letter. Standard SQL has a function that finds the first occurrence of a string within another string called POSITION(); proprietary versions of the same thing exist as CHARINDEX(), and so forth.

```
CREATE VIEW Keepers(word_key, seq)
AS
SELECT word_key, seq
  FROM Wordlist AS W, Sequence AS S
WHERE S.seq < CHARLENGTH(word_txt)
  AND POSITION (SUBSTRING (word_txt FROM S.seq FOR 1)
               IN SUBSTRING (word_txt FROM 1 FOR
               S.seq-1)) = 0;
```

A simple change would give us a table with the word and the positions of the letters to be removed:

```
CREATE VIEW Kills (word_key, seq)
AS
SELECT word_key, seq
  FROM Wordlist AS W, Sequence AS S
 WHERE S.seq < CHARLENGTH(word_txt)
   AND POSITION (SUBSTRING (word_txt FROM S.seq FOR 1)
                IN SUBSTRING (word_txt FROM 1 FOR
                S.seq-1)) <> 0;
```

The idea of both of these is to split up the string into characters and position numbers. I can use these tables to do an UPDATE to my Wordlist table. But Standard SQL does not have a lot of fancy string operators— and neither do proprietary extensions. Examining one letter at a time is difficult. This is long but easily generated with any good text editor.

```
UPDATE Wordlist
 SET word_txt
    SUBSTRING(word_txt FROM 1 FOR 1) -- always a keeper
    || CASE WHEN EXISTS
              (SELECT *
                 FROM Keepers AS K
                WHERE K.word_key = Wordlist.word_key
```

```
                          AND K.seq = 2)
            THEN SUBSTRING(word_txt FROM 2 FOR 1)
            ELSE '' END
  || CASE WHEN EXISTS
              (SELECT *
                FROM Keepers AS K
               WHERE K.word_key = Wordlist.word_key
                 AND K.seq = 3)
            THEN SUBSTRING(word_txt FROM 3 FOR 1)
            ELSE '' END

   ..
    || CASE WHEN EXISTS
              (SELECT *
                FROM Keepers AS K
               WHERE K.word_key = Wordlist.word_key
                 AND K.seq = <n>)
            THEN SUBSTRING(word_txt FROM <n> FOR 1)
            ELSE '' END;
```

The CASE expressions break up the original string; see if the position is
a keeper or a kill; replace it with itself or an empty string; and concatenate the characters back into a new string.

18.1.3 Impure SQL Solution

You can split the string into letters recursively in a CTE without using
the concatenated SUBSTRING() calls.

```
WITH Letters (place, letter)
AS (-- Break up the string into single characters
VALUES (1, SUBSTRING(:test_string FROM 1 FOR 1)
UNION ALL
SELECT place+1, SUBSTRING (:test_string FROM place FOR 1)
  FROM Wordlist
WHERE place < CHARLENGTH(:test_string)),
```

The bad news is that this works for only one string at a time, so you can
only use it in a function call.

18.2 Two Approaches to Sudoku

Sudoku, the current puzzle fad, started in the United States in 1979
in *Games* magazine, then caught on in Japan in 1986 and became

an international fad in 2005. Most newspapers today carry a daily Sudoku. You start with a nine-by-nine grid that is further divided into nine three-by-three regions. Some of the cells will hold a digit from 1 to 9 in them at the start of the puzzle. Your goal is to fill in all the cells with more digits, such that each row, column, and region contains one and only one instance of each digit.

There are two general approaches to the puzzle. One is to assume that you have a grid with all possible digits in each cell, and then remove the digits that we know cannot be there. The second approach is to copy the grid, using a place marker such as zero for the unknown digits, and then update the cells to the one allowed value.

18.2.1 Procedural Approach

There are many Sudoku solvers in open source software, and you can buy dedicated handheld devices for the puzzle.

One common procedural method is called "back tracking" to solve the puzzle. The known numbers are put into the grid, which is modeled with an array in a conventional programming language. The program looks for the row, column, or region with the most known numbers and begins trying to insert the rest of the nine digits into that row, column, or region. Each arrangement of digits is tested to see if it is legal or not. The possible legal patterns are kept and the process is repeated until a complete grid can be constructed.

If you have a programming language that supports arrays, this problem is very easy to model.

18.2.2 Data-Driven Approach

How can we do this in SQL? We can start by modeling the grid as an (i, j) array with a value in the cell. The first attempt usually does not have the region information as one of the columns. The regions do not have names in the puzzle, so we need a way to give them names or tag numbers.

```
CREATE TABLE SudokuGrid
(i INTEGER NOT NULL
  CHECK (i BETWEEN 1 AND 9),
 j INTEGER NOT NULL
  CHECK (j BETWEEN 1 AND 9),
 val INTEGER NOT NULL
  CHECK (val BETWEEN 1 AND 9),
```

```
region_nbr INTEGER NOT NULL
  CHECK (region_nbr BETWEEN 1 AND 9),
PRIMARY KEY (i, j, val));
```

A popular manual solution technique is to put nine dots in a 3×3 pattern in each empty Sudoku cell. The dots represent the digits 1 to 9, and you cross out or erase them as you eliminate a digit from that cell. Let's fill in our grid in the same way. Each (i, j) cell needs to start with all nine digits, so we build a table of the digits 1 to 9 and do CROSS JOINs.

A region number is a little harder. An obvious name would be to assign a letter like A thru I to each region. You might want to try this approach to see why I rejected it. It required too much table lookup and funny-looking joins.

Another way is the position of the region by (x, y) coordinates where x = {1, 2, 3} and y = {1, 2, 3}. We can then make them into one number by making x coordinate the tens place and y coordinate the units place, so we get {11, 12, 13, 21, 22, 23, 31, 32, 33} for the regions. The math for this depends on integer arithmetic, but it is not really hard.

If you just do integer division by 3, you get this result for the digits:

Digit	digit/3
1	0
2	0
3	1
4	1
5	1
6	2
7	2
8	2
9	3

Not quite what I would like, but close enough so I can see how to shift the results up "two slots" to get what I want.

```
INSERT INTO SudokuGrid (i, j, val, region_nbr)
SELECT D1.d, D2.d, D3.d,
       10*((D1.d+2)/3) + ((D2.d+2)/3) AS region_nbr
  FROM Digits AS D1
```

```
CROSS JOIN Digits AS D2
CROSS JOIN Digits AS D3;
```

This expression can also be put into a CHECK() constraint on the table for each row.

18.2.3 Handling the Given Digits

We will need a procedure to insert the known values and clear out that value in the rows, columns, and regions. As we removed more and more values, we hope to get a table with 81 cells that is the unique solution for the puzzle.

The first attempt is usually to write three delete statements, one for rows, one for columns, and one for the regions. The input is a triple (:my_i, :my_j, :my_val), like this:

```
BEGIN -- wrong!!
DELETE FROM SudokuGrid -- rows
WHERE :my_i = i
  AND :my_j <> j
  AND :my_val = val;

DELETE FROM SudokuGrid -- columns
WHERE :my_i <> i
  AND :my_j = j
  AND :my_val = val;

DELETE FROM SudokuGrid -- region
WHERE i <> :my_i
  AND j <> :my_j
  AND region_nbr = 10*((:my_i+2)/3) + ((:my_j+2)/3)
  AND :my_val = val);
END;
```

But this is a waste of execution time. Why use three statements, when you can write it in one? Let's do a brute force code merge.

```
DELETE FROM SudokuGrid
WHERE ((((:my_i = i AND j <> :my_j)
      OR (:my_i <> i AND j = :my_j))
    AND :my_val = val)
  OR (i <> :my_i
      AND j <> :my_j
```

```
AND region_nbr = 10*((:my_i+2)/3) + ((:my_j+2)/3)
AND :my_val = val);
```

Those nested ORs are ugly! The expression (:my_val = val) appears
twice. Step back and consider that the (i, j) pairs can relate to our
input in one of four mutually exclusive ways, which require that we
remove a value from a cell or leave it. That implies a CASE expression
instead of the nested ANDs and ORs. That gives us the second attempt.

```
DELETE FROM SudokuGrid -- wrong!!
WHERE CASE WHEN :my_i = i AND :my_j = j -- my cell
        THEN 'Keep'
        WHEN :my_i = i AND :my_j <> j -- row
        THEN 'Delete'
        WHEN :my_i <> i AND :my_j = j -- column
        THEN 'Delete'
        WHEN i <> :my_i AND j <> :my_j -- region
            AND region_nbr
              = 10*(:my_i+2)/3) + (:my_j+2)/3)
        THEN 'Delete'
        ELSE NULL END = 'Delete'
      AND :my_val = val);
```

Test it and put it in a stored procedure. It fails because it does not cover
all the possible cases. When the (i, j) coordinates match, the cell
value, that third dimension, may or may not match—two separate cases!
When I gave this as a class problem, this was the most often missed
fact by students. The val column was seen as content and not as third
dimension, so it got lost.

```
DELETE FROM SudokuGrid
WHERE CASE WHEN :my_i = i AND :my_j = j
              AND :my_val <> val -- my cell #1
          THEN 'Delete'
          WHEN :my_i = i AND :my_j = j
              AND :my_val = val -- my cell #2
          THEN 'Keep'
          WHEN :my_i = i AND :my_j <> j -- row
              AND :my_val = val -- my cell
          THEN 'Delete'
          WHEN :my_i <> i AND :my_j = j -- column
              AND :my_val = val -- my cell
```

```
              THEN 'Delete'
              WHEN i <> :my_i AND j <> :my_j -- region
                   AND region_nbr
                     = 10*(:my_i+2)/3) + (:my_j+2)/3)
                   AND :my_val = val -- my cell
              THEN 'Delete'
              ELSE NULL END = 'Delete');
```

A trick here is that the WHEN clauses are executed in the order they are written. If you can make the WHEN predicates independent of execution order, then you can place them in any order. However, you can use that order of execution to advantage. Within the known (i, j) cell, we can immediately remove eight values, so do that first. Rows and columns have about the same payoff, and then a region can only have four values to remove.

The next improvement might be to put the known cells into their own table, so we have a history of the puzzle. But let's leave that as a problem for the reader.

18.3 Data Constraint Approach

This method is due to Richard Romley. The idea is to UNION a SudokuGrid with the given digits to a constrained grid that has all the constraints imposed on each cell. The code gets a bit long, but it is repetitive and can be easily generated with a text editor. I will simply show the skeleton to save space.

But Richard also demonstrated another technique that makes many newbie SQL programmers nervous—long parameter lists.

```
CREATE PROCEDURE SolveSudoku
(IN r1c1 INTEGER, IN r1c2 INTEGER, IN r1c3 INTEGER,
 IN r1c4 INTEGER, IN r1c5 INTEGER, IN r1c6 INTEGER,
 IN r1c7 INTEGER, IN r1c8 INTEGER, IN r1c9 INTEGER,
 ..
 IN r9c1 INTEGER, IN r9c2 INTEGER, IN r9c3 INTEGER,
 IN r9c4 INTEGER, IN r9c5 INTEGER, IN r9c6 INTEGER,
 IN r9c7 INTEGER, IN r9c8 INTEGER, IN r9c9 INTEGER)

LANGUAGE SQL
DETERMINISTIC
...
```

The procedure uses one parameter for each of the 81 cells in the grid. The names are generated with the template "r#c#" for the row and column numbers. The nice part is that this lets you map the procedure call to a GUI front end where one box on the screen puts a digit into a parameter.

```
BEGIN
IF r1c1 BETWEEN 1 AND 9
 THEN UPDATE SudokuGrid
         SET val = r1c1
      WHERE (i, j) = (1, 1);
END IF;
...
IF r9c9 BETWEEN 1 AND 9
 THEN UPDATE SudokuGrid
         SET val = r9c9
      WHERE (i, j) = (9, 9);
END IF;
```

Move the values from the parameter list into the SudokuGrid table. Parameters that were not provided will be NULL.

```
-- T is a temporary table, with three integer columns
INSERT INTO T(i, j, val) -- all possible values
for each cell
SELECT i, j, val              -- known cell values
  FROM SudokuGrid
 WHERE val IS NOT NULL
UNION ALL
 SELECT S1.i, S1.j, Digits.d -- unknown cells possible values
   FROM SudokuGrid AS S1
        CROSS JOIN
        Digits
  WHERE S1.val IS NULL
    AND NOT EXISTS
          (SELECT *
             FROM SudokuGrid AS S2
            WHERE S2.val = Digits.d
              AND (S2.i = S1.i
                   OR S2.j = S1.j
                   OR S2.region_nbr = S1.region_nbr));
```

```
INSERT INTO Solution (i, j, val) -- solution values
SELECT S.i, S.j,
        CASE -- 81 cells have the proper value for (i, j)
        WHEN S.i = 1 AND S.j = 1 THEN T11.val
        WHEN S.i = 1 AND S.j = 2 THEN T12.val
        WHEN S.i = 1 AND S.j = 3 THEN T13.val
        WHEN S.i = 1 AND S.j = 4 THEN T14.val
        WHEN S.i = 1 AND S.j = 5 THEN T15.val
        WHEN S.i = 1 AND S.j = 6 THEN T16.val
        WHEN S.i = 1 AND S.j = 7 THEN T17.val
        WHEN S.i = 1 AND S.j = 8 THEN T18.val
        WHEN S.i = 1 AND S.j = 9 THEN T19.val

           . . .

        WHEN S.i = 9 AND S.j = 1 THEN T91.val
        WHEN S.i = 9 AND S.j = 2 THEN T92.val
        WHEN S.i = 9 AND S.j = 3 THEN T93.val
        WHEN S.i = 9 AND S.j = 4 THEN T94.val
        WHEN S.i = 9 AND S.j = 5 THEN T95.val
        WHEN S.i = 9 AND S.j = 6 THEN T96.val
        WHEN S.i = 9 AND S.j = 7 THEN T97.val
        WHEN S.i = 9 AND S.j = 8 THEN T98.val
        WHEN S.i = 9 AND S.j = 9 THEN T99.val
        ELSE NULL END
    FROM SudokuGrid AS S,
      -- use temp table 81 times
        T AS T11, T AS T12, T AS T13,
        T AS T14, T AS T15, T AS T16,
        T AS T17, T AS T18, T AS T19,

          . . .

        T AS T91, T AS T92, T AS T93,
        T AS T94, T AS T95, T AS T96,
        T AS T97, T AS T98, T AS T99
    WHERE T11.i = 1 AND T12.i = 1 AND T13.i = 1
--check T(i, j)
      AND T14.i = 1 AND T15.i = 1 AND T16.i = 1
      AND T17.i = 1 AND T18.i = 1 AND T19.i = 1
      AND T11.j = 1 AND T12.j = 2 AND T13.j = 3
      AND T14.j = 4 AND T15.j = 5 AND T16.j = 6
      AND T17.j = 7 AND T18.j = 8 AND T19.j = 9
    . . .
```

```
        AND T91.i = 9 AND T92.i = 9 AND T93.i = 9
        AND T94.i = 9 AND T95.i = 9 AND T96.i = 9
        AND T97.i = 9 AND T98.i = 9 AND T99.i = 9
        AND T91.j = 1 AND T92.j = 2 AND T93.j = 3
        AND T94.j = 4 AND T95.j = 5 AND T96.j = 6
        AND T97.j = 7 AND T98.j = 8 AND T99.j = 9


-- add all the row, column and region constraints
    AND T11.val -- row 1
        NOT IN (T12.val, T13.val, T14.val, T15.val, T16.val,
T17.val, T18.val, T19.val)
    AND T12.val
        NOT IN (T13.val, T14.val, T15.val, T16.val, T17.val,
T18.val, T19.val)
   AND T13.val
        NOT IN (T14.val, T15.val, T16.val, T17.val, T18.val,
T19.val)
    AND T14.val
NOT IN (T15.val, T16.val, T17.val, T18.val, T19.val)
    AND T15.val NOT IN (T16.val, T17.val, T18.val, T19.val)
    AND T16.val NOT IN (T17.val, T18.val, T19.val)
    AND T17.val NOT IN (T18.val, T19.val)


  -- column 1
  AND T11.val
        NOT IN (T21.val, T31.val, T41.val, T51.val, T61.val,
T71.val, T81.val, T91.val)
    AND T21.val
        NOT IN (T31.val, T41.val, T51.val, T61.val, T71.val,
T81.val, T91.val)
    AND T31.val
        NOT IN (T41.val, T51.val, T61.val, T71.val, T81.val,
T91.val)
    AND T41.val NOT IN (T51.val, T61.val, T71.val, T81.val,
T91.val)
    AND T51.val NOT IN (T61.val, T71.val, T81.val, T91.val)
    AND T61.val NOT IN (T71.val, T81.val, T91.val)
    AND T71.val NOT IN (T81.val, T91.val)
    AND T81.val NOT IN (T91.val)
  ...
```

```
   -- region 11
    AND T11.val
         NOT IN (T12.val, T13.val, T21.val, T22.val, T23.val,
   T31.val, T32.val, T33.val)
      AND T12.val
           NOT IN (T13.val, T21.val, T22.val, T23.val, T31.val,
   T32.val, T33.val)
      AND T13.val
           NOT IN (T21.val, T22.val, T23.val, T31.val, T32.val,
   T33.val)
      AND T21.val NOT IN (T22.val, T23.val, T31.val, T32.val,
   T33.val)
      AND T22.val NOT IN (T23.val, T31.val, T32.val, T33.val)
      AND T23.val NOT IN (T31.val, T32.val, T33.val)
      AND T31.val NOT IN (T32.val, T33.val)
      AND T32.val NOT IN (T33.val)
      ... ;

UPDATE SudokuGrid
   SET val = (SELECT val
                 FROM Solution
              WHERE i = SudokuGrid.i
                AND j = SudokuGrid.j)
     WHERE val IS NULL;
   END;
```

A version of this procedure written in SQL Server 2000 was able to
solve a puzzle in less than one second on a home computer.

18.4 Bin Packing Problems

There is a set of math problems called bin packing problems that relate to the
real world. Imagine that you have a bunch of items that you have to put into
a box to ship. Each item has a size or shipping weight expressed as an integer and the box has a capacity expressed by another integer in the same units.

I take the box and start filling it. My goal is either to fill the box to
capacity or to get as many single items as I can in the box (perhaps
without filling it all the way). A more complex version also assigns value
and item weight to each item; a very lightweight box can have a great
value—a few grams of diamonds are worth more than a ton of sand.
Another version has more than one box; another can have restrictions
(do not put the fox and goose in the same box), and so forth.

Let me give you the simplest example. I have a box that can hold 10 pounds and I have four items that weigh 1, 3, 4, and 6 pounds each. I can fill my box with (4, 6) and (1, 3, 6). Both waste no space, but the second answer gets the most items in the box.

18.4.1 The Procedural Approach

Can I do this in SQL? Sure! Should I do this in SQL? No! Why do I, a known SQL fanatic, say not to use SQL? Because SQL is a set-oriented language, it finds the entire set of answers, not just the first one that is usable. There is a class of what are called NP-complete problems. They grow in size faster than you can keep up. Let me show you what I mean by modeling my example in SQL.

```
CREATE TABLE Weights
(item_nbr INTEGER NOT NULL PRIMARY KEY,
 item_wgt INTEGER NOT NULL);

INSERT INTO Weights VALUES (1, 1);
INSERT INTO Weights VALUES (2, 3);
INSERT INTO Weights VALUES (3, 6);
INSERT INTO Weights VALUES (4, 4);
```

Now, here is the problem. There is no simple algorithm to pack the box! A greedy algorithm is one that takes the "biggest bite" each time and it can be pretty good in actual situations. But it can fail. What if my four items weighed (7, 6, 5, 4)? The best fit is (6, 4), but in a greedy algorithm, I start with 7 pounds and have to stop. With a "reverse greedy" algorithm, I start with 4, add 5, and stop at 9 pounds in the box.

The best algorithms involve "backtracking." These solutions try one answer, run into a problem, and go back to the previous step, trying and retrying answers. This is a procedural approach, and SQL is a set-oriented language.

18.4.2 The SQL Approach

What do we do in SQL? We have to materialize all the possible packing combinations and weigh in parallel. Let's do it a table of combinations of items in the box.

```
CREATE TABLE Packings
(seq INTEGER NOT NULL PRIMARY KEY,
 flag1 INTEGER DEFAULT 0 NOT NULL
   CHECK (flag1 IN (0, 1)),
```

```
flag2 INTEGER DEFAULT 0 NOT NULL
   CHECK (flag2 IN (0, 1)),
flag3 INTEGER DEFAULT 0 NOT NULL
   CHECK (flag3 IN (0, 1)),
flag4 INTEGER DEFAULT 0 NOT NULL
   CHECK (flag4 IN (0, 1)));

INSERT INTO Packings VALUES (1, 0, 0, 0, 1);
INSERT INTO Packings VALUES (2, 0, 0, 1, 0);
INSERT INTO Packings VALUES (3, 0, 0, 1, 1);
INSERT INTO Packings VALUES (4, 0, 1, 0, 0);
INSERT INTO Packings VALUES (5, 0, 1, 0, 1);
INSERT INTO Packings VALUES (6, 0, 1, 1, 0);
INSERT INTO Packings VALUES (7, 0, 1, 1, 1);
INSERT INTO Packings VALUES (8, 1, 0, 0, 0);
INSERT INTO Packings VALUES (9, 1, 0, 0, 1);
INSERT INTO Packings VALUES (10, 1, 0, 1, 0);
INSERT INTO Packings VALUES (11, 1, 0, 1, 1);
INSERT INTO Packings VALUES (12, 1, 1, 0, 0);
INSERT INTO Packings VALUES (13, 1, 1, 0, 1);
INSERT INTO Packings VALUES (14, 1, 1, 1, 0);
INSERT INTO Packings VALUES (15, 1, 1, 1, 1);
```

This is really a table of binary numbers in a thin disguise. I need the total weight of each combination so that I can find those which are less than or equal to the size of my box.

```
SELECT seq,
      SUM (CASE WHEN item_nbr = 1
     THEN (W.wgt * flag1)
     ELSE 0 END) AS item1,
      SUM (CASE WHEN item_nbr = 2
     THEN (W.wgt * flag2)
     ELSE 0 END) AS item2,
      SUM (CASE WHEN item_nbr = 3
     THEN (W.wgt * flag3)
     ELSE 0 END) AS item3,
      SUM (CASE WHEN item_nbr = 4
     THEN (W.wgt * flag4)
     ELSE 0 END) AS item4
  FROM Weights AS W,
       Packings AS P
GROUP BY seq
```

```
HAVING SUM (CASE WHEN item_nbr = 1
      THEN (W.wgt * flag1)
      ELSE 0 END) +
       SUM (CASE WHEN item_nbr = 2
      THEN (W.wgt * flag2)
      ELSE 0 END) +
        SUM (CASE WHEN item_nbr = 3
      THEN (W.wgt * flag3)
      ELSE 0 END) +
        SUM (CASE WHEN item_nbr = 4
      THEN (W.wgt * flag4)
      ELSE 0 END) <= 10;
```

If I add one more item, the query and the table double in size. See the problem? If we put this into a VIEW or a CTE, then we can use this simpler query to get both the number of items and the total weight of the items.

```
SELECT seq, (item1 + item2 + item3 + item4) AS wgt_tot,
       (SIGN(item1) + SIGN(item2) + SIGN(item3) +
SIGN(item4)) AS item_cnt
  FROM Combos
ORDER BY package_wgt DESC, item_cnt DESC;
```

This lets me filter by item count and by item weight in whatever order is most important to me. Let me make that explicit with the data from the example:

```
Results
```

Seq	wgt_tot	item_cnt	
14	10	3	<= best item_wgt, best item count
3	10	2	<= best item_wgt, second best count
6	9	2	
13	8	3	
10	7	2	
5	7	2	
2	6	1	
9	5	2	
12	4	2	
1	4	1	
4	3	1	
8	1	1	

Now put this in a VIEW called Best and use:

```
SELECT B1.*
  FROM Best AS B1
WHERE wgt_tot
       = (SELECT MAX(wgt_tot) FROM Best)
    AND item_cnt
       = (SELECT MAX(item_cnt)
            FROM Best AS B3
          WHERE wgt_tot
              = (SELECT MAX(wgt_tot) FROM Best));
```

to get your final answer that maximizes both and item counts.

This is how bad it gets with just one box and four items. Think about a real problem with multiple boxes and a lot of items.

18.5 Inventory Costs over Time

The cost of goods in inventory varies over time. Sometimes we can buy low and sell high, and other times the market works against us and the price goes down. This creates a problem in how to compute the cost of the goods sold for any given purchase.

This is easier to explain with a very simple inventory of one kind of item, widgets, to which we add stock once a day. The inventory is then used to fill orders that also come in once a day. The table looks like this:

```
CREATE TABLE WidgetInventory
(receipt_nbr INTEGER NOT NULL PRIMARY KEY,
 purchase_date TIMESTAMP DEFAULT CURRENT_TIMESTAMP NOT NULL,
 on_hand_qty INTEGER NOT NULL
   CHECK (on_hand_qty >= 0),
 unit_price DECIMAL (12, 4) NOT NULL);
```

with the following data:

WidgetInventory

receipt_nbr	purchase_date	on_hand_qty	unit_price
=============	===============	=============	============
1	'2009-08-01'	15	10.00
2	'2009-08-02'	25	12.00
3	'2009-08-03'	40	13.00

```
receipt_nbr    purchase_date    on_hand_qty    unit_price
================================================================
     4          '2009-08-04'         35          12.00
     5          '2009-08-05'         45          10.00
```

The business now sells 100 units on 2009-08-05. How do you calculate the value of the widgets sold? There is not one right answer, but here are some options:

1.   Use the current replacement cost, which is $10.00 per unit as of 2009-08-05. That would mean the sale cost us only $1,000.00 because of a recent price break.

2.   Use the current average price per unit. We have a total of 160 units in stock, for which we paid a total of $1,840.00 and that gives us an average cost of $11.50 per unit, or $1,150.00 in total inventory costs on this sale. This is a measure of what we have invested in the inventory.

3.   LIFO, which stands for "last in, first out." We start by looking at the most recent purchases and work backwards through time.

```
2009-08-05: 45 * $10.00 = $450.00 and 45 units
2009-08-04: 35 * $12.00 = $420.00 and 80 units
2009-08-03: 20 * $13.00 = $260.00 and 100
with 20 units left over
```

for a total of $1,130.00 in inventory cost.

4.   FIFO, which stands for "first in, first out." We start by looking at the earliest purchases and work forward through time.

```
2009-08-01: 15 * $10.00 = $150.00 and 15 units
2009-08-02: 25 * $12.00 = $300.00 and 40 units
2009-08-03: 40 * $13.00 = $520.00 and 80 units
2009-08-04: 20 * $12.00 = $240.00 with 15 units
left over
```

for a total of $1,210.00 in inventory costs.
The first two scenarios are trivial to program.

```
CREATE VIEW Current_Replacement_Cost (unit_cost)
AS
SELECT unit_price
```

```
       FROM WidgetInventory
WHERE purchase_date
       = (SELECT MAX(purchase_date) FROM WidgetInventory);
```

and then

```
CREATE VIEW Average_Replacement_Cost (unit_cost)
AS
SELECT SUM(unit_price * on_hand_qty)/SUM(on_hand_qty)
  FROM WidgetInventory;
```

The LIFO and FIFO are more interesting because they involve looking at matching the order against blocks of inventory in a particular order. Consider this VIEW:

```
CREATE VIEW LIFO (stock_date, unit_price, on_hand_qty_tot,
cost_tot)
AS
SELECT W1.purchase_date, W1.unit_price,
       SUM(W2.on_hand_qty),
       SUM(W2.on_hand_qty * W2.unit_price)
 FROM WidgetInventory AS W1,
       WidgetInventory AS W2
 WHERE W2.purchase_date <= W1.purchase_date
 GROUP BY W1.purchase_date, W1.unit_price;
```

A row in this VIEW tells us the total quantity on hand, the total cost of the goods in inventory, and what we were paying for items on each date. The quantity on hand is a running total. We can get the LIFO cost with this query.

```
SELECT (cost_tot - ((on_hand_qty_tot - :order_qty) *
unit_price))
       AS cost
  FROM LIFO AS L1
 WHERE stock_date
       = (SELECT MIN(stock_date)
            FROM LIFO AS L2
           WHERE on_hand_qty_tot >= :order_qty);
```

This is straight algebra and a little logic. You need to find the most recent date that we had enough (or more) quantity on hand to meet the order. If by dumb blind luck, there is a day when the quantity on hand exactly matched the order, return the total cost as the answer. If the order was for more than we have in stock, then return nothing. If we go back to a day when we had more in stock than the order was for, then look at the unit price on that day, multiply by the overage, and subtract it.

Alternatively, you can use a derived table and a CASE expression. The CASE expression computes the cost of units that have a running total quantity less than the :order_qty and then does algebra on the final block of inventory, which would put the running total over the limit. The outer query does a sum on these blocks.

```
SELECT SUM(W3.unit_cost) AS cost_tot
  FROM (SELECT W1.unit_price
               * CASE WHEN SUM(W2.on_hand_qty) <= :order_qty
                      THEN W1.on_hand_qty
                      ELSE :order_qty
                           - (SUM(W2.on_hand_qty) -
                           W1.on_hand_qty)
                      END
          FROM WidgetInventory AS W1,
               WidgetInventory AS W2
         WHERE W1.purchase_date <= W2.purchase_date
         GROUP BY W1.purchase_date, W1.on_hand_qty,
         W1.unit_price
        HAVING (SUM(W2.on_hand_qty) - W1.on_hand_qty)
        <= :order_qty)
       AS W3(unit_cost);
```

FIFO can be done with a similar VIEW, CTE, or derived table.

```
CREATE VIEW FIFO (stock_date, unit_price, on_hand_qty_tot,
cost_tot)
AS
SELECT W1.purchase_date, W1.unit_price,
       SUM(W2.on_hand_qty),
       SUM(W2.on_hand_qty * W2.unit_price)
  FROM WidgetInventory AS W1,
       WidgetInventory AS W2
 WHERE W2.purchase_date <= W1.purchase_date
 GROUP BY W1.purchase_date, W1.unit_price;
```

with the corresponding query:

```
SELECT (cost_tot - ((on_hand_qty_tot - :order_qty) *
unit_price)) AS cost
  FROM FIFO AS F1
 WHERE stock_date
       = (SELECT MIN (stock_date)
             FROM FIFO AS F2
            WHERE on_hand_qty_tot >= :order_qty);
```

These queries and VIEWs only told us what the value of the widget inventory is. Notice that we never actually shipped anything from the inventory.

18.5.1 Inventory UPDATE Statements

What we did not do in the previous section was actually update the inventory when we shipped out the widgets. Let's build another VIEW that will make life easier.

```
CREATE VIEW StockLevels (purchase_date, previous_qty,
current_qty)
AS
SELECT W1.purchase_date,
       SUM(CASE WHEN W2.purchase_date < W1.purchase_date
               THEN W2.on_hand_qty ELSE 0 END),
       SUM(CASE WHEN W2.purchase_date <= W1.purchase_date
               THEN W2.on_hand_qty ELSE 0 END)
  FROM WidgetInventory AS W1,
       WidgetInventory AS W2
 WHERE W2.purchase_date <= W1.purchase_date
 GROUP BY W1.purchase_date, W1.unit_price;
```

StockLevels

purchase_date	previous_qty	current_qty
'2009-08-01'	0	15
'2009-08-02'	15	40
'2009-08-03'	40	80
'2009-08-04'	80	115
'2009-08-05'	115	160

The use of the CASE expressions will save us a self-join.

```
CREATE PROCEDURE RemoveQty (IN my_order_qty INTEGER)
LANGUAGE SQL
BEGIN
IF my_order_qty > 0
THEN
UPDATE WidgetInventory
  SET on_hand_qty
     = CASE
       WHEN my_order_qty
            >= (SELECT current_qty
                 FROM StockLevels AS L
                WHERE L.purchase_date
                      = WidgetInventory.purchase_date)
       THEN 0
       WHEN my_order_qty
            < (SELECT previous_qty
                 FROM StockLevels AS L
                WHERE L.purchase_date
                      = WidgetInventory.purchase_date)
       THEN WidgetInventory.on_hand_qty
       ELSE (SELECT current_qty
                 FROM StockLevels AS L
                WHERE L.purchase_date = WidgetInventory.
                purchase_date)
               - my_order_qty END;
END IF;

-- remove empty bins
DELETE FROM WidgetInventory
 WHERE on_hand_qty = 0;
END;
```

18.5.2 Bin Packing Returns

Another inventory problem is how to fill an order with the smallest or greatest number of bins. This assumes that the bins have no ordering, so we are free to fill the order as we wish. Using the fewest bins would make less work for the order pickers. Using the greatest number of bins would clean out more storage in the warehouse.

For example, with this data, you could fill an order for 80 widgets by shipping out bins (1, 2, 3) or bins (4, 5). These bins happen to be in date and bin number order in the sample data, but that is not required.

As we saw in the previous section, this is not easy in SQL because it is a declarative, set-oriented language. A procedural language can stop when it has a solution that is "good enough", while an SQL query tends to find all of the correct answers no matter how long it takes.

If you can have a limit on the number of bins we are willing to visit, you can fake an array in a table.

```
CREATE TABLE Picklists
(order_nbr INTEGER NOT NULL PRIMARY KEY,
 goal_qty INTEGER NOT NULL
   CHECK (goal_qty > 0),
 bin_nbr_1 INTEGER NOT NULL UNIQUE,
 on_hand_qty_1 INTEGER DEFAULT 0 NOT NULL
   CHECK (on_hand_qty_1 >= 0),
 bin_nbr_2 INTEGER NOT NULL UNIQUE,
 on_hand_qty_2 INTEGER DEFAULT 0 NOT NULL
   CHECK (on_hand_qty_2 >= 0),
 bin_nbr_3 INTEGER NOT NULL UNIQUE,
 on_hand_qty_3 INTEGER DEFAULT 0 NOT NULL
   CHECK (on_hand_qty_3 >= 0),
 CONSTRAINT not_over_goal
   CHECK (on_hand_qty_1 + on_hand_qty_2 + on_hand_qty_3
         <= goal_qty)
CONSTRAINT bins_sorted
  CHECK (on_hand_qty_1 >= on_hand_qty_2
        AND on_hand_qty_2 >= on_hand_qty_3));
```

Now we can start stuffing bins into the table. This query will give us the ways to fill or almost fill an order with three or fewer bins. The first trick is to load some empty dummy bins into the table. If you want at most (n) picks, then add (n − 1) dummy bins.

```
INSERT INTO WidgetInventory VALUES (-1, '2006-01-01',
0 ,0.00);
INSERT INTO WidgetInventory VALUES (-2, '2006-01-02',
0 ,0.00);
```

This next is to build a CTE or VIEW with the possible pick lists:

```
CREATE VIEW PickCombos(total_pick, bin_1, on_hand_qty_1,
                  bin_2, on_hand_qty_2,
                  bin_3, on_hand_qty_3)
AS
SELECT DISTINCT
       (W1.on_hand_qty + W2.on_hand_qty + W3.on_hand_qty)
AS total_pick,
       CASE WHEN W1.receipt_nbr < 0
            THEN 0 ELSE W1.receipt_nbr END AS bin_1,
            W1.on_hand_qty,
       CASE WHEN W2.receipt_nbr < 0
            THEN 0 ELSE W2.receipt_nbr END AS bin_2,
            W2.on_hand_qty,
       CASE WHEN W3.receipt_nbr < 0
            THEN 0 ELSE W3.receipt_nbr END AS bin_3,
            W3.on_hand_qty
  FROM WidgetInventory AS W1,
       WidgetInventory AS W2,
       WidgetInventory AS W3
WHERE W1.receipt_nbr NOT IN (W2.receipt_nbr, W3.receipt_nbr)
  AND W2.receipt_nbr NOT IN (W1.receipt_nbr, W3.receipt_nbr)
  AND W1.on_hand_qty >= W2.on_hand_qty
  AND W2.on_hand_qty >= W3.on_hand_qty;
```

Now we need a procedure to find the pick combination that meet or come closest to a certain quantity.

```
CREATE PROCEDURE OverPick (IN goal_qty INTEGER)
LANGUAGE SQL
BEGIN
IF goal_qty > 0
THEN
SELECT goal_qty, total_pick, bin_1, on_hand_qty_1,
      bin_2, on_hand_qty_2,
      bin_3, on_hand_qty_3
  FROM PickCombos
 WHERE total_pick
       = (SELECT MIN (total_pick)
```

```
              FROM PickCombos
              WHERE total_pick >= goal_qty)
END IF;
END;
```

With the SQL-99 syntax, the VIEW could be put into a CTE, making this into a query without a VIEW. With the current data, and a goal of 73 widgets, we can find two picks that both total to 75, namely {3, 4} and {4, 2, 1}.

I will leave it as an exercise for the reader to find a query that underpicks a target quantity.

Index

Printed and bound by CPI Group (UK) Ltd, Croydon, CR0 4YY

03/10/2024

01040319-0011